PRAISE FOR

The ancient Prophet Ho[ ] mouth." Randy Terry has written a prophetic message on "Divine Correction" to the Church in the style of Hosea. He has put the trumpet of God's Word in terms we can understand in today's culture.

Randy clears the fog of compromise away from the "sins that cry for vengeance." His forty years of standing for truth have given him the experience to reinforce this urgent message.

Read at the risk of becoming a radical world changer.

—REV. PAUL JOHANSSON, President Emeritus,
Elim Bible Institute and College,
Lima, NY

Since 1988, I have known and respected Randall Terry as a friend and a fearless warrior in the battle for life. St. Jerome said, "Ignorance of the Scriptures is ignorance of Christ." Randall has been searching the Scriptures for many years as a true believer in the Risen Christ. His research in *Divine Correction* is extensive and worthy of the time and attention of any cleric or lay-person who is concerned about "the sins that cry for vengeance" that are rampant in formerly Christian nations.

—BISHOP JOSEPH L. COFFEY, Archdiocese
for the Military Services, USA

Abraham Lincoln, in his trademark brevity, once said, "If slavery isn't wrong, nothing is." Randall Terry stands as an outspoken reminder in our day that if sins that cry for vengeance aren't wrong, nothing is. And like Lincoln and the prophets of Israel, he is hated by many for it. But the prophets are called and equipped to speak truth regardless of the consequences.

JOHN GROOTERS, Writer, Director, *Tortured for Christ*

We are living through a perfect cultural storm of wickedness, forgetfulness, foolishness, shallowness, and pridefulness. In this sobering, substantive, must-read book, Randall Terry reminds us all that God is not mocked. We will reap what we have sown. Our longsuffering, righteous, and altogether gracious God will most assuredly bring us to the bar of justice. Lord, have mercy. Church, have courage.

—GEORGE GRANT, Parish Presbyterian Church,
Franklin, TN

So…where is God in these tumultuous times? This book digs deep to address Scripture and history combined exhaustively to answer all your questions and doubts. It did for me!

—JOSEPH COSTELLO JR.

This is the best book Randall Terry has written yet. I could not put it down. All I could think was, "How do we get this into the hands of every pastor in America?"

—REV. JOE SLOVENIC

As a Catholic author who loves Sacred Scripture, I appreciate when an expert clearly exposits from the Word of God. Randall's comprehensive knowledge of the Holy Scriptures, from his formal Bible College training to his decades of study and research, has produced this unparalleled, must-read treatise.

Prophets of old called the children of God to repentance. *Divine Correction* is a prophetic call, deriving its force and clarity from the Biblical prophets of old, who call over the centuries to us today—calling the nations back to God—and warning us of the cost of refusing God's divine correction. May we heed their call while we still can.

—BUD MACFARLANE, Bestselling Novelist;
Founder, Operation True Cross,
The Mary Foundation, CatholiCity.com

The one thing that got my attention the most in Randall Terry's *Divine Correction* is the undeniable fact that all our actions lead to very real consequences, both in the positive and negative. Therefore, we would do well in adjusting our steps according to the precepts of the Word of God—individually, in our families, church-wise, and nationally.

—Nikola Dimitrov, DMin, Pastor,
Life in Glory—Radinovo Church;
Author, *The Four in One Gospel of Jesus*

Randall Terry has been on the front battle lines of the prolife movement for decades. The fire of the Holy Spirit blows like a strong wind when Randall speaks or writes on the defense of human life. Amos 3:7 (RSV): "Surely the Lord God does nothing, without revealing his secret to his servants the prophets."

Randall Terry, in prophetic style, reminds us in this book that modern man has it all wrong when it comes to the sanctity of human life. The purpose of this book is to awaken you to the seriousness, cunning, and ferocity of Satan. Our nation is in the midst of a spiritual war, a battle we will lose if Christians don't arm themselves with God's grace, power, and knowledge of our infernal enemy and his lust for the killing of babies.

Randall Terry is a prophet for our times. Characteristics of a biblical prophet: 1) Randall speaks with moral clarity, and he speaks inconvenient truths to power. 2) He speaks about the consequences of sin. 3) He calls people to repentance. 4) He leans heavily on God's Word. 5) He has been persecuted by our own government. 6) He's been villified, calumniated, and gaslighted by the political Left. God sends prophets (the Greek word means "spokesmen"), whose role includes warning people that they are headed over the Niagara Falls. You'd think people would be grateful for the heads-up Randall Terry has been providing us. But often, people respond to bad news by killing the messenger. Let's be wise and listen to this prophet.

—Jesse Romero, M.A., Retired Los Angeles Deputy Sheriff;
Catholic Speaker; Author and Radio Talk Show Host

DIVINE
CORRECTION

DIVINE CORRECTION

HOW GOD GETS A NATION'S ATTENTION

RANDALL A. TERRY

Nordskog
Publishing inc.

VENTURA, CALIFORNIA

DIVINE CORRECTION: HOW GOD GETS A NATION'S ATTENTION
By Randall Terry • © 2023 Randall Terry
ISBN: 978-1-946497-60-4
Library of Congress Control Number: 2023931649

Aaron Ford of digicomdesigns.com, Cover Design
Ronald W. Kirk, Theology and Lead Editor
Michelle Shelfer (benediction.biz), Managing Editor, Typesetting
Nikola Dimitrov, Proofreader

Printed in the United States of America by CMYK Printing & Graphics.

Nordskog Publishing Inc.

Ventura, California
805-642-2070
NordskogPublishing.com

TABLE OF CONTENTS

FOREWORD

R andall Terry writes with an eloquence forged by fire. Some have an elegant way with words, but not the eloquence that springs from deep conviction. Randall's battle courage has been tested again and again, and by God's strength he has persevered.

My friendship with Randall Terry has spanned more than three decades. I have watched him lead Operation Rescue and have defended those who, inspired by Randall, have put their bodies on the line in defense of unborn children. Even as "respectable" pro-life leaders denounced him as too radical, Randall persevered because he knew he was doing God's will as revealed in His Word.

Now, in *Divine Correction*, Randall has risen above the moment with a call to repentance that transcends time. His basic premise is that, just as God judged Israel and Judah of old, so He will judge us today.

This is an emotion-charged theme, but Randall pursues it with cold logic. First, he establishes that there is a timeless standard for judgment—the Law of God, which, as Randall demonstrates, Jesus came not to destroy but to fulfill. He surveys Biblical judgments—weather, plague, economic ruin, the sword of foreign conquest and domestic discord—and warns that God may employ these same instruments today. For the sins of Western nations are like those of ancient Israel and the pagan Canaanites, but on a much grander scale.

And just as Israel's (and America's) sins are timeless, so is God's response and so is our remedy. Repentance—turning to Christ's finished work on the Cross for our salvation and to His Word for instruction and renewal—is the key to our hope.

Randall, thanks for writing *Divine Correction*. May God use it to bring people to their senses and draw them to Himself.

And now—let's go out and slay some dragons!

JOHN A. EIDSMOE, Chaplain (Colonel Ret),
Mississippi State Guard,
Lt. Colonel, US Air Force (Ret),
Senior Counsel, Foundation for Moral Law,
Professor of Constitutional Law, Oak Brook College of Law
& Government Policy,
Pastor, Association of Free Lutheran Congregations,
Author, *Historical and Theological Foundations of Law*

My anguish, my anguish! I writhe in pain!
Oh, the walls of my heart!
My heart is beating wildly;
I cannot keep silent;
for I hear the sound of the trumpet,
the alarm of war.
Disaster follows hard on disaster,
the whole land is laid waste.
Suddenly my tents are destroyed,
my curtains in a moment.
How long must I see the standard,
and hear the sound of the trumpet?
"For My people are foolish,
they know Me not;
they are stupid children,
they have no understanding.
They are skilled in doing evil,
but how to do good they know not."

Jeremiah 4:19–22

PREFACE

He Who Has Ears to Hear, Let Him Hear

This book is a comprehensive study of divine correction brought to bear on individuals, families, clans, and nations in this life and in this world.

The primary focus will be on nations and the sins committed in those nations, often with the approval, protection, and even promotion of their governments—sins that call for God's chastening.

Sacred Scriptures, as well as the teachings of the historic Church, demonstrate *why* nations come under divine correction—i.e., because *of sins that cry to God for vengeance*. Sacred Scriptures also explain *the means* God uses to get a nation's attention. These divine corrections are laid out in the Sacred Scriptures, recorded throughout the Sacred Scriptures, and attested to in the annals of human history since the Scriptures were canonized.

The sufferings and convulsions that nations have endured throughout history were often the chastenings of God—*temporal corrections that are thoroughly delineated* in Sacred Scriptures as the means God uses to chasten a nation and to call that nation to repentance and back to Himself.

When a nation comes under God's chastening, if it is to be healed and restored, it must "bring forth fruit in keeping with repentance" (Matthew 3:8 NASB). These "fruits of repentance" are words and deeds—*knowable* to mankind—that will often mitigate the chastenings of God and set a nation on a path of restoration.

Hence, if God is chastening any nation, the length, severity, and final outcome of His punishments are in part in the hands of its citizens. As God told the Prophet Jeremiah:

> If at any time I announce that a nation or kingdom is to be uprooted, torn down and destroyed, and if that nation I warned repents of its evil, then I will relent and not inflict on it the disaster I had planned. (Jeremiah 18:7–8 NIV)

Christians of every denomination can and should strive together against the sins and crimes in their nations that cry to God for vengeance. While there are clearly internecine theological quarrels between servants of Christ that will not be resolved in this life, it is a righteous goal for devout believers to work together to restore all nations to the Law, love, and fear of God.

Jesus said: "For he that is not against us is for us. For truly, I say to you, whoever gives you a cup of water to drink because you bear the name of Christ, will by no means lose his reward" (Mark 9:40–41).

In that spirit, may believers across cultural and denominational lines unite in "the fruits of repentance" and help restore their respective nations to justice and godliness, in the hope that the chastenings of God for national sins can be averted or mitigated—in hope that God will relent of the disasters He has threatened or has even begun to unleash.

It is especially hoped that clergy of all Trinitarian streams will embrace and then communicate the truths about divine correction to those in their charge, for the sake of spurring them on to "love and good works," to the end that their nations will be spared the impending chastening of the Almighty.

In judgment, may God remember mercy.

—RANDALL A. TERRY
Ash Wednesday 2023

ACKNOWLEDGMENTS

In writing acknowledgments, one is duty bound to look back over the journey—the happy moments, the pitfalls, the wreckage, the high points and the low—remembering those who pushed, pulled, prodded, and protested along the way, both in the book and in life.

The primary difficulties with *Divine Correction* were threefold:

1) I wanted to write a book that was not dated. That meant removing almost all references to contemporary leaders, news, and issues.

2) I wanted to write a theological work that would prove useful for clergy in whatever country in which they lived. While I am an American, this is not a book about America. This is a theological work that can be applied to America, the nations of Europe, and in many ways, all the nations of the earth. That meant keeping the references to America as few as possible and including the post-Christian nations of Europe.

3) I wanted to write a book that stayed within the theological dispositions and assumptions of all Trinitarian communities. This was perhaps the most difficult aspect of this work, and it will be up to the reader to see if I succeeded. Suffice to say, I frequently gave this book to Christians from multiple denominations and asked them to "*push back*; tell me what you *don't* like."

So, those to whom I give thanks are those who helped me overcome many difficulties.

My editor, Michelle Shelfer, had to help me through all three of these difficulties and did a fantastic and good-natured job.

My publisher, Jerry Nordskog, is a prince of a man. He and his wife, Gail, have been stalwart defenders and supporters of my work for thirty years. Moreover, Jerry waited patiently through three full rewrites and the consumption of three years of time. Having him as my publisher is a privilege, as well as a debt of honor. Thank you, Ronald W. Kirk, for the pushback I asked for that made the book better.

In addition to the mechanical parts of writing and publishing a book is the safety net—the kitchen table, the laughs, tears, family games, and prayers of men and women who keep life on track and "normal" (whatever that is).

Hence, to the friends and fellow laborers who frequently held up my weary arms and occasionally gave input on this manuscript, I express my thanks. (I fear naming some and forgetting others. Nevertheless…) Special thanks to Rob and Cyndy Shearer, and Chris and Kerry Marsh (for decades of friendship and years of editorial input, activism, and Scrabble); Colleen Orfe (for honest criticism); Dr. Evelyn McDonald (for wonderful grammatical and contextual criticism); Rev. Paul Johannson (for decades of mentoring and counsel—"How did we both get so old?"); Michael Hirsh, Esq. (for invaluable legal and theological counsel, as well as laughs); Father John Mikalajunas (Catholic) and Father Terry Gensemer (Charismatic Episcopal), who both saved my life; Eric Michaloski (my best man, with whom I learned to escape cribs before we could talk); Joe Costello (for unflinching friendship); Rev. Joe Slovenec (for memories in battle and hope for the future); Dad and Mom (who taught me to hate injustice and to fight against it); Matt Labash (who penned the best-ever biography of me); Dale and Suzzane Cooper (for refuge in a time of storm); David Long (for decades of co-belligerence); Randy Henderson (for being "The Navigator" and "Consigliere"); our circle of dear friends in Memphis, who became "community" when we had a health emergency; my daughters, Faith and Tila, who gave me the joy of being a daddy to girls.

And finally, my wife, Andrea, and our four sons, who have made life worth living.

Do not think that I have come to abolish the Law or the Prophets; I have not come to abolish them but to fulfill them. For truly I tell you, until heaven and earth disappear, not the smallest letter, not the least stroke of a pen, will by any means disappear from the Law until everything is accomplished. Therefore anyone who sets aside one of the least of these commands and teaches others accordingly will be called least in the kingdom of heaven, but whoever practices and teaches these commands will be called great in the kingdom of heaven.

Matthew 5:17–19 NIV

Do not be idolaters, as some of them were; as it is written: "The people sat down to eat and drink and got up to indulge in revelry." We should not commit sexual immorality, as some of them did—and in one day twenty-three thousand of them died. We should not test Christ, as some of them did—and were killed by snakes. And do not grumble, as some of them did—and were killed by the destroying angel. THESE THINGS HAPPENED TO THEM AS EXAMPLES AND WERE WRITTEN DOWN AS WARNINGS FOR US.

First Corinthians 10:7–11 NIV

INTRODUCTION

Does God Chasten Men and Nations in This Life?

It is clear that under the *Old Covenant*, God brought punishments on nations, families, and individuals *in this life*—nations, families, and individuals that incurred His wrath.

The question at hand is whether the Almighty sends corrections on individuals, families, and nations under the *New Covenant*. Theologians have discussed this question for centuries. That is, in the "age of grace" brought by our Lord Jesus Christ, does God bring judgments on men and nations—temporal punishments—*in this life*?

This work seeks to answer the following questions:

- Does God send correction, or judgment, on men and nations in this life today, under the New Covenant?
- If so, does He bring judgment on His people—i.e., the Church—or only on those outside the Church?
- If God visits men and nations with chastening in this life, why does He do so?
- What forms do His corrections take?
- Can anything be done to avert or mitigate His judgments?
- If so, what?

The author will provide comprehensive answers to these questions, deriving the answers from Sacred Scripture from the *Old and New Testaments*—namely, that God does bring correction to individuals, families, and nations *here and now*. Moreover, those judgments from heaven come from a large repository of chastenings that God has at His disposal. He has delineated them in great detail in Sacred Scripture and has used them since the dawn of time.

The reader will be left to judge if the case has been made that:

- God's love for mankind is expressed at times in His correction, as the Scripture says:

And have you forgotten the exhortation which addresses you as sons?—

"My son, do not regard lightly the discipline of the Lord, nor lose courage when you are punished by him.

For the Lord disciplines him whom he loves, and chastises every son whom he receives." (Hebrews 12:5, 6)

- Yes, God does bring chastenings in this life when He pleases on individuals and nations, including on those in the Church.
- Specific sins incur His judgment in this world.
- There are specific ways He threatens and brings judgment in this world.
- His corrective chastening (herein discussed) are in the temporal realm and are not necessarily indicative of *eternal* judgment.
- And finally, there are specific ways mankind can repent to avert or mitigate the judgment of God in this life.

The author will use the words *correction, chastening, punishment,* and *judgment* interchangeably in this work.

Now, to the topic at hand.

Before You punished me, I used to go wrong,
but now I obey Your word. . . .
My punishment was good for me,
because it made me learn Your commands. . . .
I know that Your judgments are righteous, LORD,
and that You punished me because You are faithful.

Psalm 119:67, 71, 75 GNT

For when Thy judgments are in the earth,
the inhabitants of the world learn righteousness.

Isaiah 26:9b

TEMPORAL CORRECTION, NOT ETERNAL DAMNATION

The Scriptures teach that there is a *final* judgment—i.e., some men and women will be with God for all eternity, and others will be separated from God for all eternity.

However, the Sacred Scriptures of the Old and New Testaments also teach that God *visits judgment* on men and nations *in time*—i.e., *in this life*. He can visit with various hardships, calamities, sorrows, and even death to individuals, communities, regions, and nations.

The Scriptures studied here will provide a comprehensive overview of divine corrections as recorded in the Old and New Testaments and as witnessed since the dawn of human history.

Divine laws and warnings are not altered by the arrogance of kings and presidents or the rebellion of judges and governors. Biblical themes do not change with political administrations. Immutable truths predate political parties, parliaments, and presidents and are not subservient to or nullified by court rulings or acts of Congress, parliament, dictators, or tyrants. The laws and judgments of Almighty God are over all men and nations for all time. As this Messianic psalm states:

Why do the heathen rage,
and the people imagine a vain thing?
The kings of the earth set themselves,
and the rulers take counsel together,
against the LORD, and against His anointed, saying,
Let us break their bands asunder,
and cast away their cords from us.
He that sitteth in the heavens shall laugh:
The LORD shall have them in derision.
Then shall He speak unto them in His wrath,
and vex them in His sore displeasure....
Be wise now therefore, O ye kings:
be instructed, ye judges of the earth.
Serve the LORD with fear,
and rejoice with trembling.
Kiss the Son, lest He be angry,
and ye perish from the way,
when His wrath is kindled but a little.
(Psalm 2:1–5, 10–12 KJV)

Psalm 110 is another Messianic psalm dealing with Christ's authority *after* His resurrection and ascension *but before* He returns at the end of time:

The LORD says to my lord:
"Sit at My right hand
until I make Your enemies
a footstool for Your feet."
The LORD will extend Your mighty scepter from Zion,
saying,
"Rule in the midst of Your enemies!"...
The Lord is at Your right hand;
He will crush kings on the day of His wrath.
He will judge the nations, heaping up the dead
and crushing the rulers of the whole earth.
(Psalm 110:1–2, 5–6 NIV)

He who sits at the right hand of God displays His sovereign power by bringing the objects of His displeasure and the targets of His wrath—whether kings and princes, men and nations—under His divine punishments *in this life*...as well as the next.

The Who, What, When, Where, and Why of Temporal Correction

Sacred Scripture provides extensive detail of the corrective measures God promises to bring on those who defy His Laws. Moreover, Scripture has an extensive record of those judgments being poured out on various individuals, families, and nations over multiple centuries. This record of judgment is for the sake of God's Church, as well as all mankind, for warning and instruction. The Apostle Paul wrote to the Corinthians:

> Nevertheless with most of them [the Israelites] God was not pleased; for they were overthrown in the wilderness. Now these things are warnings for us, not to desire evil as they did. Do not be idolaters as some of them were; as it is written, "The people sat down to eat and drink and rose up to dance." We must not indulge in immorality as some of them did, and twenty-three thousand fell in a single day. We must not put the Lord to the test, as some of them did and were destroyed by serpents; nor grumble, as some of them did and were destroyed by the Destroyer. Now these things happened to them as a warning, but they were written down for our instruction, upon whom the end of the ages has come. (First Corinthians 10:5–11)

The Apostle Peter likewise explained that the sacred history of divine judgments of the past is for the sake of those now living, to serve as a warning:

> But false prophets also arose among the people, just as there will be false teachers among you, who will secretly bring in destructive heresies, even denying the Master who

bought them, bringing upon themselves swift destruction. And many will follow their licentiousness, and because of them the way of truth will be reviled. And in their greed they will exploit you with false words; from of old their condemnation has not been idle, and their destruction has not been asleep.

For if God did not spare the angels when they sinned, but cast them into hell and committed them to pits of nether gloom to be kept until the judgment; if He did not spare the ancient world, but preserved Noah, a herald of righteousness, with seven other persons, when He brought a flood upon the world of the ungodly; if by turning the cities of Sodom and Gomor'rah to ashes He condemned them to extinction and made them an example to those who were to be ungodly; and if He rescued righteous Lot, greatly distressed by the licentiousness of the wicked (for by what that righteous man saw and heard as he lived among them, he was vexed in his righteous soul day after day with their lawless deeds), then the Lord knows how to rescue the godly from trial, and to keep the unrighteous under punishment until the day of judgment, and especially those who indulge in the lust of defiling passion and despise authority. (Second Peter 2:1–10)

This book will present the Scriptural patterns regarding *how* God sends judgment, *on whom* He sends judgment, *when* He sends judgment, and most importantly, *why* He sends judgment. It will also explore how to avert judgment, what can be done in the midst of judgment, and what actions mankind can take to deflect, mitigate, or speed the end of God's judgment. The Scripture says that men do not thresh wheat forever (see Isaiah 28:28). The judgments of God in this world are *temporal and finite*—not *eternal and infinite*—so hope can be had in the midst of judgment. As the prophet Habakkuk pleaded with God: "In wrath, remember mercy" (Habakkuk 3:2).

In whatever nation one lives and in whatever year or century one reads this, all mankind is subject to the immutable laws of God. And as Sacred Scripture declares and history bears out, "The judgments of the LORD are true and righteous altogether" (Psalm 19:9 NKJV).

Indeed I tremble for my country when I reflect that God is just: that His justice cannot sleep forever.

Thomas Jefferson, "Query XVIII,"
from *Notes on the State of Virginia*

The Lord is at your right hand; He will shatter kings on the day of His wrath. He will execute judgment among the nations, filling them with corpses; He will shatter chiefs over the wide earth.

Psalm 110:5–6 ESV

It is a dreadful thing to fall into the hands of the living God.

Hebrews 10:31 NIV

2

God Is Judge of Men and Nations—
In This Life

The *premise* of this treatise is that God is real and has given the human race His laws. If mankind obeys His laws, there are blessings to be reaped. If mankind persistently and obstinately breaks His laws, even going so far as to institutionalize abominable sins and crimes, there is a price to be paid *in this life*: divine judgment.

The exact chastenings that may be peculiar to any particular nation and time are clearly laid out in Sacred Scripture, including pandemics, violence, loss of liberty, corrupt and oppressive political leadership, rampant fear, drought, intense weather patterns, economic loss, and more.

The *purpose* of this treatise is to show what the human family—as individuals, families, communities, and nations—can and must do to mitigate God's judgment. He has outlined the path for a nation's restoration via certain concrete, visible, knowable acts of repentance. This blessed roadmap is also clearly laid out in Sacred Scripture.

God Judges Individuals—*In This Life*

God is not only the final Judge of all men's souls for eternity, but He is also the sovereign Judge of individuals in this world, in this life, in all nations and all eras.

Consider examples of divine *judgment on individuals* in the Scriptures—judgments in their bodies, their minds, their homes, their finances, or their health.

For his arrogance against God, Nebuchadnezzar was smitten with some type of insanity so that he lived like a wild beast:

> And the king said, "Is not this great Babylon, which I have built by my mighty power as a royal residence and for the glory of my majesty?" While the words were still in the king's mouth, there fell a voice from heaven, "O King Nebuchadnez'zar, to you it is spoken: The kingdom has departed from you, and you shall be driven from among men, and your dwelling shall be with the beasts of the field; and you shall be made to eat grass like an ox; and seven times shall pass over you, until you have learned that the Most High rules the kingdom of men and gives it to whom He will." Immediately the word was fulfilled upon Nebuchadnez'zar. He was driven from among men, and ate grass like an ox, and his body was wet with the dew of heaven till his hair grew as long as eagles' feathers, and his nails were like birds' claws.

Afterward, Nebuchadnezzar repented and said:

> At the end of the days I, Nebuchadnez'zar, lifted my eyes to heaven, and my reason returned to me, and I blessed the Most High, and praised and honored Him who lives for ever;
> For His dominion is an everlasting dominion,
> and His kingdom endures from generation to generation;
> all the inhabitants of the earth are accounted as nothing;
> and He does according to His will in the host of heaven

and among the inhabitants of the earth;
and none can stay His hand
or say to Him, "What doest Thou?"

When his reason returned, Nebuchadnezzar saw the world—and God—as it truly is:

At the same time my reason returned to me; and for the glory of my kingdom, my majesty and splendor returned to me. My counselors and my lords sought me, and I was established in my kingdom, and still more greatness was added to me. Now I, Nebuchadnez'zar, praise and extol and honor the King of heaven; for all His works are right and His ways are just; and those who walk in pride He is able to abase. (Daniel 4:30–37)

Another example of divine judgment on an individual is the Jewish King Saul, chosen by God to be king, who lost the kingdom and his life for his sins against God:

So Saul died for his unfaithfulness; he was unfaithful to the LORD in that he did not keep the command of the LORD, and also consulted a medium, seeking guidance, and did not seek guidance from the LORD. Therefore the LORD slew him, and turned the kingdom over to David the son of Jesse. (First Chronicles 10:13–14)

King Ahab was killed in battle as a direct judgment from God:

And Micai'ah said, "Therefore hear the word of the LORD: I saw the LORD sitting on His throne, and all the host of heaven standing beside Him on His right hand and on His left; and the LORD said, 'Who will entice Ahab, that he may go up and fall at Ra'moth-gil'ead?' And one said one thing, and another said another. Then a spirit came forward and stood before the LORD, saying, 'I will entice him.' And the LORD said to him, 'By what means?' And he said, 'I will go forth, and will be a lying spirit in the mouth of all his prophets.' And He said, 'You are to entice him, and you shall succeed; go forth and do so.' Now therefore behold, the LORD has put a lying spirit in the mouth of all these your prophets; the LORD has spoken evil concerning you." (First Kings 22:19–23)

As the prophet warned, Ahab was killed in battle by an arrow shot at random.

King David's first son, born of his sin with Bathsheba, was smitten with sickness and died (Second Samuel 12:1–23).

King Solomon had multiple rebellions raised against him because of his idolatry (First Kings 11).

King Jeroboam's hand was withered in the presence of the prophet because of his sin of idolatry (First Kings 13:1–10).

An unnamed prophet—used mightily by God—was slain by a lion because he disobeyed God's command not to eat or drink in Israel (First Kings 13:11–32).

The son of King Jeroboam died, the kingdom was wrenched from Jeroboam's family, and all his male children were slain, all because he led Israel into idolatry (First Kings 14:1–20).

The above examples comprise a small sample of the recorded judgments of God meted out on individuals *in this life*.

The majority of this work will focus on the larger theme of God judging nations.

God Judges Nations—*In This Life*

Sadly, many Christians doubt that God judges nations in their own times. They believe that God judges *individuals in eternity*. Some believe that God judges *individuals in this life*, but the concept of God judging entire *nations in this life* is foreign to them.

However, the Scriptures are replete with evidence that God is the Judge of nations in the present tense:

O LORD God, to whom vengeance belongs—O God, to whom vengeance belongs, shine forth! Rise up, O

Judge of the earth; render punishment to the proud. (Psalm 94:1–2 NKJV)

Arise, O God, *judge the earth*; for to Thee belong *all the nations*! (Psalm 82:8)

For dominion belongs to the LORD, and He rules over the nations. (Psalm 22:28)

I will gather all the nations and bring them down to the valley of Jehosh'aphat, and I will enter into judgment with them there. (Joel 3:2)

The LORD shall judge the peoples; judge me, O LORD, according to my righteousness, and according to my integrity within me. Oh, let the wickedness of the wicked come to an end, but establish the just; for the righteous God tests the hearts and minds. My defense is of God, who saves the upright in heart. *God is a just judge, and God is angry with the wicked every day.* (Psalm 7:8–11 NKJV)

But the LORD shall endure forever; He has prepared His throne for judgment. He shall judge the world in righteousness, and He shall administer judgment for the peoples in uprightness. The LORD also will be a refuge for the oppressed, a refuge in times of trouble. And those who know Your name will put their trust in You; for You, LORD, have not forsaken those who seek You.... When He avenges blood, He remembers them; He does not forget the cry of the humble.... The LORD is known by the judgment He executes; the wicked is snared in the work of his own hands.... Arise, O LORD, do not let man prevail; *let the nations be judged in Your sight. Put them in fear, O LORD, that the nations may know themselves to be but men.* (Psalm 9:7–20 NKJV)

The Canaanites and the Jews

The promised land given to the Jews—a land flowing with milk and honey—was the prior possession of pagan Canaanite nations. Those nations offended God so severely by their sins that He obliterated them, taking their land from them.

After a lengthy, specific list of the sins the Canaanite nations committed (a list of sins to be studied later), God said to the Israelites:

> Do not defile yourselves in any of these ways, for by all these practices *the nations I am casting out* before you have defiled themselves. Thus the land became defiled; and *I punished it for its iniquity, and the land vomited out its inhabitants.* (Leviticus 18:24–25 NRSV)

God declared to Israel that the pagan nations that had held the promised land forfeited the land because of their sins:

> You shall keep all My statutes and all My ordinances, and observe them, so that the land to which I bring you to settle in may not vomit you out. You shall not follow the practices of the nation that I am driving out before you. *Because they did all these things, I abhorred them.* But I have said to you: You shall inherit their land, and I will give it to you to possess, a land flowing with milk and honey. I am the LORD your God; I have separated you from the peoples. (Leviticus 20:22–24 NRSV)

Sadly, the Israelites fell into gross sin over and over. So again and again, the Lord sent judgment upon them. Here is one illustration from the book of Judges:

> The people of Israel did what was evil in the sight of the LORD; *and the LORD gave them into the hand of Mid'ian seven years.* And the hand of Mid'ian prevailed over Israel; and because of Mid'ian the people of Israel made for themselves the dens which are in the mountains, and the caves and the strongholds. For whenever the Israelites put in seed the Mid'ianites and the Amal'ekites and the people of the East would come up and attack them; they would encamp against them and destroy the produce of the land, as far

as the neighborhood of Gaza, and leave no sustenance in Israel, and no sheep or ox or ass. For they would come up with their cattle and their tents, coming like locusts for number; both they and their camels could not be counted; so that they wasted the land as they came in. (Judges 6:1–5)

The Old Testament and the New Testament Have One Voice

All of the passages quoted thus far regarding judgment on individuals and nations are from the Old Testament. That is because most of these principles are found in the Old Testament. However, the Old Testament is the Word of God just as much as the New Testament.

Some Christian preachers and teachers abandon or even decry passages of judgment from the Old Testament, claiming that because Christians are "not under law but under grace" (Romans 6:14), if a commandment or a promise or a threat comes from the Law and is *not* in the New Testament, it can be ignored. This error—or better put, this heresy—is known in theological studies as *antinomianism*—literally "anti-law" or "against the law" of God.

Being anti-law, or antinomian, is, in short, the heretical belief that Christians are not bound to any of the elements of the five books of the Law of Moses (the Pentateuch), the Ten Commandments, or the prophetic books, because those are not the New Covenant. By extension, this belief means that the Scriptural threats and warnings are not valid for today.

If the antinomians are right, nations need never fear the judgments of God, such as the sword, famine, and plague, because they are "not under law," and the Old Testament has little or no bearing on how God governs and judges this world in the age of grace brought to us by the death of Jesus Christ.

If God is no longer the "Supreme Judge of the World" (as America's founders called Him), the institutionalized crimes committed against God—the national sins that cry to heaven—will *not* lead to a national chastisement.

While correcting the error and heresy of antinomianism is not the main purpose of this book, antinomianism is a fallacy that must be confronted. Why? Because the fruit of antinomianism has poisoned so many Christians. Millions of Christians have no godly fear for the danger that present-day abominations bring on a nation. They have little or no motivation to rid the nation of these institutional sins and crimes—crimes that could lead to calamity, destruction, and unthinkable heartache from the judgment of God.

Jesus Said: "I Did Not Come to Destroy the Law"

Certain parts of the Law are clearly no longer practiced. Lambs are not sacrificed as sin offerings because the Lamb of God (Christ) has been slain for sin once and for all.

There are "types and shadows" in the Levitical system that have been fulfilled in Christ. For example, the Levitical priesthood no longer exists to sacrifice animals at the temple or to offer grain offerings, etc., "since then we have a great High Priest who has passed through the heavens, Jesus, the Son of God" (Hebrews 4:14). "He has no need, like those high priests, to offer sacrifices daily, first for His own sins and then for those of the people, since He did this once for all when He offered up Himself" (Hebrews 7:27 ESV). Likewise, certain dietary prohibitions and Sabbath regulations are no longer binding (See Colossians 2:11–23; Romans 14:14–23; Hebrews 9).

These alterations, however, in no way mean that mankind can ignore, abandon, or disobey the entire Law of God and ignore the warnings of judgment that are repeated throughout the Law and the Prophets. To do so is folly of the highest order and is not true Christianity.

Consider these two Scriptures from the mouth of Jesus to show the folly of antinomianism:

Think not that I have come to abolish the law and the prophets; I have come not to abolish them but to fulfill them. For truly, I say to you, till heaven and earth pass away, not an iota, not a dot, will pass from the law until all is accomplished. Whoever then relaxes one of the least of these commandments and teaches men so, shall be called least in the kingdom of heaven; but he who does them and teaches them shall be called great in the kingdom of heaven. (Matthew 5:17–19)

But when the Pharisees heard that He had silenced the Sad'ducees, they came together. And one of them, a lawyer, asked Him a question, to test Him. "Teacher, which is the great commandment in the law?" And He said to him, "You shall love the Lord your God with all your heart, and with all your soul, and with all your mind. This is the great and first commandment. And a second is like it, You shall love your neighbor as yourself. On these two commandments depend all the law and the prophets." (Matthew 22:34–40)

Another version translates it thus: "The whole of the Law and the Prophets *is summed up* in these two Commandments" (v. 40 WNT).

The Lord was not *abolishing the Law* in His statements, but rather, He was *summarizing the Law*. To understand how one is to love God and one's neighbor, one must know the Law of God, *not dismiss it*.

As the Apostle Paul wrote: "Do we then overthrow the law by this faith? By no means! On the contrary, we uphold the law" (Romans 3:31).

Those who insist that Jesus, the Lamb of God, would never execute judgments in this life are sadly mistaken. Consider the scene of the last judgment painted by Michelangelo in the Sistine Chapel. What does it picture? The image of Christ sending the damned into the lake of fire, as the Scriptures teach He will. If the Lord Jesus will condemn souls who reject Him to eternal punishment, why would He not chasten men and nations with temporal punishment—*a chastisement in this life that might save them in the next life?*

Has God's Character Changed?

God is One God, eternally coexistent in Three Persons: the Father, the Son, and the Holy Spirit. He is "the same yesterday and today and for ever" (Hebrews 13:8). There is "no variableness, neither shadow of turning" in Him (James 1:17 KJV). This means, among many other points of theology, that *God the Son* was present and involved, for example, in the destruction of Sodom and Gomorrah. *God the Son* was present and involved in sending the plagues on the Egyptians. *God the Son* was present and involved in the destruction of Solomon's Temple and Jerusalem. He was present sending plagues on His chosen people for their crimes against Him and against innocent blood.

God the Son was also present and involved in the mercy promised to Adam and Eve, the salvation of Noah and his family, the healing waters of Meribah, the healing of King Hezekiah, the restoration of the Jews to Jerusalem, and the rebuilding of the temple after the Babylonian captivity.

In other words, judgment and mercy, plagues and healings, blessings and chastisements were exercised by the Blessed Trinity before God the Son appeared as the Word made flesh.

Yes, the incarnation altered heaven because now a man—a God-man—sits on the throne of heaven. Jesus became man and "was in all points tempted as we are, yet without sin" (Hebrews 4:15 NKJV). He suffered mental anguish and physical pain. He experienced being human. But His divine attributes of justice and mercy did not change.

The temptation of some Christians is to believe God transformed in character after the incarnation. They base their faith on the notion that the "God of the Old Testament" was a vengeful God full of wrath, and the "God of the New Testament" is a merciful God full of love. In the Old Testament, God had rigid rules and punishments; in the New Testament, He softens the rules and never or seldom punishes anyone. This view of God is simply not borne out in Sacred Scripture.

Yes, the love of God was displayed in Christ when He bore the sins of the world in His Own body on Calvary's tree. Clearly, the punishment He bore means that eternal salvation was purchased for sinners by His shed blood. The redemption offered to mankind is His gift to undeserving rebels. But to assert that He is no longer the divine and ultimate Judge *in time and eternity* is to suggest that *He has changed*—that He has given up using His authority to judge individuals and nations in this world, as well as judge immortal souls. This is Biblically untenable.

God is the same gracious God, both Priest and Sacrifice—and Judge. In the Old Testament, God says:

> The LORD is a jealous and avenging God;
> the LORD is avenging and wrathful;
> the LORD takes vengeance on His adversaries
> and keeps wrath for His enemies. (Nahum 1:2 ESV)

In the New Testament, God says:

> Beloved, never avenge yourselves, but leave it to the wrath of God; for it is written, "Vengeance is Mine, I will repay, says the Lord." (Romans 12:19)

New Testament Examples

What follow are New Testament references to prove that God still exercises His authority as Judge in the here and now, both for individuals and nations.

When Ananias and Sapphira lied to the Holy Spirit, they were struck dead in the presence of the Apostle Peter and the Christians who were with him (see Acts 5:1–11).

When Herod Agrippa was hailed as a god, the True God sent an angel to smite him with worms, and he died:

On an appointed day Herod put on his royal robes, took his seat upon the throne, and made an oration to them. And the people shouted, "The voice of a god, and not of man!" Immediately an angel of the Lord smote him, because he did not give God the glory; and he was eaten by worms and died. (Acts 12:21–23)

The book of Acts records the Apostle Paul, operating in the authority God gave him, pronouncing the judgment of blindness on a false prophet:

When they had gone through the whole island as far as Paphos, they came upon a certain magician, a Jewish false prophet, named Bar-Jesus. He was with the proconsul, Sergius Paulus, a man of intelligence, who summoned Barnabas and Saul and sought to hear the word of God. But El'ymas the magician (for that is the meaning of his name) withstood them, seeking to turn away the proconsul from the faith. But Saul, who is also called Paul, filled with the Holy Spirit, looked intently at him and said, "You son of the devil, you enemy of all righteousness, full of all deceit and villainy, will you not stop making crooked the straight paths of the Lord? And now, behold, the hand of the Lord is upon you, and you shall be blind and unable to see the sun for a time." Immediately mist and darkness fell upon him and he went about seeking people to lead him by the hand. Then the proconsul believed, when he saw what had occurred, for he was astonished at the teaching of the Lord. (Acts 13:6–12)

Christ Himself, as recorded in the Revelation of St. John, issues judgments that echo the prophets of the Old Testament:

Nevertheless I have a few things against you, because you allow that woman Jezebel, who calls herself a prophetess, to teach and seduce My servants to commit sexual immorality and eat things sacrificed to idols. And I gave her time to repent of her sexual immorality, and she did not repent.

Indeed I will cast her into a sickbed, and those who commit adultery with her into great tribulation, unless they repent of their deeds. I will kill her children [or followers] with death, and all the churches shall know that I am He who searches the minds and hearts. And *I will give to each one of you according to your works.* (Revelation 2:20–23 NKJV)

The Holman Christian Standard Bible translates verse 23: "I will kill her children with the plague." The New English Translation Bible translates it: "Furthermore, I will strike her followers with a deadly disease."

What follows is another passage from Revelation where Christ is speaking in the first person, declaring that God will send plagues:

I Jesus have sent Mine angel to testify unto you these things in the churches. I am the root and the offspring of David, and the bright and morning star. And the Spirit and the bride say, Come. And let him that heareth say, Come. And let him that is athirst come. And whosoever will, let him take the water of life freely. For I testify unto every man that heareth the words of the prophecy of this book, If any man shall add unto these things, *God shall add unto him the plagues that are written in this book.* (Revelation 22:16–18 KJV)

Other passages in the book of Revelation show God judging nations here and now. For example:

From His mouth issues a sharp sword with which to smite the nations, and He will rule them with a rod of iron; He will tread the wine press of the fury of the wrath of God the Almighty. On His robe and on His thigh He has a name inscribed, King of kings and Lord of lords. (Revelation 19:15–16)

The following passage in Hebrews references Deuteronomy 32:31–38 and Nahum 1:2. The passages in Deuteronomy and Nahum both refer to God judging nations here and now:

For we know Him who said, *"Vengeance is Mine, I will repay,"* says the Lord. And again, *"The LORD will judge His people."* It is a fearful thing to fall into the hands of the living God. (Hebrews 10:30–31 NKJV)

Any nation is in grave danger when this element of God's nature is avoided or forgotten. "There is no fear of God before their eyes" (Roman 3:18; see also Psalm 36:1).

Psalm 2 and Psalm 110 are both Messianic psalms. They hold a critical place in understanding Christ's rule and authority, and both psalms teach that Christ judges nations now. Moreover, Psalm 2 and Psalm 110 are quoted or alluded to over a dozen times in the New Testament. Psalm 110:1 is the most frequently quoted Old Testament verse in the New Testament, quoted in full or in part over ten times:

The LORD says to my Lord:
"Sit at My right hand,
till I make Your enemies Your footstool." (Psalm 110:1)

This level of repetition, inspired by the Holy Spirit, testifies to the human race that the rule of Christ *in this world now* is a central dogma of Christianity.

God Is Love... And a Consuming Fire

Before proceeding to the punishments delineated in Sacred Scripture that God uses to judge nations, as well as facing Scriptural reasons why God may judge, one more aspect of the nature of God must be addressed.

The truth about God's judgment is for Christians of every Trinitarian tradition or denomination. Whatever tradition or denomination or independent church one belongs to, *the Bible* teaches that God is a jealous God; *the Bible* declares that God is the Judge of nations; *the Bible* warns that God will send specific judgments—fear, plagues, famines, economic calamity, the sword—and a long list of other woes when a nation turns its back on Him and spurns His laws.

It is the Bible—the Old and New Testaments—that teaches *there are sins that cry to God for vengeance.*

When a national culture disintegrates, what the faithful hold sacred is mocked and vilified. Good is called evil, evil is called good (see Isaiah 5:20), and those Christians who hold to and promote God's laws are viewed as the villains and the enemy.

Sadly, clergy and laity from every Christian denomination often shrink into the shadows at these times. In order to justify inaction, silence, or retreat, many "teachers" of the Word of God provide "spiritual cover" for their inaction and cowardice. They quote Bible passages that seem to vindicate flight from battle and surrender to evil and that falsely state that God would never judge a nation for its accumulated crimes.

Many clergy, leaders and teachers, messengers, and fundraisers focus on the more pleasant aspects of God's character and nature. They ignore or abandon other aspects of His nature. For example:

Most Christians have probably heard sermons based on the truth that "God is Love" (First John 4:16).

Most Christians have probably heard sermons on the truth that "God is light" (First John 1:5).

Many have heard sermons on the truth that "God is Spirit" (John 4:24).

But how many have heard sermons on the truth that *"God is a consuming fire"* (Deuteronomy 4:24; Hebrews 12:29)?

The context of this passage is Moses warning the children of Israel that God is a consuming fire—a jealous God—who will judge them in their land if they forsake Him and His commands:

> Be careful not to forget the covenant of the LORD your God that He made with you; do not make for yourselves an idol in the form of anything the LORD your God has forbidden. *For the LORD your God is a consuming fire, a jealous God.*

After you have had children and grandchildren and have lived in the land a long time—if you then become corrupt and make any kind of idol, doing evil in the eyes of the LORD your God and arousing His anger, I call the heavens and the earth as witnesses against you this day that *you will quickly perish from the land that you are crossing the Jordan to possess. You will not live there long but will certainly be destroyed.* (Deuteronomy 4:23–26 NIV)

Very few Christians have heard sermons from the passage, "God is a consuming fire." Even fewer have been formed or discipled, catechized or trained to remember simultaneously that "God is Love" *and* "a jealous God" *and* "a consuming fire." Believers happily talk of the love of God, and they foolishly forget the fear of God.

American and European theologians are inclined to create a God who is compatible with modern culture—a God who is never offended and rarely offends. He seldom demands, rarely condemns, and always forgives, because "God is Love."

Whether Catholic or Protestant, Evangelical or Orthodox, the overwhelming testimony of clergy and laypeople, TV and radio broadcast networks, and superstar broadcasters belies the fact that it is much more attractive to "tickle itching ears," attending only to the love and mercy of God.

God Chastens Those He Loves

Nevertheless, in the "God-is-Love" paradigm, God disciplines and chastens those He loves.

"My son, do not make light of the Lord's discipline,
and do not lose heart when He rebukes you,
because *the Lord disciplines the one He loves,*
and He *chastens everyone He accepts as His son.*"
Endure hardship as discipline; God is treating you as His children. For what children are not disciplined by their father? If you are not disciplined—and everyone undergoes

discipline—then you are not legitimate, not true sons and daughters at all. Moreover, we have all had human fathers who disciplined us and we respected them for it. How much more should we submit to the Father of spirits and live! They disciplined us for a little while as they thought best; *but God disciplines us for our good, in order that we may share in His holiness. No discipline seems pleasant* at the time, but painful. Later on, however, *it produces a harvest of righteousness* and peace for those who have been trained by it. (Hebrews 12:5–11 NIV)

The chastenings God delivers are not restrained or defined by His errant children, His arrogant enemies, or confused, misguided, or deceived theologians who dismiss that God is a "consuming fire."

He is God, and He is Judge. And He will pour out His judgments on a rebellious nation to get its attention, purge evil from its midst, and hopefully, produce a harvest of righteousness in the national life.

The Israelites groaned in their slavery and cried out, and their cry for help because of their slavery went up to God. God heard their groaning... The LORD said, "I have indeed seen the misery of My people in Egypt. I have heard them crying out because of their slave drivers, and I am concerned about their suffering. So I have come down to rescue them from the hand of the Egyptians....

"Say therefore to the people of Israel, 'I am the LORD, and I will bring you out from under the burdens of the Egyptians, and I will deliver you from their bondage, and I will redeem you with an outstretched arm and WITH GREAT ACTS OF JUDGMENT.'"

Exodus 2:23–24, 3:7–8 NIV, 6:6 RSVCE, 1400 B.C.

The fact is, the labour of slaves comes so cheap to the avaricious usurpers.... They are so happy to keep in ignorance and degradation, and to receive the homage and the labour of the slaves, they forget that God rules in the armies of heaven and among the inhabitants of the earth, having His ears continually open to the cries, tears, and groans of His oppressed people; and being a just and holy Being will at one day appear fully in behalf of the oppressed.... If God gives you peace and tranquillity, and suffers you thus to go on afflicting us, and our children, who have never given you the least provocation—would He be to us a God of justice?

David Walker, *Walker's Appeal, in Four Articles,* A.D. 1829

Fondly do we hope—fervently do we pray—that this mighty scourge of war may speedily pass away. Yet, if God wills that it continue, until all the wealth piled by the bond-man's two hundred and fifty years of unrequited toil shall be sunk, and until every drop of blood drawn with the lash, shall be paid by another drawn with the sword, as was said three thousand years ago, so still it must be said, "the judgments of the LORD, are true and righteous altogether."

Abraham Lincoln, "Second Inaugural Address," A.D. 1865

3

Déjà Vu:
Learning from the Past

Nations Reap What Nations Sow

A principle—actually, a law—repeated throughout Scripture is that of *sowing* and *reaping*. The law of sowing and reaping is engrained in the heart of man.

Daily conversation is full of the echoes of the principle of sowing and reaping:

"What goes around comes around."

"As you give, you receive."

"His actions came back to haunt him."

"There will be hell to pay for that."

"He got what was coming to him."

"His bill was due."

"We have sown the wind and reaped the whirlwind."

And of course, a more crass colloquial phrase:

"*Karma is a b*tch.*"

All these sayings communicate the notion that actions have consequences, and those consequences are waiting. Lurking... invariably...inevitably...coming.

Beyond that, they echo the idea that the principle of sowing and reaping is a cosmic law, established by the Almighty. The Scripture says: "Do not be deceived; *God is not mocked*, for whatever a man sows, that he will also reap" (Galatians 6:7).

The principle of sowing and reaping applies to nations as well as individuals. As the Biblical proverb declares:

> Justice exalteth a nation: but sin maketh nations miserable. (Proverbs 14:34 DRB)

To believe that men and nations can commit crimes against humanity and go unpunished *is to mock God*. To believe that the law of sowing and reaping does not exist is to deceive oneself and to mock God at the same time. One does not sow a seed of corn and expect to harvest a motorcycle, nor does a man commit gross acts of evil and expect to reap a harvest of peace, joy, and blessings.

Sacred Scripture and history record times that God brought great suffering and hardship, misery, and death to chasten individuals and nations who oppressed the innocent. One well-known example is Egypt.

Slavery in Egypt

The Jews held in bondage by the Egyptians provide an illustrious example of God hearing the cry of the oppressed and of the Egyptians reaping what they sowed. God heard the cry of the Israelites, and He came with an outstretched hand and mighty arm to deliver them. After many warnings to Pharaoh, who refused to repent and let the Jews go free, God broke the back of Egypt.

> Then the LORD said, "I have seen the affliction of My people who are in Egypt, and have heard their cry because of their taskmasters; I know their sufferings, and I have come down to deliver them out of the hand of the Egyptians." (Exodus 3:7–8)

> Say therefore to the people of Israel, "I am the LORD, and I will bring you out from under the burdens of the Egyptians,

and I will deliver you from their bondage, and I will redeem you with an outstretched arm and with *great acts of judgment.*" (Exodus 6:6)

O great and mighty God whose name is the LORD of hosts, great in counsel and mighty in deed; whose eyes are open to all the ways of men, *rewarding every man according to his ways and according to the fruit of his doings*; who hast shown signs and wonders in the land of Egypt, and to this day in Israel and among all mankind, and hast made thee a name, as at this day. Thou didst bring Thy people Israel out of the land of Egypt with signs and wonders, *with a strong hand and outstretched arm, and with great terror.* (Jeremiah 32:18–21)

The Egyptians sowed oppression and slavery. They reaped terror from the hand of God: ten plagues, including the death of all firstborn children. God sent them horror and sickness. He destroyed their economy, their military, their tranquility, and their families, all because God heard the cry of His suffering people. Egypt reaped what it sowed.

Judgment on America

David Walker Predicted the Civil War in 1829

With terrifying precision, David Walker, a young, highly educated black man in his thirties living as a free man in Boston, prophesied the coming of the Civil War. In 1829, Walker delivered a devastating condemnation of Christians for their part in slavery in his book, *Walker's Appeal.* He not only prophesied the coming of the Civil War thirty years before it came, he rightly warned over and over that many American Christians who participated in that demonic system of slavery would pay with their lives for their treachery against God's Law and their cruel condemnation of innocent men, women, and children. Here is an excerpt from his book:

> They tell us of the Israelites in Egypt, the Helots in Sparta, and of the Roman Slaves, which last were made

up from almost every nation under heaven, whose sufferings under those ancient and heathen nations, were, in comparison with ours, under this enlightened and Christian nation, no more than a cypher—or, in other words, those heathen nations of antiquity had but little more among them than the name and form of slavery; while wretchedness and endless miseries were reserved, apparently in a phial [a vial], to be poured out upon our fathers, ourselves, and our children, by *Christian* Americans!…

For although the destruction of the oppressors God may not effect by the oppressed, *yet the Lord our God will bring other destructions upon them—for not unfrequently, will He cause them to rise up one against another, to be split and divided, and to oppress each other, and sometimes to open hostilities with sword in hand.* Some may ask, what is the matter with this united and happy people?—Some say it is the cause of political usurpers, tyrants, oppressors, &c. But has not the Lord an oppressed and suffering people among them? Does the Lord condescend to hear their cries and see their tears in consequence of oppression? Will He let the oppressors rest comfortably and happy always? *Will He not cause the very children of the oppressors to rise up against them, and oftimes put them to death?* *"God works in many ways His wonders to perform."*[1]

David Walker was born in approximately 1797 in Wilmington, North Carolina. His father was a slave. His mother was a free woman—hence, he inherited his freedom through her. He lived in Wilmington until approximately 1815. The horror of slavery and the belligerent treatment he witnessed and experienced drove him to leave his home and family.

He settled in Boston and opened a used-clothing store. For the remainder of his life, he wrote, spoke, and agitated for the

---

1. David Walker, *Walker's Appeal, in Four Articles* (Boston: David Walker, 1830; repr., Bedford, MA: Applewood Books, 2008), 3, 5–6, emphasis added.

immediate, unconditional release of all slaves. He was a true abolitionist.

As his book, *Walker's Appeal,* proves, Walker was extremely well read and articulate. He and his book were roundly condemned in all slave states, *as well as being condemned by anti-slavery white folk in the North.* The reason he was condemned in all quarters is that part of his message was that slaves had the God-given right to defend themselves with force and to use force to secure their freedom.

A price was put on his head, and in 1830, he was found dead at the age of thirty-three. Some said he was poisoned, and others said he succumbed to tuberculosis. The truth will not be known until the next life.

Imagine meeting and hearing this young, fiery black man in 1829. Imagine him declaring that God Almighty was hearing the cries of the oppressed slaves—the cry of their innocent blood—and that this cry would result in war, massive bloodshed, and unimaginable loss of life and wealth. To many hearers and readers, his words would have seemed like the ravings of a frustrated, angry (justly so) young man.

But David Walker knew that Almighty God—the Just Judge—was seated on His throne in His heaven, hearing the cries of the oppressed and the cry of innocent blood—hearing the despairing prayers of raped women, kidnapped children, and murdered men.

God was also hearing the sermons of thousands of preachers and pastors who were using His Holy Word to justify the crime of kidnapping and the abomination of American slavery.

One must remember that American slavery was founded on "man-stealing," which is a capital offense in the Law of God.

> Kidnappers must be put to death, whether they are caught in possession of their victims or have already sold them as slaves. (Exodus 21:16 NLT)

Innocent people were kidnapped, chained, sold, taken across the ocean in horrific, hellish ships, and sold again like cattle. Let none deceive—American slavery was not based on Biblical justice in any fashion. It was a "sin that cried for vengeance."

God gave America space to repent—from the very dawn of the republic until the first shot at Fort Sumter—all the time whetting His sword of judgment to fall on America.

His judgment orchestrated the foolish and the evil, the fearful and the brave, the ignorant and the arrogant. His hand was behind the missteps of politics—the victory of Abraham Lincoln in the Republican primary (after at least three rounds of voting at the 1860 convention).

God used the insolence and arrogance of the Southern states and the unbending resolve of a new president determined to save the Union—a president fully prepared to leave the institution of slavery untouched if that's what it took to save the Union.

The Divine Hand moved the players into place, and the wild prophetic utterance of David Walker—the defiant, Christian, free young black man—leapt off the pages of his book and onto the blood-drenched fields of Antietam, Fredericksburg, Bull Run, and dozens of others, culminating with Gettysburg, with over fifty thousand casualties in that one battle.

One can see the dead, the dying, the maimed, and the wounded. History records the loss of wealth—house after house burned, plantations destroyed, Atlanta burned, the confederate dollar going from usable cash to having no value at all.

The Lord heard the cry of the slaves. He heard the cry of their blood that had been shed, and He brought devastation and death to the United States because of this national sin. America sowed kidnapping, rape, murder, brutality, and generational slavery. America reaped the Civil War, with five hundred thousand dead and wounded on both sides and the devastation of Southern wealth and cities.

Abraham Lincoln—Prophesying the Truth

In this light, read the words of President Lincoln, who originally had no intention of ending slavery, slowly realizing that this horror was an edict of judgment from the hand of God for the crime of American slavery:

> If God now wills the removal of a great wrong [slavery], and wills also that we of the North, as well as you of the South, shall pay fairly for our complicity in that wrong, impartial history will find therein new cause to attest and revere the justice and goodness of God.[2]

In his Second Inaugural Address, President Lincoln stated—prophesied, to be more precise—that the Civil War was the judgment of Almighty God against the entire nation—a judgment that came on Christians in the North and the South for participating in and tolerating the abomination of American slavery:

> Both read the same Bible, and pray to the same God; and each invokes His aid against the other. It may seem strange that any men should dare to ask a just God's assistance in wringing their bread from the sweat of other men's faces; but let us judge not that we be not judged. The prayers of both could not be answered; that of neither has been answered fully. *The Almighty has His own purposes. . . . If God wills that it continue, until all the wealth piled by the bond-man's two hundred and fifty years of unrequited toil shall be sunk, and until every drop of blood drawn with the lash, shall be paid by another drawn with the sword, as was said three thousand years ago, so still it must be said, "the judgments of the LORD, are true and righteous altogether."*[3]

---

2. Letter from Abraham Lincoln to Albert G. Hodges, April 4, 1864.

3. Abraham Lincoln, "Second Inaugural Address," March 4, 1865, *The Avalon Project* at Yale Law School, avalon.law.yale.edu/19th_century/lincoln2.asp.

Scripture clearly shows that there was a direct connection between the evil of the Egyptians holding the Israelites as slaves and God judging Egypt. It is clearly spelled out. The Scriptures teach that slavery is one of the sins that cries to God for vengeance (see Exodus chapters 2 and 3).

Sadly, America did not repent in time to avert the Civil War and the horrors that flowed from it. The abominable crime of kidnapping and slavery that was allowed by Christians in the North and practiced by Christians in the South led to the judgment of God.

When one looks at the Civil War, one sees the hand of God—the judgment of God—on a nation that betrayed God and man with the abominable crime of slavery. And hopefully, in the fear of God, one can examine America, Canada, and European nations today and see that they are committing crimes and sins as nations *that exceed the crime of American and European slavery.*

It is to be hoped that the Christian community in America and Europe sees the storms approaching, like David Walker saw the storm of the Civil War approaching in America, and that those who love and fear God give Him a reason to show mercy in the midst of judgment.

The slaves in America suffered generations of unrequited toil before the nation reaped the Civil War. The Jews endured four hundred years of slavery before the Egyptians reaped the ten plagues and suffered the devastation of their country. In Jerusalem, the Jews sowed centuries of rebellion and then finally reaped death by the sword, famine, and the plague, the destruction of Solomon's Temple, and the leveling of Jerusalem. Oftentimes, judgment is a long time in coming.

Perspective

The Jews were singularly chosen by God as a people to receive the Law of God through Moses and to bring forth the Savior of the world—our Lord Jesus Christ—through the lineage of David.

Yet, in spite of this glorious and unique calling, the Israelites betrayed God, worshipped idols, became entrenched in multiple perversions, and offered their children in sacrifice to demons.

Because of those sins, God brought years of terrifying punishment on the Israelites. In many ways, what the Jews suffered was even worse than what the Egyptians suffered. (This work will look in depth at those sins and punishments.)

Ponder this: is any nation higher, better, or even equal to ancient Israel—God's chosen people—through whom He gave us the Law and our Savior? If the nation of Israel, chosen and blessed by Almighty God, suffered unthinkable misery and sorrow under the judgment of God, how can any nation be so deluded as to believe itself exempt from similar judgments for their national sins?

Christians and pagans alike are warned by the Jews, warned by the Egyptians, and warned by the antebellum American South of the judgments that are coming. Woe unto those who are deaf to the lesson or oblivious to the threats.

This work will prove from Sacred Scripture that certain sins and crimes against God and man in the Americas and their European progenitors far exceed the evils of slavery. Worse still: modern sins rival—and even surpass—the crimes committed by ancient Israelites and pagan nations millennia ago—crimes that resulted in devastation and death for pagans and Jews alike.

Nations sow sins; God causes them to reap certain punishments. There are times when a nation will reap what it has sown, *no matter how many individuals pray and beg for forgiveness.* A nation can reach a threshold where judgment is inevitable because that nation, in its laws and institutions, has embraced evil and oppression.

This work will show that North America and Europe are in grave danger—that the Almighty is again whetting His sword of judgment.

Woe to those who call evil good
and good evil,
who put darkness for light
and light for darkness,
who put bitter for sweet
and sweet for bitter!
Woe to those who are wise in their own eyes,
and shrewd in their own sight!
Woe to those who are heroes at drinking wine,
and valiant men in mixing strong drink,
who acquit the guilty for a bribe,
and deprive the innocent of his right!

Isaiah 5:20–23

The look on their faces testifies against them;
they parade their sin like Sodom;
they do not hide it.
Woe to them!
They have brought disaster upon themselves.

Isaiah 3:9 NIV

I charge you in the presence of God and of Christ Jesus who is to judge the living and the dead, and by His appearing and His Kingdom: preach the word, be urgent in season and out of season, convince, rebuke, and exhort, be unfailing in patience and in teaching. For the time is coming when people will not endure sound teaching, but having itching ears they will accumulate for themselves teachers to suit their own likings, and will turn away from listening to the truth and wander into myths.

Second Timothy 4:1–4

4

BEING "HANDED OVER"—
THE BEGINNING OF SORROWS

The sinister lights of the pagan past cast an eerie shadow over the present. History has witnessed eras when the human race fell into a chasm of evil. There comes a point when nations cross into uncharted ethical and political waters.

One can know the future from seeing the past. One can predict where one is headed by seeing from whence one has come. In his letter to the Romans, St. Paul the Apostle writes of rebels—strident pagans of the lowest order who knowingly rebel against the Maker of heaven and earth. These arrogant monsters of iniquity know "the truth of God." They know His laws and make open, repeated decisions to defy His Divine Majesty and break His laws. These men and nations endure specific punishments as a result of their defiance—visible, quantifiable catastrophes.

But before the sword, famine, and plague fell upon these rebels, a different judgment was poured on them—a judgment in their minds and souls—a corruption of thought so malignant that it took from them their ethical and familial sense of duty. It removed common decency and honor.

Namely, *they were handed over*—not to a foreign power (that came later) or to the worst of violence or the ravages of famine and plague (that also came later). Rather, they were handed over to the violence of the soul. Their minds were ravaged and plagued by the fruit of their own evils, and that fruit went to seed, growing darker and more plentiful crops of abominations. They were handed over to a famine of decency and kindness, of mercy, faith, and trust.

Their very ability to think and perceive with "light" was taken from them, as their foolish minds were darkened. They craved debauchery and feasted on it until they vomited the refuse they ingested, and finally, the very land on which they committed their crimes *vomited them out.*

St. Paul makes it clear that this handing over of evildoers to the fruits of their ways *is the judgment of God Himself.* Note the progression of this malady of mind: *God Himself hands them over to their own evil thoughts and vile imaginations.* Note also *why* He does it:

> The wrath of God is indeed being revealed from heaven against every impiety and wickedness of *those who suppress the truth by their wickedness.* For what can be known about God is evident to them, because God made it evident to them. Ever since the creation of the world, His invisible attributes of eternal power and divinity have been able to be understood and perceived in what He has made. As a result, they have no excuse; for although they knew God they did not accord Him glory as God or give Him thanks. Instead, they *became vain in their reasoning, and their senseless minds were darkened. While claiming to be wise, they became fools* and exchanged the glory of the immortal God for the likeness of an image of mortal man or of birds or of four-legged animals or of snakes.
>
> *Therefore, God handed them over* to impurity through the lusts of their hearts for the mutual degradation of their bodies. *They exchanged the truth of God for a lie* and revered and worshiped the creature rather than the Creator, who is blessed forever. Amen.

Therefore, God handed them over to degrading passions. Their females exchanged natural relations for unnatural, and the males likewise gave up natural relations with females and burned with lust for one another. Males did shameful things with males and thus received in their own persons the due penalty for their perversity.

And since they did not see fit to acknowledge God, *God handed them over to their undiscerning mind* to do what is improper. They are filled with every form of wickedness, evil, greed, and malice; full of envy, murder, rivalry, treachery, and spite. They are gossips and scandalmongers and they hate God. They are insolent, haughty, boastful, ingenious in their wickedness, and rebellious toward their parents. They are senseless, faithless, heartless, ruthless. ALTHOUGH THEY KNOW THE JUST DECREE OF GOD THAT ALL WHO PRACTICE SUCH THINGS DESERVE DEATH, THEY NOT ONLY DO THEM BUT GIVE APPROVAL TO THOSE WHO PRACTICE THEM. (Romans 1:18–32 NABRE)

This passage of Scripture pronounces a dreadful judgment. Evildoers love their sin so much that God hands them over to it.

Consider those in recent times who "suppress the truth by their wickedness." Consider those who are "vain in their reasoning." Consider those whose "senseless minds" are "darkened." Or consider those who claim "to be wise" but have become "fools." Consider those who "exchanged the truth of God for a lie."

They are all being handed over by God to an "undiscerning mind." They are filled with every form of wickedness, evil, greed, and malice. They are full of envy, murder, rivalry, treachery, and spite. They are gossips and scandalmongers. They love scandal. And for many of them, as Paul wrote, *they hate God.*

These enemies of truth who suppress the truth in ungodliness are senseless, faithless, heartless, and ruthless. And they have been handed over to an *undiscerning mind.*

The RSVCE translates "undiscerning mind" as "base mind." The NKJV translates it "debased mind." The Douay-Rheims version translates it "reprobate sense," and the Geneva Bible and the King James version translate it "reprobate mind."

Proof of their reprobate minds is seen in their debauched and wicked behavior. Furthermore, the speed of their degradation and the degradation of the cultures they pollute is seen in this: the deeds they commit and promote were unthinkable and unspeakable in generations past, but the reprobate now herald those deeds as normal and good, and anyone who opposes their godless agenda is the oppressor and villain. What is unthinkable and unspeakable today that will be normal and good in another generation? How can any thinking, logical person tell a young boy or girl that they can mutilate their genitals—chemically or surgically—and thereby change genders? How can they say with a brazen face that a woman can have a penis or that a man can have a baby? They say this *because they have been handed over.* The transgender lie is an assault from hell on the human race, especially the young.

What causes this trend? It happens in large part when religious, cultural, and political leaders have been handed over by God to a reprobate mind and lead their followers into an ethical hell—a City of Darkness that their debased minds construct against the City of God. Those leaders who are silent only serve to embolden the wicked and disembowel those who would stand and fight...*if only leaders emerged to lead them into battle.*

This itself is the judgment of God on a nation. Reprobates sweep away societal and ethical norms that are based in the Christian religion and Law of God. They then create new societal and ethical norms that are spawned from hell. The damage they do in time and eternity is beyond calculation.

Consider those who are given over to "degrading passions" and "the mutual degradation of their bodies." Just one example of this can be seen in popular American and European superhero comic books of the 2020s. What happens when Marvel and DC comics introduce a homosexual Captain America, a homosexual Green Lantern, a lesbian Wonder Woman, a homosexual Superman, and multiple new "heroes" that are transgender—all of which is geared to corrupting and seducing young people?

Millions of young people turn to Marvel or DC comic books—young boys and girls with their iPads or tablets or laptops or smart phones, lying in bed, secretly exploring the sexual lives of these depraved superheroes. What toll does this take on the young? How many are seduced into experimentation and temptation to dishonor their bodies because of comic heroes that glorify and lionize abominable perversions?

As alluded to earlier, media "stars" in formerly Christian nations encourage young boys and girls to mutilate their bodies chemically or surgically so that they can "change genders." This is a crime against humanity—an insidious evil that rivals the greatest perversions and crimes of all human history. Are they ashamed? No. As St. Paul said, they revel in their evil. Where and when will this spiral into an ethical abyss end? When will they be sated with hitherto unimaginable evil?

Can any Christian of any background doubt that this is the judgment of God on their depraved spirits and minds and that these crimes will end in the physical chastenings found in "the sword, famine, and plague"?

Sin has within it the seeds of its own punishment. As God said through Jeremiah:

> "Your wickedness will punish you; your backsliding will rebuke you. Consider then and realize how evil and bitter it is for you when you forsake the LORD your God and have no awe of Me," declares the Lord, the LORD Almighty. (Jeremiah 2:19 NIV)

As the following chapters will demonstrate, being handed over is just the beginning of sorrows. God has multiple hardships and sorrows at His disposal to chasten His people as well as the heathen. And He has laid out those judgments in specific detail.

The wicked flee when no one pursues.

Proverbs 28:1

Is a trumpet blown in a city,
And the people are not afraid?
Does evil befall a city,
Unless the LORD has done it?

Amos 3:6

I will mock when panic strikes you,
when panic strikes you like a storm,
and your calamity comes like a whirlwind,
when distress and anguish come upon you.

Proverbs 1:26–27

5

FEAR

Again and again, the Scriptures promise that the people of God can have peace and be free of fear. Here are a few beloved and better-known examples:

> Be strong and courageous. Do not be afraid or terrified because of them, for the LORD your God goes with you; He will never leave you nor forsake you. (Deuteronomy 31:6 NIV)

> Even though I walk through the valley of the shadow of death, I will fear no evil, for You are with me; Your rod and Your staff, they comfort me. (Psalm 23:4 ESV)

> The LORD is my light and my salvation—whom shall I fear? The LORD is the stronghold of my life—of whom shall I be afraid? (Psalm 27:1 NIV)

> The angel of the LORD encamps around those who fear Him, and He delivers them. (Psalm 34:7 NIV)

And perhaps the most beloved psalm about fear:

> He who dwells in the shelter of the Most High,
> who abides in the shadow of the Almighty,
> will say to the LORD, "My refuge and my fortress;
> my God, in whom I trust."

For He will deliver you from the snare of the fowler
and from the deadly pestilence;
He will cover you with His pinions,
and under His wings you will find refuge;
His faithfulness is a shield and buckler.
You will not fear the terror of the night,
nor the arrow that flies by day,
nor the pestilence that stalks in darkness,
nor the destruction that wastes at noonday.
(Psalm 91:1–6)

And lastly, from the Apostle Paul:

For God hath not given us the spirit of fear: but of power,
and of love, and of sobriety. (Second Timothy 1:7 DRB)

These passages are known and loved by billions of Christians across the world and provide confidence and peace. Many Christians hold fast to these Scriptures during turbulent times.

The Gospels record the words of Jesus during His earthly ministry. He repeatedly tells His disciples, "Do not be afraid."

Therefore do not worry about tomorrow, for tomorrow will worry about itself. Each day has enough trouble of its own. (Matthew 6:34 NIV)

Immediately He spoke to them and said, "Take courage! It is I. Don't be afraid." (Mark 6:50 NIV)

Jesus told him, "Don't be afraid; just believe." (Mark 5:36 NIV)

God Struck the Hearts of the Ungodly with the Fear of His People

Not only did God encourage His people to "fear not," He also promised the Jews that He would *strike fear* in the hearts of their enemies:

Rise up, take your journey, and go over the valley of the Arnon; behold, I have given into your hand Sihon the

Amorite, king of Heshbon, and his land; begin to take possession, and contend with him in battle. *This day I will begin to put the dread and fear of you upon the peoples that are under the whole heaven, who shall hear the report of you and shall tremble and be in anguish because of you.* (Deuteronomy 2:24–25)

And this:

Every place on which the sole of your foot treads shall be yours; your territory shall be from the wilderness and Lebanon and from the River, the river Euphra'tes, to the western sea. No man shall be able to stand against you; the LORD your God will lay the fear of you and the dread of you upon all the land that you shall tread, as He promised you. (Deuteronomy 11:24–25)

When King David won a great victory, God struck fear in the hearts of other nations:

So David did as God commanded him, and they struck down the Philistine army, all the way from Gibeon to Gezer. So David's fame spread throughout every land, *and the LORD made all the nations fear him.* (First Chronicles 14:16–17 NIV)

These passages and promises—and scores like them—give believers confidence in God's protection and boldness in His service.

But what about when God sends fear *in the hearts of His people* or *in the hearts of nations that previously claimed to honor Him?*

When Fear Is the Punishment for Disobedience

Fear as a judgment can be understood as the reversal of God's promise of peace. This notion may seem odd, especially since the Scriptures say so many times, "Fear not." Nevertheless, as a chastening, God can remove peace and replace it with fear.

Scripture teaches that Almighty God can and will send fear to a people as a punishment turning their backs on Him. God uses gripping fear or terror as a judgment against a sinner or a sinful nation. The same God who promises His people that they can live free of fear also warns them that He will *use fear* as a part of His punishments. For example:

> The LORD has mingled within her a spirit of confusion;
> and they have made Egypt stagger in all her doings
> as a drunken man staggers in his vomit.
> And there will be nothing for Egypt
> which head or tail, palm branch or reed, may do.
> *In that day the Egyptians will be like women,*
> *and tremble with fear* before the hand
> which the LORD of hosts shakes over them.
> (Isaiah 19:14–16)

As seen in the following passage, fear is the result of disobedience to the commands of God:

> Because I have called and you refused to listen,
> have stretched out My hand and no one has heeded,
> and you have ignored all My counsel
> and would have none of My reproof,
> I also will laugh at your calamity;
> *I will mock when panic strikes you,*
> *when panic strikes you like a storm,*
> *and your calamity comes like a whirlwind,*
> *when distress and anguish come upon you.*
> (Proverbs 1:24–27)

Earlier, we looked at Deuteronomy 11:25. Now let us look at it in context and see the conditional nature of this promise:

> Every place on which the sole of your foot treads shall be yours; your territory shall be from the wilderness and Lebanon and from the River, the river Euphra'tes, to the western sea. No man shall be able to stand against you; *the LORD your God will lay the fear of you and the dread of you upon all the land that you shall tread, as He promised you.*

Behold, I set before you this day a blessing and a curse: the blessing, if you obey the commandments of the LORD your God, which I command you this day, *and the curse, if you do not obey the commandments of the LORD your God,* but turn aside from the way which I command you this day, to go after other gods which you have not known. (Deuteronomy 11:24–28)

The promise that God's people will prevail against their enemies and that their enemies will fear them is conditioned on God's people obeying God's commandments. But if His people do not obey Him, *He will send them fear as part of their chastening.*

But if you will not obey the voice of the LORD your God or be careful to do all His commandments and His statutes which I command you this day,…a people whom you do not know shall eat up the fruit of your ground and of all your labors; you shall be continually abused and crushed, *and driven mad by the sight that your eyes shall see.…*

Among those nations you shall find no ease, no resting place for the sole of your foot. *There the LORD will give you a trembling heart,* failing eyes, and a languishing spirit. *Your life shall hang in doubt before you; night and day you shall be in dread,* with no assurance of your life. *In the morning you shall say, "If only it were evening!" and at evening you shall say, "If only it were morning!"—because of the dread that your heart shall feel and the sights that your eyes shall see.* (Deuteronomy 28:15 RSVCE, 33–34, 65–67 NRSVCE)

These warnings were not idle threats from the Almighty. The Jews betrayed God and His Law, committing horrific sins and crimes. The stench of those evils rose to the heavens, and God brought the punishments on them that He had promised. Ezekiel preached these words from Babylon in the final days of Judah's treachery, just before all of Judah was taken and Jerusalem was destroyed:

Because the land is full of bloody crimes and the city is full of violence, I will bring the worst of the nations to take possession of their houses; I will put an end to their proud might, and their holy places shall be profaned. *When anguish comes, they will seek peace, but there shall be none.* Disaster comes upon disaster, *rumor follows rumor*; they seek a vision from the prophet, but the law perishes from the priest, and counsel from the elders. The king mourns, the prince is wrapped in despair, *and the hands of the people of the land are palsied by terror.* According to their way I will do to them, and according to their own judgments I will judge them; and they shall know that I am the LORD. (Ezekiel 7:23–27)

The prophets Jeremiah and Ezekiel were contemporaries. Ezekiel was prophesying from Babylon, Jeremiah from Jerusalem. In spite of their distance and the minimal communication these men could have had, Jeremiah's and Ezekiel's messages were eerily similar.

Both Jeremiah and Ezekiel were from Levitical priestly families, both men were trained in the Law of God, both were devout men of prayer, and both were delivering the message of judgment and doom on an unrepentant, rebellious nation. Those judgments were clearly spelled out in the Law of God.

Moses received the Law directly from Almighty God. Moses spoke with God as a man speaks with his friend (Exodus 33:11). The Law that God gave Moses was perfect, instructing the simple (Psalm 19). As we can see in Leviticus 26, Deuteronomy 28, and many other passages in the Pentateuch, Moses promised blessings from God if the Israelites obeyed God's commands, and judgments from God if the Israelites abandoned God and His Law. Jeremiah, Ezekiel, and many other prophets announced that God was making good on His promises—the promises of judgment.

During the ministry of the prophet Jeremiah, God announced through him that Jerusalem and Solomon's Temple would be destroyed. The book of Lamentations records the remorse, anguish, and fear that gripped God's people, echoing and living out the exact punishment we see threatened in Deuteronomy chapter 28:

Is it not from the mouth of the Most High
that both calamities and good things come?
Why should the living complain
when punished for their sins?
Let us examine our ways and test them,
and let us return to the LORD.
Let us lift up our hearts and our hands
to God in heaven, and say:
"We have sinned and rebelled
and You have not forgiven.
You have covered Yourself with anger and pursued us;
You have slain without pity.
You have covered Yourself with a cloud
so that no prayer can get through.
You have made us scum and refuse
among the nations.
All our enemies have opened their mouths
wide against us.
We have suffered terror and pitfalls,
ruin and destruction."
Streams of tears flow from my eyes
because my people are destroyed.
(Lamentations 3:38–48 NIV)

However, God also uses fear to draw His people back to Himself. The psalmist writes:

Some went down to the sea in ships,
doing business on the great waters;
they saw the deeds of the LORD,
His wondrous works in the deep.
For He commanded, and raised the stormy wind,
which lifted up the waves of the sea.

They mounted up to heaven, they went down to the
depths;
their courage melted away in their evil plight;
they reeled and staggered like drunken men,
and were at their wits' end.
Then they cried to the LORD in their trouble,
and He delivered them from their distress;
He made the storm be still,
and the waves of the sea were hushed.
Then they were glad because they had quiet,
and He brought them to their desired haven.
Let them thank the LORD for His steadfast love,
for His wonderful works to the sons of men!
(Psalm 107:23–31)

Coronavirus and Fear

While most people have never felt this crippling type of fear or
experienced this type of loss and grief from national calamity,
the seeds of crippling fear were planted and grew in millions of
hearts around the world with the COVID pandemic.

When people are afraid, their minds are prone to confusion, bad decisions, mistrust, and alienation. The first fruits of
fear were seen at the outset of the COVID pandemic as people hoarded toilet paper and food and other items. Many were
afraid to leave their homes. In some cities, neighbors "snitched"
on neighbors to the police. Nations that pride themselves in
freedom allowed multiple freedoms to be swept away because
of fear. The fear of the coronavirus quickly paved the way for
Americans, Canadians, and European nations to submit to an
unimaginable loss of civil liberties—and even oppression and
jail—without a shot being fired.

The assault on those liberties continued to grow like a poisonous weed. Fear of societal meltdown in some major cities—with
violence, looting, murder, hunger, disease, and more—gripped
the hearts of millions of people. That fear was palpable and

debilitating. Multitudes left the major cities, relocating to areas that were statistically and palpably safer.

The fear was not unfounded—the policies of many political leaders, supported by the media, in effect encouraged riots and looting. Moreover, the incessant degrading of law enforcement (because of a very few bad apples) emboldened criminal activity and inspired wanton criminal acts. This was arguably part of the "debased thinking" of the moment.

The Slow-Eating Cancer of Fear

The tidal wave of fear during the coronavirus years was in many ways without equal for America and Europe since the outbreak of WWII or the great Depression. However, there had already been a steady rise in fear starting with the prior generation.

Since the 1970s, a steady decline of courage and a corresponding climb in fear and cowardice were observable in the Christian community, especially in many leaders—a fear expressed in silence, inaction, and craven subservience to the governing authorities of the Western democracies. Literally tens of thousands of churches closed—without a fight.

Again and again, believers are commanded by God to speak and to act in His Name for the good of others, for the cause of justice, for the sake of immortal souls, and for the lives of the innocent. Yet the silence of millions of Christians and tens of thousands of clergy was deafening.

Inaction and the sins of omission—"the things I have failed to do," as so many confessions of sin state—are sins that are rank to the heavens. In this light, silence and cowardice resulting from fear can be a *sin* as well as a *judgment*.

Courage is the chief virtue, because courage propels all other virtues into action in the hour they are needed. If one knows the right thing to do, or what is needed to be said, but one does not have the courage to take action or say what is needed, what value is one's knowledge of what is right or understanding of what is needed?

Questions regarding Clergy in Europe, Canada, and America

Let the reader ponder the question: how often do pastors, priests, bishops, evangelists, and TV or radio personalities preach sermons or do broadcasts confronting the sins of their nations? How often do they proclaim the Scriptural theme of judgment? How often do they declare that God hears the cry of the oppressed or the cry of innocent blood?

How often do they call on their flocks to repent of inactivity and silence? When was the last time they took a public stand against any political issue or government official that is clearly in defiance of God's Law?

And how much has this "silence of the shepherds" demoralized, scandalized, and disemboweled the faithful parishioners who endure this silence?

God spoke thought the prophet Isaiah regarding the loathsome state of His leaders and shepherds, saying:

His watchmen are blind,
they are all without knowledge;
they are all dumb dogs,
they cannot bark;
dreaming, lying down,
loving to slumber.
The dogs have a mighty appetite;
they never have enough.
The shepherds also have no understanding;
they have all turned to their own way,
each to his own gain, one and all. (Isaiah 56:10–11)

Thoughts for Laymen

Laymen, as well as clergy, are required to be witnesses for the Lord Jesus Christ and His holy laws. All Christians should consider the level at which fear has controlled their actions and words, humbly asking when the last time was they stood for God's truth and justice at work or with friends, neighbors, or family.

Courage is not the absence of fear; courage is doing what is right in spite of fear. God is able to give strength to overcome fears.

The Lord encourages His people to be brave. May all generations implore Him to keep at bay the judgment of fear and the shackles of fear, remembering the words of Jesus to His followers:

> The student is not above the teacher, nor a servant above his master. It is enough for students to be like their teachers, and servants like their masters. If the head of the house has been called Beelzebul, how much more the members of his household!
>
> *So do not be afraid of them*, for there is nothing concealed that will not be disclosed, or hidden that will not be made known. What I tell you in the dark, speak in the daylight; what is whispered in your ear, proclaim from the roofs. *Do not be afraid of those who kill the body but cannot kill the soul. Rather, be afraid of the One who can destroy both soul and body in hell.* (Matthew 10:24–28 NIV)

Are there any among the idols of the nations that can cause rain? Or can the heavens give showers? Are You not He, O LORD our God? Therefore we will wait for You, Since You have made all these.

Jeremiah 14:22 NKJV

"And I also withheld the rain from you
when there were yet three months to the harvest;
I would send rain upon one city,
and send no rain upon another city;
one field would be rained upon,
and the field on which it did not rain withered;
so two or three cities wandered to one city
to drink water, and were not satisfied;
yet you did not return to Me,"
says the LORD.

Amos 4:7–8

I will break the pride of your power, and I will make your heavens like iron and your earth like brass.

Leviticus 26:19

6

DROUGHT, FLOODS, AND OTHER WEATHER CHASTENINGS

The Scripture teaches that the weather is a part of God's creation, squarely in His hand, under His authority, and to be used for mercy, *or correction*:

When He utters His voice there is a tumult of waters in the heavens,
and He makes the mist rise from the ends of the earth.
He makes lightnings for the rain,
and He brings forth the wind from His storehouses.
(Jeremiah 10:13)

He who builds His layers in the sky, and has founded His strata in the earth; who calls for the waters of the sea, and pours them out on the face of the earth—the LORD is His name. (Amos 9:6 NKJV)

Also with moisture He saturates the thick clouds; He scatters His bright clouds. And they swirl about, being turned by His guidance, that they may do whatever He commands them on the face of the whole earth. *He causes it to come, whether for correction, or for His land, or for mercy.* (Job 37:11–13 NKJV)

A simple fact of God's creation is that the earth must have proper moisture for man and beast to drink, as well as for the food supply for all living things. Scriptural passages regarding God's control of weather are frequently connected to food:

> Sing to the LORD with thanksgiving;
> make melody to our God upon the lyre!
> He covers the heavens with clouds,
> He prepares rain for the earth,
> He makes grass grow upon the hills.
> He gives to the beasts their food,
> and to the young ravens which cry. (Psalm 147:7–9)

> From Thy lofty abode Thou waterest the mountains;
> the earth is satisfied with the fruit of Thy work.
> Thou dost cause the grass to grow for the cattle,
> and plants for man to cultivate,
> that he may bring forth food from the earth,
> and wine to gladden the heart of man,
> oil to make his face shine,
> and bread to strengthen man's heart. (Psalm 104:13–15)

The Scriptures teach specifically there is a connection between obedience to God's laws and *rain*—especially rainwater associated with food production:

> *And if you will obey My commandments* which I command you this day, to love the LORD your God, and to serve Him with all your heart and with all your soul, *He will give the rain for your land in its season, the early rain and the later rain, that you may gather in your grain and your wine and your oil. And He will give grass in your fields for your cattle, and you shall eat and be full.* (Deuteronomy 11:13–15)

> The LORD will establish you as a people holy to Himself, as He has sworn to you, if you keep the commandments of the LORD your God, and walk in His ways.... And the LORD will make you abound in prosperity, in the fruit of

your body, and in the fruit of your cattle, and in the fruit of your ground, within the land which the L ORD swore to your fathers to give you. *The L ORD will open to you His good treasury the heavens, to give the rain of your land in its season and to bless all the work of your hands*; and you shall lend to many nations, but you shall not borrow. (Deuteronomy 28:9–12)

If you walk in My statutes and observe My commandments and do them, then *I will give you your rains in their season, and the land shall yield its increase, and the trees of the field shall yield their fruit.* (Leviticus 26:3–4)

The Judgment of Drought

However, just as rain is in the hand of God to *bless* a nation, drought is in His hand to *chasten* a nation for grievous sins. God gives these warnings:

A drought is against her waters, and they will be dried up. For it is the land of carved images, and they are insane with their idols. (Jeremiah 50:38 NKJV)

He turns rivers into a desert,
springs of water into thirsty ground,
a fruitful land into a salty waste,
because of the wickedness of its inhabitants.
(Psalm 107:33–34)

Take heed lest your heart be deceived, and you turn aside and serve other gods and worship them, and the anger of the L ORD be kindled against you, and *He shut up the heavens, so that there be no rain, and the land yield no fruit*, and you perish quickly off the good land which the L ORD gives you. (Deuteronomy 11:16–17)

But if you will not obey the voice of the L ORD your God or be careful to do all His commandments and His statutes which I command you this day, then all these curses shall come upon you and overtake you. Cursed shall you be in the city, and cursed shall you be in the field. *Cursed shall be your basket and your kneading-trough. Cursed shall be the fruit of your body, and the fruit of your ground, the increase of your cattle, and the young of your flock....*

The LORD will smite you with consumption, and with fever, inflammation, and fiery heat, and *with drought, and with blasting, and with mildew; they shall pursue you until you perish. And the heavens over your head shall be brass, and the earth under you shall be iron. The LORD will make the rain of your land powder and dust; from heaven it shall come down upon you until you are destroyed.* (Deuteronomy 28:15–24)

But if you will not hearken to Me, and will not do all these commandments, if you spurn My statutes, and if your soul abhors My ordinances, so that you will not do all My commandments, but break My covenant, I will do this to you:... *I will break the pride of your power, and I will make your heavens like iron and your earth like brass; and your strength shall be spent in vain, for your land shall not yield its increase, and the trees of the land shall not yield their fruit.* (Leviticus 26:14–20)

A favorite verse of many believers, oft quoted in recent decades, is Second Chronicles 7:14:

If My people who are called by My name humble themselves, and pray and seek My face, and turn from their wicked ways, then I will hear from heaven, and will forgive their sin and heal their land.

As dear to Christians as this promise may be, before this verse is a threat that provides the context. Second Chronicles 7:14 is a passage relating the dedication of Solomon's Temple to Almighty God. God appeared to Solomon and told him that if the Israelites turned away from God, *He would cut off the rain*:

Thus Solomon finished the house of the LORD and the king's house; all that Solomon had planned to do in the house of the LORD and in his own house he successfully accomplished. Then the LORD appeared to Solomon in the night and said to him: "I have heard your prayer, and have chosen this place for Myself as a house of sacrifice. *When I shut up the heavens so that there is no rain*, or command the locust to devour the land, or send pestilence among My people, if My people who are called by My name humble themselves, and pray and seek My face, and turn from their wicked ways, then I will hear from heaven, and will forgive their sin and heal their land." (Second Chronicles 7:11–14)

Sadly, these warnings went unheeded. The Northern Tribes and Judah went into heinous sins, and God made good on His promises to Moses and to Solomon regarding drought and other punishments.

The book of the prophet Amos was likely the first *written* prophetic book. He was among many of the prophets to proclaim the dreadful message that God was punishing His people through the elements:

"I also withheld rain from you, when there were still three months to the harvest. I made it rain on one city, I withheld rain from another city. One part was rained upon, and where it did not rain the part withered. So two or three cities wandered to another city to drink water, but they were not satisfied; yet you have not returned to Me," says the LORD. (Amos 4:7–8 NKJV)

In the days of Elijah the prophet, during the wicked reign of Ahab and Jezebel, God brought drought as a punishment for the Israelites' sins of idolatry:

Now Eli'jah the Tishbite, of Tishbe in Gilead, said to Ahab, "As the LORD the God of Israel lives, before whom I stand, there shall be neither dew nor rain these years, except by my word." (First Kings 17:1)

After three and a half years, the drought was ended when Elijah had 450 prophets of Ba'al executed in a miraculous show-down on Mt. Carmel (see First Kings 17–18).

The prophet Jeremiah declared this frightful judgment from God to Judah:

"Judah wilts;
commerce at the city gates grinds to a halt.
All the people sit on the ground in mourning,
and a great cry rises from Jerusalem.
The nobles send servants to get water,
but all the wells are dry.
The servants return with empty pitchers,
confused and desperate,
covering their heads in grief.
The ground is parched
and cracked for lack of rain.
The farmers are deeply troubled;
they, too, cover their heads.
Even the doe abandons her newborn fawn
because there is no grass in the field.
The wild donkeys stand on the bare hills
panting like thirsty jackals.
They strain their eyes looking for grass,
but there is none to be found."
The people say, "*Our wickedness has*
caught up with us, Lord,
but help us for the sake of Your own reputation.
We have turned away from You
and sinned against You again and again.
O Hope of Israel, our Savior in times of trouble,
why are You like a stranger to us?
Why are You like a traveler passing through the land,
stopping only for the night?
Are You also confused?

Is our champion helpless to save us?
You are right here among us, LORD.
We are known as Your people.
Please don't abandon us now!"
So this is what the LORD says to His people:
"You love to wander far from Me
and do not restrain yourselves.
Therefore, I will no longer accept you as My people.
Now I will remember all your wickedness
and will punish you for your sins."
(Jeremiah 14:1–10 NLT)

Again, God revealed to Jeremiah the direct connection between national sins and drought:

But this people has a stubborn and rebellious heart;
they have turned aside and gone away.
They do not say in their hearts,
"Let us fear the LORD our God,
who gives the rain in its season,
the autumn rain and the spring rain,
and keeps for us
the weeks appointed for the harvest."
Your iniquities have turned these away,
and your sins have kept good from you.
(Jeremiah 5:23–25)

Wildfires

The natural—and supernatural—result of drought is crop failure and fires. These, too, are parts of the judgments God has reserved for Himself against an iniquitous people:

Upon the wicked He will rain coals; fire and brimstone
and a burning wind shall be the portion of their cup.
(Psalm 11:6 NKJV)

Praise the LORD from the earth, you great sea creatures and all the depths; fire and hail, snow and clouds; stormy wind, fulfilling His word. (Psalm 148:7–8 NKJV)

Behold, He scatters His lightning about Him,
and covers the roots of the sea.
For by these He judges peoples;
He gives food in abundance.
He covers His hands with the lightning,
and commands it to strike the mark.
Its crashing declares concerning Him,
who is jealous with anger against iniquity.
(Job 36:30–33)

But the multitude of your foes shall be like small dust,
and the multitude of the ruthless like passing chaff.
And in an instant, suddenly,
you will be visited by the LORD of hosts
with thunder and with earthquake and great noise,
with whirlwind and tempest, and *the flame of a devouring fire*. (Isaiah 29:5–6)

God has lightning, including lightning to start wildfires:

The LORD will cause people to hear His majestic voice and will make them see His arm coming down with raging anger and *consuming fire*, with cloudburst, thunderstorm and hail. (Isaiah 30:30 NIV)

Other Cataclysmic Weather

In addition to drought and fire, God clearly defines other weather-related chastisements He can use to judge a nation. God said to Job:

Have you entered the storehouses of the snow,
or have you seen the storehouses of the hail,
which I have reserved for the time of trouble,
for the day of battle and war? (Job 38:22–23)

Scripture spells out the weather elements God has at His disposal to chasten nations.

God has hail:

Have you entered the treasury of snow, or have you seen the *treasury of hail*, which I have reserved for the time of trouble, for the day of battle and war? (Job 38:22–23 NKJV)

Therefore thus says the Lord GOD: I will make a stormy wind break out in My wrath; and there shall be a deluge of rain in My anger, and *great hailstones* in wrath to destroy it. (Ezekiel 13:13)

I smote you and all the products of your toil with blight and mildew and *hail*; yet you did not return to Me, says the LORD. (Haggai 2:17)

God has hurricanes and tornados:

You will be punished by the LORD of hosts with thunder and earthquake and great noise, with *storm and tempest* and the flame of devouring fire. (Isaiah 29:6 NKJV)

The LORD will cause people to hear His majestic voice and will make them see His arm coming down with raging anger and consuming fire, with *cloudburst, thunderstorm* and hail. (Isaiah 30:30 NIV)

With pestilence and bloodshed I will enter into judgment with him, and I will rain upon him and his hordes and the many peoples who are with him *torrential rains* and hailstones, fire and sulfur. So I will show My greatness and My holiness and make Myself known in the eyes of many nations. Then they will know that I am the LORD. (Ezekiel 38:22–23 ESV)

God has earthquakes:

Then *the earth shook and trembled; the foundations of the hills also quaked and were shaken,* because He was angry. (Psalm 18:7 NKJV)

God has floods:

Also I will make justice the measuring line, and righteousness the plummet; the hail will sweep away the refuge of lies, and *the waters will overflow the hiding place.* (Isaiah 28:17 NKJV)

The LORD is good,
a stronghold in the day of trouble;
He knows those who take refuge in Him.
But with an overflowing flood
He will make a full end of His adversaries,
and will pursue His enemies into darkness.
(Nahum 1:7–8)

Consider America and other nations in the light of these principles, passages, promises, and threats. Reflect on the droughts, fires, and devastating weather patterns. As Job says, can it be for correction? Could it be to *chasten* and *awaken* and call a nation back to Him?

The New Testament

To the Christian who asks, "Where is this in the New Testament?" one only need read the judgments promised in the book of Revelation to understand that these rods of discipline are still among the options God uses:

When He opened the fourth seal, I heard the voice of the fourth living creature say, "Come!" And I saw, and behold, a pale horse, and its rider's name was Death, and Hades followed him; and they were given power over a fourth of the earth, to kill with sword and with famine and with pestilence and by wild beasts of the earth. (Revelation 6:7–8)

I looked when He broke the sixth seal, and there was a great earthquake; and the sun became as black as sackcloth made of hair, and the whole moon became like blood. (Revelation 6:12 NASB)

Then the angel took the censer and filled it with the fire of the altar, and hurled it to the earth; and there were peals of thunder and sounds, and flashes of lightning and an earthquake. (Revelation 8:5 NASB)

And at that hour there was a great earthquake, and a tenth of the city fell. Seven thousand people were killed in the earthquake, and the rest were terrified and gave glory to the God of heaven. (Revelation 11:13 ESV)

And there were flashes of lightning and sounds and peals of thunder; and there was a great earthquake, such as there had not been since mankind came to be upon the earth, so great an earthquake was it, and so mighty. (Revelation 16:18 NASB)

Weather Calamities Are Not from the Devil

The calamitous weather judgments—in the past and today—are not from Satan. It is disheartening and alarming how many Christians give improper credit and authority to the devil.

Yes, the devil is real, and he wants to "steal and kill and destroy." He prowls about seeking whom he may devour—primarily *through temptation to sin that we willfully commit*. But Satan is *not* the maker of the universe, nor the maker of the clouds.

The earth is the LORD's and the fulness thereof,
the world and those who dwell therein. (Psalm 24:1)

The earth and the waters and winds do not belong to Satan but to God. To assert that the devil brings all these calamities is to deny the plain teaching of Scripture and to ascribe to the devil the power and authority that are God's alone.

"What about Job?" one might ask. Doesn't the Scripture say that Satan attacked Job, including bringing weather that claimed the lives of his children?

Answer: God gave Satan the authority to torment Job, including the storm that hit and killed Job's children. Nevertheless, the *authority* to affect the weather came from God:

And the LORD said to Satan, "Have you considered My servant Job, that there is none like him on the earth, a blameless and upright man, who fears God and turns away from evil? He still holds fast his integrity, *although you MOVED ME against him, to destroy him without cause.*" (Job 2:3)

To use the book of Job to claim that the devil controls the weather is specious. This is *not* the devil's world, and if in any situation the devil is given authority to use weather to wreak havoc, it is because God gave it to him. God is still the ruler of the elements.

Timing Is Everything—God Is "Slow to Anger"

In the majority of threats—and cases recorded in Scripture where those threats were carried out—where cataclysmic weather was used as a judgment, *the judgments of the Lord were a long time coming.* God is patient and longsuffering. Consider Noah's day. God was forbearing for decades before His judgment fell.

The pattern in Scripture is that weather judgments are usually reserved for entire nations or large parts of nations, and they come after a long season of sin and rebellion against God.

A nation—such as America, or formerly Christian nations in Europe—can reach a point where aggregated sins and crimes against God cry to heaven, and God responds by sending judgment through the elements.

These evils that cry for divine vengeance may be codified by wicked legislative measures (laws passed), demonic state or federal court decisions (such as *Roe* or *Obergefell* in the Supreme Court of the United States), or executive orders from governors or presidents (such as orders codifying the demonic perversion and crime against children called "transgenderism").

When sins reach the boiling point—a point known to God—just as the Lord "sends rain on the good and the bad," He will withhold rain from the good and the bad. Or He will send whatever dreadful weather patterns He sees fit to call a nation to repentance or to punish a nation for refusing to repent. In those times, virtually everyone suffers…the just and the unjust.

A Storehouse of Trouble

God's power is limitless. The Scriptures show the elements as being God's "storehouse." If a nation does not respond to the "first fruits" of judgment, God has much more calamity at His disposal to judge rebellion.

Remember: *God has more disaster than any government entity has relief.*

While weather chastenings have brought hardship to many millions, and even death to a few (and for those thus bereaved, grief is the proper response), most of the world has not responded to chastenings in the weather. Prognosticators and false prophets continue ignoring God, blaming "climate change" or chalking it up to random chance, foreign volcanoes, or burning oil fields.

Many rebels refuse to acknowledge that God rules the elements. And sadly, many Christians have forgotten this truth. This arrogance and folly do not bode well for any nation. God will continue to call, rebuke, and chasten nations through weather. Then He will use other means of judgment He has threatened in His Word and used throughout history.

Then the LORD will bring on you and your offspring extraordinary afflictions, afflictions severe and lasting, and sicknesses grievous and lasting.

Deuteronomy 28:59

"I sent a plague among you as in Egypt.... And I made the stench of your camp rise up in your nostrils; Yet you have not returned to Me," declares the LORD.

Amos 4:10 NASB

7

PLAGUES

Does the Almighty use sickness to chasten a nation? God is a healer, but does He ever send sickness?

For many Christians, these questions may be difficult to answer. Very few want to conceive, much less believe, that a loving God—our Heavenly Father—would send a disease that makes people sick, such as the coronavirus or any number of plagues recorded in the Scriptures.

One can understand someone—Christian or not—recoiling at the notion, especially in the light of the heartache and misery disease causes. Moreover, many Scriptures declare God is healer. These Scriptures confirm that God is the God who heals. He is Jehovah Rapha, "the LORD, your healer." We read in the Scriptures that Jesus "went about doing good and healing all that were oppressed by the devil, for God was with Him" (Acts 10:38).

The Old and New Testaments give assurance that "by His stripes we are healed" (Isaiah 53:5; First Peter 2:24 NKJV). Psalm 91 promises God's children:

For He will deliver you from the snare of the fowler
and from the deadly pestilence;
He will cover you with His pinions,
and under His wings you will find refuge;
His faithfulness is a shield and buckler.

You will not fear the terror of the night,
nor the arrow that flies by day,
nor the pestilence that stalks in darkness,
nor the destruction that wastes at noonday. (vv. 3–6)

Scripture promises that "they shall lay hands on the sick, and they shall recover" (Mark 16:18 KJV). The Apostle James writes:

Is any among you sick? Let him call for the elders of the church, and let them pray over him, anointing him with oil in the name of the Lord; and the prayer of faith will save the sick man, and the Lord will raise him up; and if he has committed sins, he will be forgiven. (James 5:14–15)

These Scriptures are the Word of God. God *is* our healer. Jesus *did* heal people with His touch or with a word. God *does* answer prayer today, and people *are* raised up from their sick beds—often with a miraculous healing.

How, then, could the God who heals diseases be the same God who sends diseases? How could the Lord Jesus—so kind and merciful and gracious to the sick and suffering—send sickness and suffering?

The answer lies in part with His intention. Sometimes, He sends sickness as *justice*—as a temporal punishment for sin on the person or people being afflicted. Other times, He sends an illness for the purpose of *restoration* of someone's soul or a nation to righteousness.[1] Within the scope of restoration, God may send sickness for *correction*, as a disciplining parent might do.

Plagues for Justice, Restoration, or Correction

Justice. In the Scriptures, there are times when God sends sickness and death as a direct punishment—His *justice*—on men and nations because of sins they have committed. Here are two examples of when God brings punishment for justice, with no

---

1. Jesus even says in one instance that illness was allowed for the purpose of glorifying God (John 9:2–3).

apparent hope of redemption or restoration in this life. (Again, this does not refer to eternal redemption). First, consider Egypt:

> This is what the LORD, the God of the Hebrews, says: Let My people go, so that they may worship Me, or this time *I will send the full force of My plagues against you and against your officials and your people*, so you may know that there is no one like Me in all the earth. For by now I could have stretched out My hand and *struck you and your people with a plague that would have wiped you off the earth.* (Exodus 9:13–15 NIV)

Next, consider Israel. Jeremiah repeatedly predicts horrific punishments on the Jews, including plagues, with no hope of earthly redemption:

> I will send the sword, famine, *and plague* against them until they have perished from the land I gave to them and their ancestors. (Jeremiah 24:10 HCSB)

The Lord speaks a similar judgment through Ezekiel in the same era:

> Thus says the Lord GOD: Clap your hands, stamp your feet, and cry "Alas!" for all the evil abominations of the house of Israel! They shall fall by the sword, starvation, *and disease. Those far off shall die of disease*, those nearby shall fall by the sword, and those who survive and are spared shall perish by starvation; *thus will I spend My fury upon them.* (Ezekiel 6:11–12 NABRE)

And this:

> Therefore, as I live, says the Lord GOD, because you have defiled My sanctuary with all your atrocities and all your abominations, *I will surely withdraw and not look upon you with pity nor spare you. A third of your people shall die of disease* or starve to death within you; another third shall fall by the

sword all around you; a third I will scatter to the winds and pursue them with the sword. (Ezekiel 5:11–12 NABRE)

As stated before, one cannot presume to know the eternal abode of those who thus perished. That is not the point of this study. The point is that there are times when God chastens His people with sickness *in this life* to bring justice.

Restoration. Sometimes God sends sickness *to call people back* to Himself—to restore a person or nation to righteousness. Psalm 107 states:

> Some were *sick through their sinful ways,*
> *and because of their iniquities suffered affliction*;
> they loathed any kind of food,
> and they drew near to the gates of death.
> Then they cried to the LORD in their trouble,
> and He delivered them from their distress;
> *He sent forth His word, and healed them,*
> *and delivered them from destruction.*
> *Let them thank the LORD for His steadfast love,*
> for His wonderful works to the sons of men!
> And let them offer sacrifices of thanksgiving,
> and tell of His deeds in songs of joy! (vv. 17–22)

Correction. God's disciplinary actions may be compared to parental discipline, exemplified in the relationship between parents and children. Sometimes parents bring discipline to children as a punishment—solely for justice—for an offense committed. And sometimes it is for the children's formation, molding, and development of their character, so that they become better people or so that they remain safe. Parents discipline for past sins to modify future behavior. God can do the same thing. Job speaks of fatherly discipline as applied to individuals:

> Behold, happy is the man whom God reproves;
> therefore despise not the chastening of the Almighty.

For He wounds, but He binds up;
He smites, but His hands heal. (Job 5:17–18)

As for the discipline of nations, Jeremiah warns Judah while also outlining behaviors that God is looking for in His people, just as a father would do in correcting his children:

"Thus says the LORD: Behold, I set before you the way of life and the way of death. He who stays in this city shall die by the sword, by famine, *and by pestilence*; but he who goes out and surrenders to the Chalde'ans who are besieging you shall live and shall have his life as a prize of war."… And to the house of the king of Judah say, "Hear the word of the LORD, O house of David! Thus says the LORD:

"Execute justice in the morning,
and deliver from the hand of the oppressor
him who has been robbed,
lest My wrath go forth like fire,
and burn with none to quench it,
because of your evil doings." (Jeremiah 21:8–12)

God has given human beings free will to act. But He also has "free will to act" in any situation He chooses. This is seen not only in "His will," or "His general will" for all mankind, as laid down in the directives of His Law.

Obviously, He has a will for the entire human race. The prayer "*Thy will* be done, on earth as it is in heaven" reflects that God has a will in heaven that He wants done on earth. The easiest place to find His general will for all mankind is in the Ten Commandments and the Gospel. No one needs to pray, "Lord, is it your will for me to steal this car?"

But beyond the general will of God for all mankind, He has a will as an actor. He can choose to act as the all-powerful First Cause of good or ill whenever He so chooses.

Said differently, the Eternal One, who has all power and knowledge, is free to act and able to exert His will whenever

He chooses, for whatever reason He chooses, and on whomever He chooses. No man can say to Him, just as the clay cannot say to the potter, "What are you doing?" (Isaiah 45:9 NASB).

Clearly, God exercises His will in the use of sickness as a means of justice as well as restoration and correction.

Plagues against Individuals

Some cases in Scripture record that God sent a disease to an individual. The Jewish King Uzziah was a good man—a devout Jew who served the Lord.

> And he did what was right in the eyes of the LORD, according to all that his father Amazi'ah had done. He set himself to seek God in the days of Zechari'ah, who instructed him in the fear of God; and as long as he sought the LORD, God made him prosper. (Second Chronicles 26:4–5)

But when he sinned by going into the temple to burn incense to the Lord contrary to the Law of God, God struck him with leprosy:

> But when he was strong he grew proud, to his destruction. For he was false to the LORD his God, and entered the temple of the LORD to burn incense on the altar of incense. But Azari'ah the priest went in after him, with eighty priests of the LORD who were men of valor; and they withstood King Uzzi'ah, and said to him, "It is not for you, Uzzi'ah, to burn incense to the LORD, but for the priests the sons of Aaron, who are consecrated to burn incense. Go out of the sanctuary; for you have done wrong, and it will bring you no honor from the LORD God." Then Uzzi'ah was angry. Now he had a censer in his hand to burn incense, and when he became angry with the priests *leprosy broke out on his forehead*, in the presence of the priests in the house of the LORD, by the altar of incense. And Azari'ah the chief priest, and all the priests, looked at him, and behold, he was leprous in his forehead! And they thrust him out quickly, and he himself

hastened to go out, *because the LORD had smitten him*. (Second Chronicles 26:16–20)

When Nabal unjustly reviled David in the wilderness, "the LORD smote Nabal; and he died" (see First Samuel 25:36–38).

When Aaron and Miriam, Moses's brother and sister, spoke against Moses, "The anger of the LORD was kindled against them, and He departed; and when the cloud removed from over the tent, behold, Miriam was leprous, as white as snow" (Numbers 12:9–10).

When Herod Agrippa was hailed as a god, the True God sent an angel who smote him with worms, and he died:

> On an appointed day Herod put on his royal robes, took his seat upon the throne, and made an oration to them. And the people shouted, "The voice of a god, and not of man!" Immediately an angel of the Lord smote him, because he did not give God the glory; and he was eaten by worms and died. (Acts 12:21–23)

Also in the book of Acts, the Apostle Paul, operating in the authority God gave him, pronounced the judgment of blindness on a false prophet:

> When they had gone through the whole island as far as Paphos, they came upon a certain magician, a Jewish false prophet, named Bar-Jesus. He was with the proconsul, Sergius Paulus, a man of intelligence, who summoned Barnabas and Saul and sought to hear the word of God. But El'ymas the magician (for that is the meaning of his name) withstood them, seeking to turn away the proconsul from the faith. But Saul, who is also called Paul, filled with the Holy Spirit, looked intently at him and said, "You son of the devil, you enemy of all righteousness, full of all deceit and villainy, will you not stop making crooked the straight paths of the Lord? And now, behold, the hand of the Lord is upon you, and you shall be blind and unable to

see the sun for a time." Immediately mist and darkness fell upon him and he went about seeking people to lead him by the hand. Then the proconsul believed, when he saw what had occurred, for he was astonished at the teaching of the Lord. (Acts 13:6–12)

These passages from the Old and New Testaments show that God uses sickness to punish individual rebellious humans.

Plagues against Pagan Nations

Egypt is the clearest starting point to show that God punished pagan nations with disease. He punished Egypt because they oppressed the children of Israel.

In reading of the ten plagues that God sent against the Egyptians, it is noteworthy that most of the plagues *were not* sicknesses. The frogs, lice, hail, darkness, etc., were considered plagues but were not specifically diseases in the bodies of the Egyptians. God *did* send disease against the livestock of Egypt, causing massive death of herds, but this was still not against the bodies of the Egyptians.

However, two plagues clearly were diseases of the body. First, boils:

> Then the LORD said to Moses and Aaron, "Take handfuls of soot from a furnace and have Moses toss it into the air in the presence of Pharaoh. It will become fine dust over the whole land of Egypt, and festering boils will break out on people and animals throughout the land."
>
> So they took soot from a furnace and stood before Pharaoh. Moses tossed it into the air, and festering boils broke out on people and animals. The magicians could not stand before Moses because of the boils that were on them and on all the Egyptians. (Exodus 9:8–11 NIV)

The second devastating plague was when God killed all the firstborn of the Egyptians:

Now the LORD had said to Moses, "I will bring one more plague on Pharaoh and on Egypt. After that, he will let you go from here, and when he does, he will drive you out completely."...

So Moses said, "This is what the LORD says: 'About midnight I will go throughout Egypt. Every firstborn son in Egypt will die, from the firstborn son of Pharaoh, who sits on the throne, to the firstborn son of the female slave, who is at her hand mill, and all the firstborn of the cattle as well. There will be loud wailing throughout Egypt—worse than there has ever been or ever will be again.'"...

At midnight the LORD smote all the first-born in the land of Egypt, from the first-born of Pharaoh who sat on his throne to the first-born of the captive who was in the dungeon, and all the first-born of the cattle. And Pharaoh rose up in the night, he, and all his servants, and all the Egyptians; and there was a great cry in Egypt, for there was not a house where one was not dead. (Exodus 11:1, 4–6 NIV, 12:29–30 RSVCE)

Note again that God pronounced this punishment and carried it out without mercy on the Egyptians, except for those who sought refuge under the blood of the Passover lamb.

Many other examples of God punishing pagan nations with sickness are found in the Scriptures. For example, the Philistines defeated the Jews in battle and captured the Ark of the Covenant. They viewed this as a great triumph for themselves and their gods, but their rejoicing soon turned to terror *when God sent them disease.*

When the Philistines captured the ark of God, they carried it from Ebene'zer to Ashdod; then the Philistines took the ark of God and brought it into the house of Dagon and set it up beside Dagon....

The hand of the LORD was heavy upon the people of Ashdod, and He terrified and afflicted them with tumors, both Ashdod and its territory. And when the men of Ashdod saw how things were, they said, "The ark of the God of Israel must not remain with us; for His hand is heavy upon us and upon Dagon our god." So they sent and gathered together all the lords of the Philistines, and said, "What shall we do with the ark of the God of Israel?" They answered, "Let the ark of the God of Israel be brought around to Gath." So they brought the ark of the God of Israel there. But after they had brought it around, the hand of the LORD was against the city, causing a very great panic, and He afflicted the men of the city, both young and old, so that tumors broke out upon them....

They sent therefore and gathered together all the lords of the Philistines, and said, "Send away the ark of the God of Israel, and let it return to its own place, that it may not slay us and our people." For there was a deathly panic throughout the whole city. The hand of God was very heavy there; the men who did not die were stricken with tumors, and the cry of the city went up to heaven. (First Samuel 5:1–2, 6–12)

The ark was ultimately restored to the Jews, and the plague was stopped.

Generations later, Sennacherib, the king of the Assyrians, laid siege to Jerusalem. He delivered belligerent words against the Jews and blasphemous words against God. The anger of the Lord was stirred, and He responded by slaying 185,000 soldiers in one night (see Isaiah chapters 36–37). The means by which God slew this army are not spelled out specifically, but clearly they were dead because they had been judged by God.

Disease—Sent to God's People?

The fact that Sacred Scripture teaches that God judges pagan nations would not cause much alarm to the people of God. Believers might be tempted to think that because those nations were pagan, they *may have* deserved it.

However, to assert that God uses plagues and diseases to chasten and judge His people—and more specifically, modern nations that have a Judeo-Christian consensus and history or claim to be Christian—this causes some Christians a great deal of consternation and distress. Some are tempted to dismiss such a thought out of hand. Others are enraged at the notion.

The Scriptures clearly teach that God uses disease to judge and chasten pagans, and when He chooses, *He uses the same punishments to judge His people.*

> For we know Him who said, "Vengeance is Mine, I will repay." And again, *"The Lord will judge His people."* (Hebrews 10:30)

Shortly after God frees the Jews from Egypt, having devastated Egypt by plagues, He warns the Jews:

> If you will listen carefully to the voice of the LORD your God, and do what is right in His eyes, and pay attention to His commands, and keep all His statutes, *then I will not bring on you any of the diseases I inflicted on the Egyptians.* For I am the LORD who heals you. (Exodus 15:26 BSB)

Inherent in this warning is not only that God brought disease on the Egyptians, but also that He holds those same diseases as an option to punish His people. In short form, God is saying: "Obey Me and you'll be healthy. Disobey Me, and I'll afflict you with the same diseases I used to judge the Egyptians."

Here is another Scripture showing that God can and will punish His chosen people as He punished the Egyptians:

> If you do not carefully follow all the words of this law, which are written in this book, and do not revere this glorious and awesome name—the LORD your God—*the LORD will send fearful plagues on you and your descendants, harsh and prolonged disasters, and severe and lingering illnesses.* He will bring on you *all the diseases of Egypt that you dreaded, and they will cling to you.* The LORD will also *bring on you every kind of sickness*

and disaster not recorded in this Book of the Law, until you are destroyed. (Deuteronomy 28:58–61 NIV)

Over time, the Jews ignored these warnings and rebelled against God's Law. So God brought upon them these exact punishments, including disease. Before the city of Jerusalem and Solomon's Temple were totally destroyed, the prophets Jeremiah and Ezekiel prophesied over and over again that God would judge them in accordance with the warnings of His Law, including plagues.

Here are three examples from Jeremiah:

I [God] Myself will fight against you with an outstretched hand and a mighty arm in furious anger and in great wrath. I will strike down those who live in this city—both man and beast—*and they will die of a terrible plague.* (Jeremiah 21:5–6 NIV)

I [God] will send the sword, famine, and *plague* against them until they have perished from the land I gave to them and their ancestors. (Jeremiah 24:10 HCSB)

Now therefore, this is what the LORD, the God of Israel, says to this city about which you said, "It has been handed over to Babylon's king through sword, famine, and *plague*." (Jeremiah 32:36 HCSB)

And this dreadful condemnation was sent by God through Ezekiel:

Then they shall know that *I the LORD did not threaten in vain to inflict this evil on them.*

Thus says the Lord GOD: Clap your hands, stamp your feet, and cry "Alas!" for all the evil abominations of the house of Israel! *They shall fall by the sword, starvation, and disease. Those far off shall die of disease,* those nearby shall fall by the sword, and those who survive and are spared shall perish by starvation; thus will I spend My fury upon them. They shall know that I am the LORD, when their slain lie among their idols, all around their altars, on every high hill and mountaintop, beneath every green tree and leafy oak—any place they offer sweet-smelling oblations to all their idols. *I will stretch out My hand against them; I will make the land a desolate waste,* from the wilderness to Riblah, wherever they live. Thus they shall know that I am the LORD. (Ezekiel 6:10–14 NABRE)

As stated earlier, Second Chronicles 7:14, "If My people…will humble themselves and pray," is a favorite passage among many Christians, as one would expect. It is a beautiful promise that God will hear the prayers of His people. But look again at the entire context of this verse, through another translation, focusing on disease:

If I [God] shut up the heavens so that there is no rain, or if I command the locust swarms to eat up all of your crops, *or if I send an epidemic among you,* then *if My people will humble themselves and pray, and search for Me, and turn from their wicked ways, I will hear them from heaven and forgive their sins and heal their land.* (Second Chronicles 7:13–14 TLB)

Christians are too often fond of taking Bible verses out of context and ignoring or abandoning the passages that are disturbing. This passage is a case in point. Second Chronicles 7:14 is set in the context of judgment, *including disease.*

Just How Special Is America? Or England, or France?

Many Christians in America and across the world believe that America has a special destiny among nations—a special blessing and calling from God. Whether true or not, America has indeed been blessed on many levels above all the nations of the earth in recent history.

Others, historians and patriots of European powers, focus on England and France, or Spain, Holland, Italy, and Germany, for the critical roles they played in European or world leadership over the past two thousand years.

Granting that the great European powers played indispensable roles in the development of Christian civilization, and granting that America has had a special and unique season of blessing and leadership, should any of these nations fancy themselves better than Israel, the chosen people of God?

Are these world powers—nuclear powers, engines of finance and medicine, fountains of learning—*immune to the judgments of Almighty God?* Are they out of the reach of Him who brought devastation and ruin upon His chosen race—*the very people through whom He gave the Ten Commandments and the Savior of the world?*

Do Christians foolishly believe that God would punish the children of Israel with sickness but would not punish today's great powers in like manner?

If Jehovah would bring the temporal chastisement of sickness to His chosen people for chastisement, repentance, and restoration, why would He not chasten current nations with this same temporal punishment to inspire repentance and restoration?

As explored in an earlier chapter, Christ Himself issues judgments that echo the prophets of the Old Testament regarding sickness:

> Nevertheless I have a few things against you, because you allow that woman Jezebel, who calls herself a prophetess, to teach and seduce My servants to commit sexual immorality and eat things sacrificed to idols. And I gave her time to repent of her sexual immorality, and she did not repent. Indeed I will *cast her into a sickbed*, and those who commit adultery with her into great tribulation, unless they repent of their deeds. And I will strike her children [or followers] dead. And all the churches shall know that I am He who searches mind and heart, and I will give to each of you as your works deserve. (Revelation 2:20–22 NKJV, 23 RSVCE)

The New American Bible Revised Edition translates verse 23: "*I will also put her children* [or followers] *to death.* Thus shall

all the churches come to know that I am the searcher of hearts and minds and that *I will give each of you what your works deserve.*" The Hollman Christian Standard Bible translates it: "I will kill her children with the plague." The New English Translation Bible translates it: "Furthermore, I will strike her followers with a deadly disease."

What follows is the passage from Revelation where Christ is speaking in the first person, declaring that God will send plagues:

> For I testify unto every man that heareth the words of the prophecy of this book, If any man shall add unto these things, *God shall add unto him the plagues that are written in this book.* (Revelation 22:18 KJV)

Finally, perhaps the most well-known passage showing that God might chasten His people with sickness—specifically Christians—is First Corinthians 11:27–32:

> Whoever, therefore, eats the bread or drinks the cup of the Lord in an unworthy manner will be guilty of profaning the body and blood of the Lord. Let a man examine himself, and so eat of the bread and drink of the cup. For any one who eats and drinks without discerning the body eats and drinks judgment upon himself. *That is why many of you are weak and ill, and some have died.* But if we judged ourselves truly, we should not be judged. *But when we are judged by the Lord, we are chastened* so that we may not be condemned along with the world.

Note that this passage connects the idea of judgment in the body with a chastening. Also note it is redemptive: "*So that we may not be condemned along with the world.*" That is, the sicknesses and deaths associated with the specific chastenings regarding Holy Communion do not in and of themselves mean that someone is condemned to hell.

Those who insist God would never use sickness as a chastisement must deliberately ignore or deny the clear warnings of

Sacred Scripture. Are the clear words of Jesus in Revelation to be dismissed? Are the clear words of the Apostle Paul regarding God's judgment by sickness and death to those who take communion unworthily to be explained away or ignored? Are all these warnings to be scorned or not believed? God is "the same yesterday and today and for ever" (Hebrews 13:8). There is "no variableness, neither shadow of turning" in Him (James 1:17 KJV). Consider this full passage from the book of Hebrews:

> For if we go on sinning deliberately after receiving the knowledge of the truth, there no longer remains a sacrifice for sins, but a fearful expectation of judgment, and a fury of fire that will consume the adversaries. Anyone who has set aside the law of Moses dies without mercy on the evidence of two or three witnesses. How much worse punishment, do you think, will be deserved by the one who has trampled underfoot the Son of God, and has profaned the blood of the covenant by which he was sanctified, and has outraged the Spirit of grace? For we know Him who said, "Vengeance is Mine; I will repay." And again, "The Lord will judge His people." It is a fearful thing to fall into the hands of the living God. (Hebrews 10:26–31 ESV)

Nearly twenty times in the New Testament, sickness is shown to be a judgment from heaven. The book of Revelation alone says at least ten times that God sends plagues. (The book of Revelation and the concept of "end times" will be examined a little later in this book.)

A Recent Example of the Judgment of Plague?

The COVID-19, or coronavirus, pandemic fits the pattern revealed in Scripture of God chastening nations with sickness. The loss of life was tragic. Millions of people died, many perhaps unnecessarily because they were denied the treatments that were available at the time.

Consider the controversies surrounding the pandemic. Firstly, fierce and well-founded debate swirled around the true depth of danger that COVID presented to various age groups. Those with preexisting conditions, especially the elderly, were hit particularly hard. But some doctors argued that the virus, even at its worst, was of no more danger to most people than the flu.[2]

Undeniably, political tyrants used the pandemic to steal the God-given rights of individuals and seize more government control over citizens. Businesses and the families that owned those businesses were ravaged. Many of their employees were gravely harmed. Livelihoods were needlessly destroyed. Child abuse, drug use, and alcoholism skyrocketed while civil liberties were trampled on—even crushed.

Churches were closed, while most of the clergy, with a few notable exceptions, were like sheep led to the slaughter. Those clergy who dared to push back were threatened. Some clergy were arrested and even jailed.

Perhaps worse still, almost all dissent and debate were systematically silenced. Hard questions about the communist Chinese were ignored; those who questioned the duplicity and possible conflict of interest of so-called experts were ignored; skeptics were labeled conspiracy theorists; doctors who were successfully treating COVID were called "quacks" and were virtually drummed out of practicing medicine.

The full list of ways in which the pandemic was used by political tyrants and intrusive government agencies seeking to control people's lives may never be known.

In Conclusion

The Scriptures teach that God is the God who heals us. But the Old and New Testaments clearly teach that God does at times

---

2. Kit Knightly, "WHO (Accidentally) Confirms Covid is No More Dangerous than Flu," *Off-Guardian*, October 8, 2020, off-guardian.org/2020/10/08/who-accidentally-confirms-covid-is-no-more-dangerous-than-flu/.

use sickness or plagues on individuals and nations as a punishment or to call them back to Himself.

Do His people hear Him? What does it take for believers to bring forth the deeds He demands for true repentance rather than stumbling into darker and darker chasms of immorality, callousness, and judgment?

You will build a house, but you will not live in it. You will plant a vineyard, but you will not even begin to enjoy its fruit....

All these curses will come on you.

Deuteronomy 28:30, 45 NIV

Just as it pleased the LORD to make you prosper and increase in number, so it will please Him to ruin and destroy you.

Deuteronomy 28:63 NIV

Your wealth and all your treasures I will give for spoil as the price of your sin throughout all your territory.

Jeremiah 17:3

8

Economic Ruin

Destroying the Golden Calf

One of the ways that God judges a nation is by destroying or removing its wealth. The threat of such judgment is found throughout the Law and the Prophets. The pattern of such judgment is recorded not only in the Scriptures but throughout human history.

The solemn conclusion is inescapable, based upon the threats found in Scripture, that if a nation does not repent and turn to God, its collective wealth will be severely diminished or destroyed. This chapter will discuss with broad strokes how such wealth is gained and how it can be lost.

Perhaps the topic of God's judgment on wealth can be more readily understood if it is viewed in the framework of idolatry—idolatry practiced by pagans and Christians alike. Idolatry in modern times rarely resembles the idolatry of the pagan past. Most idolaters today in what was once known as Christendom do not burn incense or bow in front of pagan idols made of wood and stone, gold and silver. The names of Baal, Molech, Apollo, Zeus, or Jupiter are rarely invoked.

Though it may be that a handful of idol worshippers exists—practitioners of "dark arts," witchcraft, etc.—these rebellious, lost souls remain the exception—a queer freak show trapped in devilish lies. Additionally, the vast nation of India and a handful of Asian and African nations yet lie in the grip of demonic superstition and idolatry, serving hundreds of false gods and pagan deities. For them, believers should grieve and do their part to help evangelize.

But belief in the false gods of pagan antiquity, which once cursed Europe, Russia, the Near East, the Americas, and North Africa, has been all but obliterated. The names of pagan deities such as Nike, Saturn, Caesar, etc., no longer arouse fear and trembling. They would be forgotten if they had not been retrieved to name sneakers, cars, and dogs.

But sadly, another idolatry, perhaps nearly as vile and deadly, exists throughout North America, Europe, and the pseudo-Christian world: namely, *covetousness*—the unholy love of money, wealth, and things. The Apostle Paul wrote:

> Put to death therefore what is earthly in you: immorality, impurity, passion, evil desire, *and covetousness, which is idolatry*. (Colossians 3:5)

> Be sure of this, that no immoral or impure man, *or one who is covetous (that is, an idolater)*, has any inheritance in the kingdom of Christ and of God. (Ephesians 5:5)

The Old Testament contains the record of God's destruction of pagan idols, usually through His people and via military conquest. In the time of the early Church, pagan Roman and Grecian idolatry was defeated through the preaching of the Gospel, the "decriminalization" of Christianity, and lastly the criminalization of public idol worship in the Roman Empire (and later in other nations).

The Pantheon in Rome used to hold the most revered pagan idols of that era. After the public worship of pagan gods was outlawed, the Pantheon building was given to the Church. It has been a functioning church for over 1,400 years.

Pagan idolatry required pagan idols—i.e., physical statues in physical locations where worshippers could worship the false deity. The idolatry of covetousness, on the other hand, originates from within, and the object of worship could be anything, found anywhere, or found everywhere. Those enslaved to covetousness, which is idolatry, take their greed and lust with them everywhere they go at all times and in all places.

An idolater can covet money, a car, a guitar, a TV, a woman, a man, a gun, a dog, fame, or praise and adulation—literally anything. Because the objects of worship are everywhere to be seen, the practice of idolatry can literally carry on unabated in every waking hour. To make matters worse, the objects of modern idolatry are available anytime on TVs, computers, smart devices, etc.

Regarding idolatry's subtle influence, one of the ways people can see how their "worship of the golden calf" has affected them is by what they *don't do* and what they *don't say*. Many men and women—from individuals of modest income to the fabulously wealthy—do not say the truth and do not publicly fight for the truth because they are afraid of the impact such words and actions will have on their wealth and livelihoods. Many Christians and other people of good will have equivocated or remained silent in the face of grave evil because they fear the economic impact or the loss of stature or respectability they might suffer if they follow and obey Christ (or promote the truth) in a fashion that the enemies of truth will find offensive or militant. They fear what the "cancel culture" will do to them if they boldly proclaim the truth. Consider the fear that exists among people in many formerly Christian nations regarding transvestism and the drag-queen movement. Many of the powerful, the wealthy, the broadcasters, writers, and politically powerful are afraid to say these two phrases: 1) Men cannot have babies. 2) Women do not have a penis.

The sheer terror of saying these simple truths has multitudes embracing a lie, often fueled by idolatry—the love of self and the love of things.

Consider the many businesses, as well as men and women from various fields—education, entertainment, and politics—who have bowed before the cancel culture. This powerful system of control seeks to destroy individuals and businesses that do not go along with the new regime of godlessness, hedonism, and Marxism. There is a price to be paid for boldness in the cause of truth and holiness.

The questions all must ask themselves are these:

Who is to be more feared—God or man?

Whose praise is to be more sought after—God's or man's?

What is more valuable—eternal truth and eternal souls or comfort and wealth?

Who is to be worshipped—the Almighty or the golden calf?

No man can serve two masters. Jesus said, "You cannot serve God and mammon" (Luke 16:13). Moreover, when a nation turns its back on God and His Laws, He has the ability to destroy the golden calf if He so chooses.

The Richest Nation in the World

The United States of America is currently the wealthiest nation in the world. The factors allowing this on a physical, human level are manifold. The nation has massive natural resources, from gold and silver to timber and metals; lush farmlands and the climate to grow and harvest virtually every crop known to mankind; millions upon millions of acres of grazing land for cattle and other domestic animals; vast sums of oil, natural gas, and coal; and the third-largest population in the world, which provides a massive workforce.

And to whom much is given, much is required.

Beyond the extensive natural resources found in America, one key element that sets America apart is its *creed*—that is, the religious, "theocentric" nature of its founding and laws. America's founding document—the Declaration of Independence—has four references to God. The Founders claimed their efforts were based on His Law, His justice, and the inalienable rights He had given to man. America has experienced more codified liberty—"liberty under law"—than any nation since ancient Israel, a liberty based squarely in Christian ethics and law. This liberty has allowed an entrepreneurial genius and natural aristocracy to emerge that has created more first-generation wealth (vs. inherited wealth) than possibly any nation in the history of the world.

Hence, on a spiritual level, many have made the argument that America's unique wealth and freedom are directly connected to the blessing of God—that His blessing has been on America in a unique way because of its Founders' self-conscious effort (albeit flawed and hideously marred by slavery) to form a nation "under God." The Pilgrims, the Puritans, and the signers of the Declaration all had this in common: the belief that government and liberty were defined and limited by God's laws and the Gospel.

It is a historical fact that America's Founders sought to build "A City on a Hill," "One Nation, Under God," with currency claiming, "In God We Trust." It is a current fact that presidents, governors, judges, etc., *swear their oath of office with their hand on a Bible.* In all of this and more, American culture and traditions invoke the name and blessing of God on that republic.

Ironically, *the invocation of God's name and Law may bring down His displeasure* more severely when a nation mocks His name and spurns His Law, embracing and glorifying evils that rival the worst pagan nations in the history of mankind.

Again, *to whom much is given, much is required.*

The Law of God in America

Research shows that in American Revolutionary literature, the book most frequently quoted to justify the revolution was the Bible, particularly the book of Deuteronomy.[1]

Since the dawn of the American republic, Christians there have embraced the promises of wealth and blessings God gave to the Hebrews as promises for them:

> For the LORD your God is bringing you into a good land, a land of brooks of water, of fountains and springs, flowing forth in valleys and hills, a land of wheat and barley, of vines and fig trees and pomegranates, a land of olive trees and honey, a land in which you will eat bread without scarcity, in which you will lack nothing, a land whose stones are iron, and out of whose hills you can dig copper. And you shall eat and be full, and you shall bless the LORD your God for the good land He has given you. (Deuteronomy 8:7–10)

> And if you obey the voice of the LORD your God, being careful to do all His commandments which I command you this day, the LORD your God will set you high above all the nations of the earth. And all these blessings shall come upon you and overtake you, if you obey the voice of the LORD your God. Blessed shall you be in the city, and blessed shall you be in the field. Blessed shall be the fruit of your body, and the fruit of your ground, and the fruit of your beasts, the increase of your cattle, and the young of your flock. Blessed shall be your basket and your kneading-trough. Blessed shall you be when you come in, and blessed shall you be when you go out. (Deuteronomy 28:1–6)

---

1. Donald S. Lutz, "The Relative Influence of European Writers on Late Eighteenth-Century American Political Thought," *American Political Science Review* 78, no. 1 (1984): 189–97; Charles S. Hyneman and Donald S. Lutz, *American Political Writing During the Founding Era* (Indianapolis: Liberty Press, 1983), vols. I & II.

The Promise of Economic Ruin

Just as with plagues and fear, economic hardship and ruin are punishments God specifically says He'll use to chasten His people. But even if an economy survives a pandemic and restabilizes, if a people remains unrepentant for its national sins, economic ruin will come.

Scripture shows that God promises His people prosperity if they obey Him, and He also promises His people that He will take away their wealth if they rebel against Him:

> But if you will not obey the voice of the LORD your God or be careful to do all His commandments and His statutes which I command you this day, then all these curses shall come upon you and overtake you. Cursed shall you be in the city, and cursed shall you be in the field. Cursed shall be your basket and your kneading-trough. Cursed shall be the fruit of your body, and the fruit of your ground, the increase of your cattle, and the young of your flock. Cursed shall you be when you come in, and cursed shall you be when you go out.
>
> The LORD will send upon you curses, confusion, and frustration, in all that you undertake to do, until you are destroyed and perish quickly, on account of the evil of your doings, because you have forsaken Me....
>
> You shall build a house, and you shall not dwell in it; you shall plant a vineyard, and you shall not use the fruit of it. Your ox shall be slain before your eyes, and you shall not eat of it; your ass shall be violently taken away before your face, and shall not be restored to you; your sheep shall be given to your enemies, and there shall be no one to help you....
>
> You shall carry much seed into the field, and shall gather little in; for the locust shall consume it. You shall plant vineyards and dress them, but you shall neither drink of the wine nor gather the grapes; for the worm shall eat them. You shall have olive trees throughout all your territory, but

you shall not anoint yourself with the oil; for your olives shall drop off....

The sojourner who is among you shall mount above you higher and higher; and you shall come down lower and lower. He shall lend to you, and you shall not lend to him; he shall be the head, and you shall be the tail....

And as the LORD *took delight in doing you good and multiplying you, so the* LORD *will take delight in bringing ruin upon you and destroying you.* (Deuteronomy 28:15–20, 30–31, 38–40, 43–44, 63)

Sadly, after the Israelites were planted in the promised land, slowly and steadily, they turned their backs on God, committing horrific acts of evil, including offering their babies as sacrifices to demons and establishing idols and cult homosexual prostitution booths in Solomon's Temple. God sent prophets to warn them and to call them back to Him, but they hardened their hearts and grew more and more wicked.

As a result, God kept His promise to punish them with the loss of their wealth. The following passages are samples of scores of such verses in the Scriptures. Ezekiel declared:

Behold, the day! Behold, it comes! Your doom has come, injustice has blossomed, pride has budded. Violence has grown up into a rod of wickedness; none of them shall remain, nor their abundance, nor their wealth; neither shall there be pre-eminence among them. The time has come, the day draws near. Let not the buyer rejoice, nor the seller mourn, for wrath is upon all their multitude. For the seller shall not return to what he has sold, while they live. For wrath is upon all their multitude; it shall not turn back; and because of his iniquity, none can maintain his life. (Ezekiel 7:10–13)

Jeremiah prophesied:

Your wealth and your treasures
I will give as plunder, without charge,
because of all your sins
throughout your country....
For My anger will kindle a fire
that will burn against you. (Jeremiah 15:13–14 NIV)

Your wealth and all your treasures I will give for spoil
as the price of your sin throughout all your territory.
(Jeremiah 17:3)

Zephaniah's prophecy of economic ruin came straight from
the Law of God:

"On that day," says the LORD,
"a cry will be heard from the Fish Gate,
a wail from the Second Quarter,
a loud crash from the hills.
Wail, O inhabitants of the Mortar!
For all the traders are no more;
all who weigh out silver are cut off.
At that time I will search Jerusalem with lamps,
and I will punish the men
who are thickening upon their lees,
those who say in their hearts,
'The LORD will not do good,
nor will He do ill.'
Their goods shall be plundered,
and their houses laid waste.
Though they build houses,
they shall not inhabit them;
though they plant vineyards,
they shall not drink wine from them."
(Zephaniah 1:10–13)

These warnings from God came true, and Judah was devastated financially.

Economic Judgment on Pagan Nations

Oddly, some Christians in America have behaved as if God would *bless* people financially but He would not *punish* people financially. Others have believed that the threats and warnings of the Old Testament regarding finances only applied to the Israelites.

Even a cursory overview of the Old Testament shows that God brought economic judgment on pagan nations just as He threatened He would do with His own people. For example, the Egyptians were ruined financially because of God's judgment on them for enslaving the Jews. After sending plagues on the Egyptians, including the death of their firstborn, God also stripped them of their wealth:

> The Israelites did as Moses instructed and asked the Egyptians for articles of silver and gold and for clothing.... And they gave them what they asked for; so they plundered the Egyptians. (Exodus 12:35–36 NIV)

The seven pagan Canaanite nations had all their wealth taken from them—their houses, lands, vineyards, etc.—because of their sins. God specifically said to the Israelites:

> Hear, O Israel; you are to pass over the Jordan this day, to *go in to dispossess nations* greater and mightier than yourselves.... Know therefore this day that He who goes over before you as a devouring fire is the LORD your God; He will destroy them and subdue them before you; so you shall drive them out, and make them perish quickly, as the LORD has promised you.
>
> Do not say in your heart, after the LORD your God has thrust them out before you, "It is because of my righteousness that the LORD has brought me in to possess this land"; whereas it is *because of the wickedness of these nations that the LORD is driving them out before you. Not because of your righteousness or the uprightness of your heart are you going in to possess their land; but because of the wickedness of these nations*

the LORD your God is driving them out from before you, and that He may confirm the word which the LORD swore to your fathers, to Abraham, to Isaac, and to Jacob.

Know therefore, that the LORD your God is not giving you this good land to possess because of your righteousness. (Deuteronomy 9:1–6)

The prophet Zephaniah predicted the ruin of Philistia, Moab, and Nineveh. Ezekiel predicted the ruin of Tyre at the hand of Nebuchadnezzar, King of the Babylonians:

> With the hoofs of his horses he will trample all your streets; he will slay your people with the sword; and your mighty pillars will fall to the ground. They will make a spoil of your riches and a prey of your merchandise; they will break down your walls and destroy your pleasant houses; your stones and timber and soil they will cast into the midst of the waters. And I will stop the music of your songs, and the sound of your lyres shall be heard no more. I will make you a bare rock; you shall be a place for the spreading of nets; you shall never be rebuilt; for I the LORD have spoken, says the Lord GOD. (Ezekiel 26:11–14)

Jeremiah prophesied the economic and military ruin of Babylon:

> For behold, I am stirring up and bringing against Babylon a company of great nations, from the north country; and they shall array themselves against her; from there she shall be taken. Their arrows are like a skilled warrior who does not return empty-handed. Chalde'a shall be plundered; all who plunder her shall be sated, says the LORD....
>
> A sword upon all her treasures,
> that they may be plundered!
> A drought upon her waters,
> that they may be dried up!

> For it is a land of images,
> and they are mad over idols. (Jeremiah 50:9–10,
> 37–38)

This brief focus on these nations of the past proves the point that in the past, God used economic punishment on pagan nations as well as on His covenant people. The promises of prosperity and threats of ruin are for the entire human race.

All would do well to take warning from this Scriptural history. Whether one believes that America is a blessed nation, a covenant nation, or a pagan nation, the Scriptures teach that God will economically chasten *any nation He chooses*. And America is not exempt from these chastenings from the Almighty.

Remember This: God Has More Disaster than Any Government Has Relief

God has more disaster than any government has relief. Jeremiah said with weeping:

> Have you not brought this upon yourself
> by forsaking the LORD your God…?
> Your wickedness will chasten you,
> and your apostasy will reprove you.
> Know and see that it is evil and bitter
> for you to forsake the LORD your God;
> the fear of Me is not in you,
> says the Lord GOD of hosts. (Jeremiah 2:17–19)

> Your ways and your doings
> have brought this upon you.
> This is your doom, and it is bitter. (Jeremiah 4:18)

America's Loss of Wealth

Ponder the wealth lost in America because of the War Between the States, in both the North and the South. The economic impact of the Civil War was catastrophic. Many families and areas of the South never recovered.

With the coronavirus pandemic, we again witnessed the loss of trillions of dollars, without a shot being fired. The most prosperous nations in the history of the world bled financially and went deeper and deeper into debt. All of the "stimulus packages" intended to prop up the American economy were loans—borrowed money—against a future when the bill comes due and America will be unable to pay it.

Consider this: most Western nations function economically with "fiat currency"—i.e., paper currency with no inherent value (contrasted with real silver and gold, which have inherent value and served as money for most of human history).

Add to this the emergence of "crypto currency," which is mostly unregulated by government, and one can see that with the right circumstances—the right political climate, the right war, the right "shortage," the right government policies, or the right corrupt individuals in banking, stocks, or crypto currency, vast sums of wealth can be shrunk or eliminated virtually overnight. And such loss could be the corrective hand of God.

Look at these warnings God gave in another passage from Deuteronomy:

> Take heed lest you forget the LORD your God, by not keeping His commandments and His ordinances and His statutes, which I command you this day: *lest, when you have eaten and are full, and have built goodly houses and live in them, and when your herds and flocks multiply, and your silver and gold is multiplied, and all that you have is multiplied, then your heart be lifted up, and you forget the LORD your God....*
>
> Beware lest you say in your heart, "My power and the might of my hand have gotten me this wealth." You shall remember the LORD your God, for it is He who gives you power to get wealth; that He may confirm His covenant which He swore to your fathers, as at this day. And if you forget the LORD your God and go after other gods and serve them and worship them, I solemnly warn you this day

that you shall surely perish. Like the nations that the LORD makes to perish before you, so shall you perish, because you would not obey the voice of the LORD your God. (Deuteronomy 8:11–20)

Several more passages of Scripture prove the premise that God chastens economically nations that rebel against Him morally.

I will give away all the wealth of this city—all its products and valuables, and all the treasures of the kings of Judah—to their enemies. They will plunder them, seize them, and carry them off to Babylon. (Jeremiah 20:5 BSB)

Our inheritance has been turned over to strangers, our houses to foreigners. (Lamentations 5:2 BSB)

You will sow but not reap; you will press olives but not anoint yourselves with oil; you will tread grapes but not drink the wine. (Micah 6:15 BSB)

Now therefore, thus says the LORD of hosts: "Consider your ways!
You have sown much, and bring in little;
you eat, but do not have enough;
you drink, but you are not filled with drink;
you clothe yourselves, but no one is warm;
and he who earns wages,
earns wages to put into a bag with holes."
(Haggai 1:5–6 NKJV)

And you shall grope at noonday, as a blind man gropes in darkness; you shall not prosper in your ways; you shall be only oppressed and plundered continually, and no one shall save you. (Deuteronomy 28:29 NKJV)

And your strength shall be spent in vain; for your land shall not yield its produce, nor shall the trees of the land yield their fruit. (Leviticus 26:20 NKJV)

The following passage sounds like a report from the *Wall Street Journal*:

> The alien who is among you shall rise higher and higher above you, and you shall come down lower and lower. He shall lend to you, but you shall not lend to him; he shall be the head, and you shall be the tail. (Deuteronomy 28:43–44 NKJV)

America went from being the world's largest lender nation to the world's largest debtor nation, enabling the Chinese to position themselves to bring great economic hardship on America. God is able to humble America in poverty before foreign nations, whether friend or foe:

> Because you did not serve the LORD your God with joy and gladness of heart, for the abundance of everything, therefore you shall serve your enemies, whom the LORD will send against you, in hunger, in thirst, in nakedness, and in need of everything; and He will put a yoke of iron on your neck until He has destroyed you. (Deuteronomy 28:47–48 NKJV)

In Nehemiah's day, the Israelites were punished for their idolatry, and their chastening included the surrender of their wealth.

> Here we are, servants today!
> And the land that You gave to our fathers,
> to eat its fruit and its bounty,
> here we are, servants in it!
> And it yields much increase to the kings
> You have set over us,
> because of our sins;
> also they have dominion over our bodies and our cattle
> at their pleasure;
> and we are in great distress. (Nehemiah 9:36–37 NKJV)

What did Judah do that provoked the wrath of God with such ferocity? Exactly what crimes and sins did they commit that caused God to wipe out their wealth and send them into exile?

The economic ruin Judah endured ranks amongst the worst in all human history. These were God's chosen, covenant people. It was through Israel that God gave the world the Ten Commandments and the Savior of the world. There was never a tribe of the earth that had such a unique call from and relationship with God.

Yet God judged them fiercely. Why? *Because of the sins that cried for vengeance.*

A related question is this: If God is trying to get America's and Western nations' attention—if He is chastening them—what have they done to warrant His displeasure? What crimes and sins have happened on American and European soil that would cause the Almighty to turn His face from them and bring grievous hardships and loss to their shores?

The answers lie in Sacred Scripture and can be studied first in the ancient city of Jerusalem, and then—for a recent example—in modern New York City, to which we will turn shortly. But first, we turn our attention to the sword.

"*Thus says the LORD: Behold, I am against you, and will draw forth My sword out of its sheath, and will cut off from you both righteous and wicked. Because I will cut off from you both righteous and wicked, therefore My sword shall go out of its sheath against all flesh from south to north; and all flesh shall know that I the LORD have drawn My sword out of its sheath; it shall not be sheathed again. Sigh therefore, son of man; sigh with breaking heart and bitter grief before their eyes. And when they say to you, 'Why do you sigh?' you shall say, 'Because of the tidings. When it comes, every heart will melt and all hands will be feeble, every spirit will faint and all knees will be weak as water. Behold, it comes and it will be fulfilled,'" says the Lord GOD....*

*"A sword, a sword is sharpened
and also polished,
sharpened for slaughter,
polished to flash like lightning!"*

Ezekiel 21:3–10

I will send the sword, famine, and plague against them until they have perished from the land I gave to them and their ancestors.

Jeremiah 24:10 HCSB

Then I said: "Ah, Lord GOD, behold, the prophets say to them, 'You shall not see the sword, nor shall you have famine, but I will give you assured peace in this place.'" And the LORD said to me: "The prophets are prophesying lies in My name; I did not send them, nor did I command them or speak to them. They are prophesying to you a lying vision, worthless divination, and the deceit of their own minds. Therefore thus says the LORD concerning the prophets who prophesy in My name although I did not send them, and who say, 'Sword and famine shall not come on this land': By sword and famine those prophets shall be consumed. And the people to whom they prophesy shall be cast out in the streets of Jerusalem, victims of famine and sword, with none to bury them—them, their wives, their sons, and their daughters. For I will pour out their wickedness upon them."

Jeremiah 14:13–16

9

THE SWORD

The sword in judgment can take many forms:

- Foreign powers—i.e., Russia, China, Iran, Saudi Arabia
- Terrorist groups—i.e., Hezbollah, Al-Qaeda, the Taliban, the Islamic State
- Gangs—i.e., in the U.S., Canada, and European nations there are thousands of gangs, most of which commit acts of severe violence and murder
- Random violence—i.e., carjackings, "smash and grabs," random killings, punchings, kickings, and beatings for no apparent reason

The sword is a potent and fearful punishment against any nation that has rejected God's Law and committed sins that cry for vengeance. The Scripture delineates "the sword"—whether random violence or military conquest from an outside power—as a definitive and terrifying step in the judgment of God.

> Your ox shall be slaughtered before your eyes, but you shall not eat of it; your donkey shall be violently taken away from before you, and shall not be restored to you; your sheep shall be given to your enemies, and you shall have no one to rescue them. (Deuteronomy 28:31 NKJV)

And if you despise My statutes, or if your soul abhors My judgments, so that you do not perform all My commandments, but break My covenant, I also will do this to you: I will even appoint terror over you, wasting disease and fever which shall consume the eyes and cause sorrow of heart....

And I will bring a sword against you that will execute the vengeance of [My] covenant; when you are gathered together within your cities I will send pestilence among you; and you shall be delivered into the hand of the enemy. (Leviticus 26:15–16, 25 NKJV)

The Muslim threat of terrorism has perennially loomed large on the world horizon. God has thousands of Middle East radicals at His disposal, men who passionately hate America and the once-Christian West. As God lifts His providential, protecting hand to allow the advance of the sword, what can we expect?

The LORD will bring a nation against you from afar, from the end of the earth, as swift as the eagle flies, a nation whose language you will not understand, a nation of fierce countenance, which does not respect the elderly nor show favor to the young. (Deuteronomy 28:49–50 NKJV)

In the light of Scripture, the future can be predicted, sometimes with terrifying accuracy, simply by knowing the promises and threats God has made. The solemn threats and warnings—to punish nations that commit and institutionalize evils and abominations against Him and His laws—are clear and unambiguous.

The coming of the sword—i.e., violence sweeping through nations from within or from outside forces—can be predicted by knowing the Law of God and the prophetic books of Scripture. The sheer number of references to *the sword* as a punishment from God in the Scriptures is staggering and frightening.

The Sword Takes Many Forms

As alluded to above, the sword can take many forms, from acts of violence, cruelty, or barbarism—whether random violence in our cities, gang wars, or terrorism—to civil war, defeat on the field of battle, or conquest and occupation from a foreign foe—and rarely, the total destruction of a major city.

Many areas of historic American and European cities, once known for beauty, stability, and vibrant local culture, have been devastated. Whole sections of major urban areas that were once alive and safe have come to look like third-world nations or cities devastated by war. These cities are slowly being laid waste before the eyes of the world. This is the fruit of nations that have turned their backs on God and are under God's judgment:

> How the faithful city has become a harlot!
> It was full of justice;
> righteousness lodged in it,
> but now murderers.
> Your silver has become dross,
> your wine mixed with water.
> Your princes are rebellious,
> and companions of thieves;
> everyone loves bribes,
> and follows after rewards.
> They do not defend the fatherless,
> nor does the cause of the widow come before them.
> (Isaiah 1:21–23 NKJV)

> I will lay your cities waste and bring your sanctuaries to desolation, and I will not smell the fragrance of your sweet aromas. (Leviticus 26:31 NKJV)

Consider specific passages of Scripture in relation to the sword coming as a judgment.

Insolent and Violent Youth

The following threat from the Prophet Isaiah is being played out in hundreds of cities:

And I will make boys their princes,
and babes shall rule over them.
And the people will oppress one another,
every man his fellow
and every man his neighbor;
the youth will be insolent to the elder,
and the base fellow to the honorable.
(Isaiah 3:4–5)

In some communities, the elderly do not dare leave their homes at certain times for fear of disrespectful, violent youths. This is the fruit of the rejection of God's laws. God hands communities and nations over to violence, and nations reap the violence they have sown.

Defeat in Battle

Another part of the judgment of the sword is defeat in battle. The first war with Iraq was a great military success for the United States and her allies. But the second Iraq war and the war in Afghanistan dragged on and on. They cost thousands of American lives, hundreds of the lives of her allies, and billions of dollars. For what? A new wave of Islamic terrorism was birthed, and thousands of people died in various nations as Muslims launched their bloody attacks.

Likewise, the war in Vietnam was a humiliating defeat. The U.S. was disgraced in Beirut and in Somalia. Do more Vietnams, Beiruts, and Somalias await America on the field of battle?

Will America and European nations enter a conflict with Iran, China, Russia, or some unforeseen adversary, in which extensive life will be lost?

"Your young men I killed with a sword, along with your captive horses; I made the stench of your camps come up into your nostrils; yet you have not returned to Me," says the LORD. (Amos 4:10 NKJV)

The LORD will cause you to be defeated before your enemies; you shall go out one way against them and flee seven ways before them; and you shall become troublesome to all the kingdoms of the earth. Your carcasses shall be food for all the birds of the air and the beasts of the earth, and no one shall frighten them away. (Deuteronomy 28:25–26 NKJV)

Enemy Occupation, or Defeat on Domestic Shores

Perhaps the worst form of earthly judgment that God could bring against a nation is the defeat, occupation, and even the destruction of that nation by a foreign enemy.

The sheer geography and continental vastness of the U.S. and Canada make such scenarios unlikely, and the (current) combined strength of NATO would make the occupation of Europe all but unthinkable. However, a nuclear strike is not out of the question from China or Russia.

Worse yet is the reality that a nuclear attack need not come from a Russian or Chinese missile.

For example, if a nuclear weapon from Pakistan or Iran were to be placed on or in an oil tanker that docked in a major North American or European port and the nuclear device detonated, the loss of life would be unimaginable. Moreover, the economic meltdown and the chaos of infrastructure would be immediate and devastating. If an attack resulted in the disruption of food and/or fuel distribution—two indispensable items for a nation to survive and live in peace—life as known would cease to exist for millions. Farmers and ranchers in rural areas would fare well, but many cities could descend into chaos and burn to the ground.

God announced a judgment of this nature to the Jews:

And I will bring you out of its midst, and deliver you into the hands of strangers, and execute judgments on you. You shall fall by the sword. I will judge you at the border of Israel. Then you shall know that I am the LORD. (Ezekiel 11:9–10 NKJV)

Throughout history, God has judged nations by the sword. The seven Canaanite nations of antiquity had become so vile and corrupt before God that His intention was to obliterate them with the sword.

The thought of a foreign enemy occupying the United States, Canada, or a European nation may seem absurd. But before the Nazi blitzkrieg of 1939, France was believed to have had the greatest army on earth. In 1936, the thought of Germany conquering France was inconceivable.

A more likely scenario would be a nuclear strike against America or a NATO member, coupled with nuclear blackmail, combined with the occupation of a capital or major city. Such a scenario may seem to border on the insane, but other vast empires have fallen over the centuries. Today, one can wander the ruins of Delphi, the Forum, Nineveh, and Babylon and see the seats of power that ruled the then-known world—now heaps of rubble and the haunts of wild animals at night.

Also consider Israel and the prophet Amos. When Amos prophesied the destruction of Israel—drought, famine, plague, and the sword—Israel was in a state of great wealth and prosperity. Her enemies, the Syrians and the Assyrians, were in disarray and not a threat to her security. Amos's predictions of military conquest must have seemed laughable then, too. But before fifty years had elapsed, the Assyrians came and obliterated the Ten Northern Tribes in a crushing military conquest. The conquerors scattered their survivors to the wind and transplanted other pagan peoples into the land of Israel (from whence came the despised Samaritans). Israel never recovered from this fatal blow (see Second Kings 17, Amos, and Hosea).

America and Europe are foolish to think that their prosperity, military standing in the world, and the disarray of many of their enemies make them as safe as an eagle in a mountain crag. If Almighty God decrees destruction, all the patriot missiles and stealth bombers in the world will not protect a nation from defeat or devastating injury at the hands of its enemies. God will aid the enemies in that nation's injury or defeat just as surely as He brought down the "impenetrable walls" of Jericho so that the Israelites could destroy them.

Furthermore, even if an enemy never invades, the forces of terrorism—foreign and domestic—can continue to raise their horrifying heads. The threat of Muslim terrorism is not merely a threat. Thousands of lives have been lost in North America and Europe—and many African and Asian nations—to the sword of Islam. There are thousands of Middle East terrorists who passionately hate America and the once-Christian West. As God lifts His providential, protecting hand to allow the advance of the sword, what can we expect?

The fact that Muslim terrorists are evil murderers and do not serve the true God is of little import if they are used to bring chastening to a nation that has offended Almighty God. The prophet referred to Babylon as "the worst of the nations":

> Because the land is full of bloody crimes and the city is full of violence, I will bring the worst of the nations to take possession of their houses; I will put an end to their proud might, and their holy places shall be profaned. (Ezekiel 7:23–24)

Babylon was brutal and despicable. And ultimately, God destroyed them, turning their capital into an uninhabited ruin, as it is to this day. But before that dreadful day, He used them to punish the Jews for their abominations.

The violence and riots that mar the cities of the world will continue. The first bitter fruits of the violence that has been sown are being eaten across the globe, and more is coming. God has unsheathed His sword.

We see in Matthew chapters 23 and 24 the Lord Jesus grieving the violent fall of Jerusalem because God is punishing the city for all the blood of the righteous that has been shed there. Here is a quote from our Lord from the Gospel of Luke:

> Then let those who are in Judea flee to the mountains, and let those who are inside the city depart, and let not those

who are out in the country enter it; *for these are days of vengeance, to fulfil all that is written.* Alas for those who are with child and for those who give suck in those days! *For great distress shall be upon the earth and wrath upon this people; they will fall by the edge of the sword, and be led captive among all nations.* (Luke 21:21–24)

This falling of the sword in judgment against Jerusalem—the "City of Blood"—was what Jesus meant by the "days of vengeance." It was the wrath of God poured out on Jerusalem, the city that stoned its prophets and rejected the Son of God. The Lord spoke a similar judgment through Ezekiel:

Thus says the Lord GOD: Clap your hands, stamp your feet, and cry "Alas!" for all the evil abominations of the house of Israel! They shall fall by the sword, starvation, and disease. Those far off shall die of disease, *those nearby shall fall by the sword,* and those who survive and are spared shall perish by starvation; *thus will I spend My fury upon them.* (Ezekiel 6:11–12 NABRE)

Therefore, as I live, says the Lord GOD, because you have defiled My sanctuary with all your atrocities and all your abominations, *I will surely withdraw and not look upon you with pity nor spare you.* A third of your people shall die of disease or starve to death within you; *another third shall fall by the sword all around you; a third I will scatter to the winds and pursue them with the sword.* (Ezekiel 5:11–12 NABRE)

With the exception of the Civil War, until recently, America's history has been graced with an incredible legacy of domestic peace and stability. Its borders have not been breached by a foreign power since the war of 1812. Until the close of the last millennium, its cities were among the safest in the world. During the Great Depression, people went to bed with their doors unlocked. Not long ago, parents felt secure knowing their children were playing "somewhere in the neighborhood."

The stability and peace Americans once enjoyed, and perhaps even our military victories in WWI and WWII, were part of the blessing of God:

> I will give peace in the land, and you shall lie down, and none will make you afraid; I will rid the land of evil beasts, and the sword will not go through your land. You will chase your enemies, and they shall fall by the sword before you. (Leviticus 26:6–7 NKJV)

But like all the other blessings that were taken for granted, the blessing of peace and safety was wrenched from America's grasp. The sword replaced peace in much of the nation, and its reach continues to grow.

Sadly, too few recognize that this is the law of God at work—the law of sowing and reaping. Sow violence and oppression as a nation, and reap the rancid fruit.

Major European cities are writhing under similar punishments of violence—the sword. When will the direct connection between rebellion against God as a nation and His outpoured judgment of the sword be accepted for what it is? Some *can't* see it because they *refuse* to see it.

> "Thus says the LORD: *Behold, I am against you, and will draw forth My sword out of its sheath, and will cut off from you both righteous and wicked.* Because I will cut off from you both righteous and wicked, therefore My sword shall go out of its sheath against all flesh from south to north; *and all flesh shall know that I the LORD have drawn My sword out of its sheath; it shall not be sheathed again.* Sigh therefore, son of man; sigh with breaking heart and bitter grief before their eyes. And when they say to you, 'Why do you sigh?' you shall say, 'Because of the tidings. When it comes, every heart will melt and all hands will be feeble, every spirit will faint and all knees will be weak as water. Behold, it comes and it will be fulfilled,'" says the Lord GOD....

"A sword, a sword is sharpened
and also polished,
sharpened for slaughter,
polished to flash like lightning!

"*Or do we make mirth? You have despised the rod, My son,
with everything of wood. So the sword is given to be polished,
that it may be handled; it is sharpened and polished to be given
into the hand of the slayer. Cry and wail, son of man, for it is
against My people; it is against all the princes of Israel; they
are delivered over to the sword with My people.* Smite therefore
upon your thigh. For it will not be a testing—what could it
do if you despise the rod?" says the Lord GOD.

"*Prophesy therefore, son of man; clap your hands and let the
sword come down twice, yea thrice, the sword for those to be slain;
it is the sword for the great slaughter, which encompasses them,
that their hearts may melt, and many fall at all their gates.* I have
given the glittering sword; ah! it is made like lightning, it is
polished for slaughter. Cut sharply to right and left where
your edge is directed. I also will clap My hands, and I will
satisfy My fury; I the LORD have spoken." (Ezekiel 21:3–17)

The judgment of violence—the sword—nations reaping
what they have sown—has been rising in a steady crescendo
for fifty or sixty years. If nations are to be spared further horrors
of the sword and the violence, bloodshed, and death it brings,
they must repent of the evils and sins that cry to heaven—the
evils that have opened the door to these punishments.

If they do not—if they harden their hearts or lie to themselves
by ignoring the connection between sins that cry to heaven and
the ever-growing violence that is cursing their nations—then
they will reap whatever violence and bloodshed the Almighty
decrees they deserve.

Now the question must be answered: What "sins that cry
to heaven" are America, Canada, and European nations

committing? What crimes against God and man have been institutionalized and protected in these foolish nations? What seeds have been sown to bring a harvest of violence?

The first: *The shedding of innocent blood—the murder of innocent children.*

What have you done? The voice of YOUR BROTHER'S BLOOD IS CRYING
TO ME FROM THE GROUND.

Genesis 4:10

*You shall not give any of your children to devote them by fire to Molech,
and so profane the name of your God: I am the* LORD.

Leviticus 18:21

The LORD *said to Moses, "Say to the Israelites: 'Any Israelite or any
foreigner residing in Israel who sacrifices any of his children to Molek
is to be put to death.'"*

Leviticus 20:1–2 NIV

*They did not destroy the peoples,
as the* LORD *commanded them,
but they mingled with the nations
and learned to do as they did.
They served their idols,
which became a snare to them.
They sacrificed their sons
and their daughters to the demons;
they poured out innocent blood,
the blood of their sons and daughters,
whom they sacrificed to the idols of Canaan;
and the land was polluted with blood.
Thus they became unclean by their acts,
and played the harlot in their doings.
Then the anger of the* LORD *was kindled against His people,
and He abhorred His heritage;
He gave them into the hand of the nations,
so that those who hated them ruled over them.
Their enemies oppressed them,
and they were brought into subjection under their power.*

Psalm 106:34–42

10

DON'T KILL CHILDREN

The following chapters deal with the *why?* of judgment, based on extensive Sacred Scripture references, which are best considered slowly, thoughtfully, and prayerfully. These Scriptures have a powerful, timeless message for all nations. Moreover, if the teachings and conclusions of these chapters are correct, the formerly Christian nations of the West are in grave danger.

God gave multiple warnings of judgment against Judah. Jeremiah and Ezekiel announced those judgments were at hand. Those terrifying punishments were finally fulfilled against Jerusalem.

But what crimes did the Jews commit that brought plagues, fear and terror, and economic collapse? What exactly were their national sins that were so outrageous to God that He sent the sword against them? What did they do that so enraged God that He orchestrated the destruction of their—and His—beloved temple and the holy city of Jerusalem, sending the scant survivors into captivity in Babylon?

The most egregious crime that the Jews committed was the "shedding of innocent blood." They literally killed their own offspring, *"and the LORD would not forgive."*

To set the stage of Israel's doom, one must examine the nations that predated the Jews: the Canaanites.

Why Did God Destroy the Canaanite Nations?

When God delivered the Jews from Egypt, He led them to the promised land, which was occupied by seven Canaanite nations. He commanded the Jews to defeat the Canaanites, dispossess them, and utterly destroy them. Why?

God told the Israelites He was giving the Jews the promised land not because the Jews were good, but rather, God was removing the Canaanites from the face of the earth because the Canaanites were evil:

> Hear, O Israel; you are to pass over the Jordan this day, to go in to dispossess nations greater and mightier than yourselves, cities great and fortified up to heaven, a people great and tall.... *Know therefore this day that He who goes over before you as a devouring fire is the* LORD *your God; He will destroy them and subdue them before you*; so you shall drive them out, and make them perish quickly, as the LORD has promised you.

> Do not say in your heart, after the LORD your God has thrust them out before you, "It is because of my righteousness that the LORD has brought me in to possess this land"; whereas *it is because of the wickedness of these nations that the* LORD *is driving them out before you*. Not because of your righteousness or the uprightness of your heart are you going in to possess their land; *but because of the wickedness of these nations the* LORD *your God is driving them out from before you,* and that He may confirm the word which the LORD swore to your fathers, to Abraham, to Isaac, and to Jacob.

> Know therefore, that *the* LORD *your God is not giving you this good land to possess because of your righteousness; for you are a stubborn people.* (Deuteronomy 9:1–6)

What specifically were the Canaanites doing that caused God to hurl them from their habitations? God gave a concise list of the sins—the "abominations," as He called them—that the Canaanites had committed that brought the wrath of God on them. Here is an example:

You shall not give any of your children to devote them by fire to Molech, and so profane the name of your God: I am the LORD. You shall not lie with a male as with a woman; it is an abomination. And you shall not lie with any beast and defile yourself with it, neither shall any woman give herself to a beast to lie with it: it is perversion.

Do not defile yourselves by any of these things, for by all these the nations I am casting out before you defiled themselves; and the land became defiled, so that I punished its iniquity, and the land vomited out its inhabitants. But you shall keep My statutes and My ordinances and do none of these abominations, either the native or the stranger who sojourns among you (for all of these abominations the men of the land did, who were before you, so that the land became defiled); lest the land vomit you out, when you defile it, as it vomited out the nation that was before you. (Leviticus 18:21–28)

God singled out one crime that rose as a stench in His nostrils more than all the other crimes—namely, the Canaanites were killing their children.

When the LORD your God cuts off before you the nations whom you go in to dispossess, and you dispossess them and dwell in their land, take heed that you be not ensnared to follow them, after they have been destroyed before you, and that you do not inquire about their gods, saying, "How did these nations serve their gods?—that I also may do likewise." You shall not do so to the LORD your God; *for every abominable thing which the LORD hates they have done for their gods; for they even burn their sons and their daughters in the fire to their gods.* (Deuteronomy 12:29–31)

The crime of offering and slaying their children as burnt offerings was an evil that the Lord detested.

Before going further, let it be clearly established that the commands against slaying children encompass born and *unborn* children. In the Old Testament, the Hebrew word for "children" is *ben*, which is used interchangeably to depict a person already born—including adults—with a child yet in his mother's womb. For example, when Rebecca was pregnant with Esau and Jacob, Genesis 25:22 says, "The children struggled together within her [womb]." The Hebrew is the word *ben*.

Likewise, in the New Testament, the word for a born baby or an unborn baby is the same Greek word: *brephos*. In Luke 18:15 (NASB), it says, "And they were bringing even their babies to Him [Jesus] so that He might touch them." The word "babies" is the Greek word *brephos*. In Luke chapter 1, verse 41 (NASB), the record of Mary and Elizabeth's meeting states: "And it came about that when Elizabeth heard Mary's greeting, the baby leaped in her womb." This is again the Greek word *brephos*.

Throughout the Scriptures, one sees the consistent teaching that the born and the unborn are human beings, known by God. And clearly, all scientific evidence proves that from the moment of conception onward, a new and distinct human being exists, with its own DNA, completely separate from that of the mother. Yes, the child resides in the mother, but it is not "her body" that is being hunted and killed; it is the life of the child—the *brephos*, the *ben*—that is being snuffed out. "Abortion," as it is euphemistically called, is murder.

And murder—the deliberate shedding of innocent blood—is a crime that is first recorded and condemned in Genesis, with the condemnation of shedding innocent blood carried all the way through Sacred Scripture.

Blood Talks to God

The first instance of this crime was when Cain killed his brother Abel.

> Now Abel was a keeper of sheep, and Cain a tiller of the ground. In the course of time Cain brought to the LORD an offering of the fruit of the ground, and Abel brought of the firstlings of his flock and of their fat portions. And

the LORD had regard for Abel and his offering, but for Cain and his offering He had no regard. So Cain was very angry, and his countenance fell. The LORD said to Cain, "Why are you angry, and why has your countenance fallen? If you do well, will you not be accepted? And if you do not do well, sin is couching at the door; its desire is for you, but you must master it."

Cain said to Abel his brother, "Let us go out to the field." And when they were in the field, Cain rose up against his brother Abel, and killed him. Then the LORD said to Cain, "Where is Abel your brother?" He said, "I do not know; am I my brother's keeper?" And the LORD said, "What have you done? *The voice of your brother's blood is crying to Me from the ground*. And now you are cursed from the ground, which has opened its mouth to receive your brother's blood from your hand. When you till the ground, it shall no longer yield to you its strength; you shall be a fugitive and a wanderer on the earth." (Genesis 4:2–12)

The sin of shedding innocent blood ranks in a singular way with God. This can be seen in the instructions that God gave Noah. After being saved from judgment, Noah and his family disembarked from the ark, and God gave them these specific instructions:

And God blessed Noah and his sons, and said to them, "Be fruitful and multiply, and fill the earth. The fear of you and the dread of you shall be upon every beast of the earth, and upon every bird of the air, upon everything that creeps on the ground and all the fish of the sea; into your hand they are delivered. Every moving thing that lives shall be food for you; and as I gave you the green plants, I give you everything. Only you shall not eat flesh with its life, that is, its blood. *For your lifeblood I will surely require a reckoning; of every beast I will require it and of man; of every man's brother I will require the life of man. Whoever sheds the blood of man, by*

man shall his blood be shed; for God made man in His own image.
And you, be fruitful and multiply, bring forth abundantly
on the earth and multiply in it." (Genesis 9:1–7)

Centuries before God gave the Law to Moses—centuries
before the Canaanites brought the curse of God on themselves—God told Noah: "For your lifeblood I will surely require
a reckoning." God proceeded to command that murderers be
put to death by other humans. Why? Because man is made in
the image of God, and because of this, murder is an assault on
the image of God and, therefore, an assault on God Himself.

Note that this is the only negative, *punishable deed* God spoke
of after the Flood—that is, murder and the death sentence for
the murderer. While Genesis 9:1–7 has several instructions, only
one punishment is listed: the execution of a murderer. This
shows how heinous the crime of murder is to God. God *hates*
the shedding of innocent blood.

Do Not Shed Innocent Blood

God especially detests the killing of children. As will be shown,
the phrase "the shedding of innocent blood" became synony-
mous with killing children in Biblical literature.

God gave the Ten Commandments to Moses and, through
him, to the world. The Ten Commandments are the unchange-
able bedrock for law and the requirements for human behavior. In addition to the Ten Commandments, in the books of
Exodus, Leviticus, Numbers, and Deuteronomy, the specifics
of how those commandments applied to all aspects of life were
laid out in great and glorious detail.[1] The laws of God and His

---

1. The Law of God regarding such things as wells, human waste, disease,
purification, quarantine, burning of clothes, etc., makes for worthwhile study.
Why did God order certain steps to be taken regarding water, waste, and
the sick or diseased? He understood germs, bacteria, viruses, etc., as being
contagious. Only a Divine Being who knew these details could have inspired
those instructions at that point in human history—before microscopes, etc.

various prohibitions and punishments make it clear that all sins
are *not equal.*

All Sin Is Sin, but Not All Sin Is Equal

One pernicious lie has cursed certain fields of thought in Protestant theology—namely, that all sins are equal in the eyes of
God. This is an absurdity that can be quickly put aside by using
some "earthy" illustrations and Scriptural reasoning.

What sin would a wife find more devastating: her husband
committing the sin of drunkenness at a party, or her husband
committing adultery at that party?

What sin would a parent find more horrifying: a teenage boy
telling a lie, or a teenage boy raping a girl?

What sin would destroy a husband's life: a thief stealing his
wife's purse, or someone murdering his wife?

Apart from plain common sense, the fact that not all sins
are equal to God is clear in the punishments God requires for
various sins and crimes. For example, covetousness is a sin, but
no earthly punishment is mandated for covetousness. Laziness
is a sin, but again, God does not mandate any punishment from
earthly civil authorities for this sin.

Theft is a sin, and the punishment mandated by God is restitution. Murder is a sin, and the punishment prescribed in the
laws of Noah and Moses is *death.*

God does not talk about "covetousness crying from the
ground," or "theft crying from the ground." He speaks of *blood
crying from the ground.*

If the shedding of innocent blood is no bigger or more rep-
rehensible a sin to God than covetousness, an unholy devotion
to sports, or someone cheating on their taxes, then America
and the formerly Christian nations of the world have little to
worry about. But if the shedding of innocent blood demands
God's special attention because He has declared it will have His
special attention, then those nations are in critical danger of the
judgment of God.

Better to Be Drowned
than to Harm or Corrupt Children

It is clear in the Scriptures that God has a special place in His heart and Law for children. One of the few times in the New Testament our Lord Jesus became angry was when His disciples tried to keep small children away from Him.

> And they were bringing children to Him, that He might touch them; and the disciples rebuked them. *But when Jesus saw it He was indignant,* and said to them, "Let the children come to Me, do not hinder them; for to such belongs the kingdom of God. Truly, I say to you, whoever does not receive the kingdom of God like a child shall not enter it." And He took them in His arms and blessed them, laying His hands upon them. (Mark 10:13–16)

The Greek word used here for *indignant* means to be sore displeased, vexed, moved, and grieved with indignation. Jesus had such love for children that He was *grieved* by His closest disciples simply because they sought to keep children away from Him. They would have seen—and felt—His deep displeasure; they knew He was indignant with them. This would have made a huge impact on them because they so rarely saw Him moved with indignation at them.

On another occasion, Jesus revealed how much He loathes the harming of children. He gave this chilling warning:

> Whoever causes one of these little ones who believe in Me to sin [Greek, "stumble"], it would be better for him if a great millstone were hung round his neck and he were thrown into the sea. (Mark 9:42)

This too would have made a searing imprint on the disciples and all His listeners. All three of the synoptic Gospels—Matthew, Mark, and Luke—record these words. The Lord Jesus uses the strongest language to draw a graphic comparison, weighing the harming of children (and presumably the divine punishment that follows) against violent drowning, which He suggests is a kinder fate. Luke records it this way:

> And He said to His disciples, "Temptations to sin are sure to come; but woe to him by whom they come! It would be better for him if a millstone were hung round his neck and he were cast into the sea, than that he should cause one of these little ones to sin. (Luke 17:1–2)

Matthew provides this remembrance:

> At that time the disciples came to Jesus, saying, "Who is the greatest in the kingdom of heaven?" And calling to Him a child, He put him in the midst of them, and said, "Truly, I say to you, unless you turn and become like children, you will never enter the kingdom of heaven. Whoever humbles himself like this child, he is the greatest in the kingdom of heaven.
>
> "Whoever receives one such child in My name receives Me; but whoever causes one of these little ones who believe in Me to sin, it would be better for him to have a great millstone fastened round his neck and to be drowned in the depth of the sea. (Matthew 18:1–6)

Here is a paraphrase of Jesus's words in the Luke passage above:

> There will always be temptations to sin,...but woe to the man who does the tempting. If he were thrown into the sea with a huge rock tied to his neck, he would be far better off than facing the punishment in store for those who harm these little children's souls. I am warning you! (Luke 17:1–3 TLB)

Jesus is saying that the sin of causing a child to stumble is *so heinous that it would be better to be violently drowned than to face the judgment of God for harming children.* Imagine the scene Jesus painted for His listeners. A millstone was a large, round stone chiseled into a wheel, which was used to grind wheat at a wheat mill. The weight of a millstone would usually exceed three thousand pounds. Imagine the guilty soul taken out to sea in a large vessel. The millstone is connected to his neck by a chain or a rope. Would the villain be thrown into the water, and while he is swimming frantically, the sailors push over the millstone? Does it snap his neck as it drags him under the water? Whatever picture someone has in mind, it is disturbing. It is violent. It is fearsome—even terrifying. *It is meant to instill fear.*

Jesus spoke against many sins, but it's clear that harm to children brings unique anger from the Lord. To say that all sins are equal in the eyes of God is an absurdity.

Thus Saith the Lord: Don't Kill Your Children

God decreed annihilation for the Canaanites because of their crimes, singling out the crime of child killing as demanding this severe judgment.

The Canaanite crime of killing their children was happening before God gave the Ten Commandments and the Law through Moses. The Canaanites were violating the command God gave Noah. When God finally gave His Law through Moses, He affirmed the command He had given to Noah with these simple words: *Thou shalt not murder.*

How is *murder* to be defined from the perspective of the Law of God? Murder is the planned, deliberate destruction of a judicially innocent human life in a time of peace.

An accident is not murder; killing in a time of war is not murder; capital punishment is not murder; a crime of passion is not murder; self-defense is not murder; the taking of an animal's life is certainly not murder—one cannot murder a lion or an elephant.

Murder is *lying in wait for a judicially innocent human being* with malice and forethought. This definition is critical in our understanding of blood crying from the ground.

Again, *murder is the planned, deliberate destruction of a judicially innocent human life in a time of peace.*

Murder and Child Killing

The commandment *You shall not murder* should suffice as a prohibition against killing children. But God went beyond His overarching command to not commit murder. He specifically and repeatedly commanded: *don't sacrifice your children*. For example:

> Do not give any of your children to be sacrificed to Molek, for you must not profane the name of your God. I am the LORD. (Leviticus 18:21 NIV)

> You must not worship the LORD your God in their way [the way of pagans], because in worshiping their gods, they do all kinds of detestable things the LORD hates. They even burn their sons and daughters in the fire as sacrifices to their gods. (Deuteronomy 12:31 NIV)

Those who have raised children know that training includes repetition. And when some behavior is particularly important—"don't hit your sister," or "don't touch that light socket"—that instruction may be repeated many times over. Repetition indicates that something is important to our Heavenly Father as well. He is committed to training and leading His people in the path of righteousness. In that light, note how many times the Scriptures forbid and later condemn the killing of children.

In Deuteronomy chapter 18, child killing appears at the head of a list of satanic practices and demonic rituals:

> When you come into the land which the LORD your God gives you, you shall not learn to follow the *abominable practices* of those nations. *There shall not be found among you any one who burns his son or his daughter as an offering, any one who practices divination, a soothsayer, or an augur, or a sorcerer, or a charmer, or a medium, or a wizard, or a necromancer. For whoever does these things is an abomination to the LORD; and because of these abominable practices the LORD your God is driving them out before you.* (Deuteronomy 18:9–12)

In the following passage, God not only forbids and condemns child killing, He specifically calls for the execution of a child killer. Beyond that, He threatens to punish those who allow the crime of child killing to go unpunished—i.e., those who stand idly by and do not stop child killing. Also note that God considers child killing a personal affront to Himself. It defiles His sanctuary. It profanes His Holy Name.

> The LORD said to Moses, "Say to the Israelites: 'Any Israelite or any foreigner residing in Israel who sacrifices any of his children to Molek is to be put to death. The members of the community are to stone him. I Myself will set My face against him and will cut him off from his people; for by sacrificing his children to Molek, he has defiled My sanctuary and profaned My holy name. If the members of the community close their eyes when that man sacrifices one of his children to Molek and if they fail to put him to death, I Myself will set My face against him and his family and will cut them off from their people together with all who follow him in prostituting themselves to Molek. (Leviticus 20:1–5 NIV)

The following passage from the book of Proverbs puts the principle of Leviticus 20 into a command form, along with a warning of judgment for those who fail to act:

> Rescue those who are being taken away to death;
> hold back those who are stumbling to the slaughter.
> If you say, "Behold, we did not know this,"
> does not He who weighs the heart perceive it?
> Does not He who keeps watch over your soul know it,
> and will He not requite man according to his work?
> (Proverbs 24:11–12)

God commanded: don't kill your children. And if someone kills his children, deal with that person. He is to be executed.

God's words might be paraphrased as follows: "*If you hide your eyes—if you pretend you don't see it—if you fail to put him to death,* YOU ARE PLAYING THE HARLOT AFTER MOLEK, *and I am going to deal with all of you for letting this crime take place.*"

The Jews Killed Their Babies

One would think that with such clear commands from God, coupled with the knowledge that the Canaanites were judged for killing their children, the Jews would have stayed away from that abominable practice. Yet horrifyingly, they slowly embraced this crime against God and children. And more horrifically, *it started with King Solomon.*

Solomon was the wisest man to ever live, until Christ came. God appeared to him in a dream and promised he would receive wisdom like no other man in human history. He wrote lengthy passages of Sacred Scripture. He built the temple, and God manifested Himself at the dedication of the temple in ways that were truly miraculous. Nations brought tribute to him and came to hear his wisdom.

Yet it was Solomon who built a filthy pagan altar for child killing in Jerusalem. How did this happen? Solomon had seven hundred wives and three hundred concubines, many from pagan nations, and they turned his heart from the Lord. When he was old, Solomon built altars for his pagan wives to the false gods Ashtoreth and Chemosh—and worst of all, to Molech, the false god to whom the Canaanites sacrificed children:

> Now King Solomon loved many foreign women: the daughter of Pharaoh, and Moabite, Ammonite, E'domite, Sido'nian, and Hittite women, from the nations concerning which the LORD had said to the people of Israel, "You shall not enter into marriage with them, neither shall they with you, for surely they will turn away your heart after their gods"; Solomon clung to these in love. He had seven hundred wives, princesses, and three hundred concubines; and his wives turned away his heart. For when Solomon

was old his wives turned away his heart after other gods; and his heart was not wholly true to the LORD his God, as was the heart of David his father. For Solomon went after Ash'toreth the goddess of the Sido'nians, and after Milcom the abomination of the Ammonites. So Solomon did what was evil in the sight of the LORD, and did not wholly follow the LORD, as David his father had done. *Then Solomon built a high place for Chemosh the abomination of Moab, and for Molech the abomination of the Ammonites, on the mountain east of Jerusalem.* And so he did for all his foreign wives, who burned incense and sacrificed to their gods. (First Kings 11:1–8)

The passage is unclear as to whether or not Solomon himself offered one of his own children as a sacrifice or allowed any of his wives to do so, but one thing is certain: that pagan altar of child killing was built by Solomon and was used to kill children. It remained in Jerusalem for hundreds of years, until King Josiah destroyed it in his desperate attempt to save Judah from the judgment of God because of child killing (see Second Kings 23:13–14).

Sadly, the crime of child killing took root and grew like Satanic weeds in Judah. In the end, *the innocent blood of children crying out to God is why God sent Chaldean armies to break down the wall of Jerusalem, burn Jerusalem's great buildings with fire, and destroy Solomon's Temple.*

Scripture records the terrifying judgment that befell Judah because of the rampant practice of child killing. This happened after the bloody reign of King Manasseh:

And the LORD...sent them against Judah to destroy it, according to the word of the LORD which He spoke by His servants the prophets. Surely this came upon Judah at the command of the LORD, to remove them out of His sight, for the sins of Manas'seh, according to all that he had done, *and also for the innocent blood that he had shed; for he filled Jerusalem with innocent blood, AND THE LORD WOULD NOT PARDON.* (Second Kings 24:2–4)

Judah shed so much innocent blood—the blood of children—and thus angered God so much that the Lord was not going to turn away from the punishment He had determined against them. *"The LORD would not pardon."*

They sacrificed their sons
and their daughters to the demons;
they poured out innocent blood,
the blood of their sons and daughters,
whom they sacrificed to the idols of Canaan;
and the land was polluted with blood....
Then the anger of the LORD was kindled *against His people,*
and He *abhorred His heritage;*
He gave them into the hand of the nations,
so that those who hated them ruled over them.
(Psalm 106:37–41)

Note that the anger of the Lord was kindled against *His people,* not the pagans. Note that He *abhorred His heritage.* Earlier, God abhorred the Canaanites for killing their children. Now, God abhorred His heritage—*His own people*—because they were killing their sons and daughters, and the land was polluted with blood.

The crime of child killing, coupled with the refusal of the people of God to put an end to the slaughter, puts a nation in the crosshairs of Almighty God. He hears the blood of children crying out, and He sees the gross negligence of His people who allow the crime to continue without trying to stop it—or worse yet, *who help the murderous practice to continue unabated.*

God sees the "sins of omission," like the warning issued in Leviticus 20:4: "And if the people of the land do at all hide their eyes from that man, when he gives one of his children to Molech..." God sees that His people in North America and Europe have made a "covenant of silence and inaction"—literally *a covenant with hell*—to "hide their eyes" from child killing and thereby "play the harlot" with the child killers.

God sees the vast number of Christians from all denominations in North America and Europe that have self-knowingly voted for baby killers to get into office. Christians have literally cast votes for men and women who vowed to keep child killing "safe and legal."

This is an affront to God and a sin against Christ Himself. Jesus said, "Whatever you did for one of the least of these brothers and sisters of Mine, you did for Me." And conversely, "Whatever you did not do for one of the least of these, you did not do for me." (See Matthew 25 NIV.) Voting for baby killers is like voting for someone who would kill Christ. Does this not incur the displeasure of the Lord God?

Would God punish the Canaanites for killing their children, and then punish His chosen people for shedding the innocent blood of children, but *not* judge America and the once-Christian West for the same crime?

America has sown the blood of over sixty-five million innocent human beings, wantonly slaughtered for no legitimate reason. Nearly two million babies have been murdered in Canada. Tens of millions of babies have been slaughtered in European nations, with Great Britain being the most likely place a child will be killed.

The blood of these innocents is crying from the ground—from sewers, landfills, and ghoulish laboratories where the remains of their lifeless bodies are often sold to the highest bidder.

As a consequence, North America and European nations are reaping more and more random violence. They see a steady meltdown of major cities. They suffer brutality and murder, gang violence, and more. When a nation commits grievous crimes and the sword of the Lord falls, the signs are unmistakable.

God commands mankind: "Do not murder your children." If a nation spurns this command, a dreadful punishment equal to the crime of shedding innocent blood awaits. This judgment may be a long time in coming, but it eventually comes. Judah provides a sobering record of warnings, crimes, and punishments that came upon them for slaughtering their children. Judah serves as a warning to all the nations of the earth.

Therefore thus says the Lord GOD: WOE TO THE BLOODY CITY!

Ezekiel 24:9

Moreover the word of the LORD came to me, saying, "And you, son of man, will you judge, will you judge THE BLOODY CITY? Then declare to her all her abominable deeds. You shall say, Thus says the Lord GOD: A CITY THAT SHEDS BLOOD IN THE MIDST OF HER, THAT HER TIME MAY COME.

Ezekiel 22:1–3

Because the people have forsaken Me, and have profaned this place by burning incense in it to other gods whom neither they nor their fathers nor the kings of Judah have known; and BECAUSE THEY HAVE FILLED THIS PLACE WITH THE BLOOD OF INNOCENTS, and have built the high places of Ba'al TO BURN THEIR SONS IN THE FIRE AS BURNT OFFERINGS TO BA'AL, which I did not command or decree, nor did it come into My mind;…I WILL MAKE THIS CITY A HORROR, A THING TO BE HISSED AT; EVERY ONE WHO PASSES BY IT WILL BE HORRIFIED AND WILL HISS BECAUSE OF ALL ITS DISASTERS.

Jeremiah 19:4–5, 8

For they have committed adultery, and blood is upon their hands; with their idols they have committed adultery; and they have even offered up to them for food the sons whom they had borne to Me. Moreover this they have done to Me: they have defiled My sanctuary on the same day and profaned My sabbaths. For when they had slaughtered their children in sacrifice to their idols, on the same day they came into My sanctuary to profane it. And lo, this is what they did in My house.

Ezekiel 23:37–39

11

THE BLOODY CITY

Whearl the defining trait of a city, from God's point of view,
is the shedding of innocent blood, severe judgment is not
far off. This is because *blood demands a reckoning from Almighty God.*

One of the greatest attestations to this principle comes from
the words of Jesus Himself. Shortly before His crucifixion,
knowing He would be unjustly arrested, tried, and killed, Jesus
declared these words of judgment on Jerusalem and the Jewish
leaders for the *righteous blood* that had been shed:

> Therefore I send you prophets and wise men and scribes,
> some of whom you will kill and crucify, and some you will
> scourge in your synagogues and persecute from town to
> town, *that upon you may come all the righteous blood shed on
> earth, from the blood of innocent Abel to the blood of Zechari'ah
> the son of Barachi'ah*, whom you murdered between the
> sanctuary and the altar. Truly, I say to you, all this will come
> upon this generation.
>
> *O Jerusalem, Jerusalem*, killing the prophets and stoning
> those who are sent to you! How often would I have gathered
> your children together as a hen gathers her brood under
> her wings, and you would not! *Behold, your house is forsaken
> and desolate.* (Matthew 23:34–38)

Jesus went on to prophesy the destruction of the temple: "Truly, I say to you, there will not be left here one stone upon another, that will not be thrown down." (Matthew 24:2)

Luke records the Lord's frightening words thus:

> Therefore, the wisdom of God said, "I will send to them prophets and apostles; some of them they will kill and persecute" in order that *this generation might be charged with the blood of all the prophets shed since the foundation of the world, from the blood of Abel to the blood of Zechariah* who died between the altar and the temple building. Yes, I tell you, *this generation will be charged with their blood*! (Luke 11:49–51 NABRE)

As a rebuke to the people of God, even the pagan governor Pilate feared shedding the innocent blood of Jesus before His crucifixion:

> So when Pilate saw that he was gaining nothing, but rather that a riot was beginning, he took water and washed his hands before the crowd, saying, "I am innocent of this man's blood; see to it yourselves." And all the people answered, "His blood be on us and on our children!" (Matthew 27:24–25 ESV)

This was their way of saying, "We take responsibility for His death!"

After Christ's resurrection, the apostles were preaching boldly to the Jewish leaders who orchestrated the unjust killing of Christ. Those leaders arrested the apostles and, in a moment of naked honesty, expressed their fear of bloodguilt:

> "We strictly charged you not to teach in this name, yet here you have filled Jerusalem with your teaching, and *you intend to bring this man's blood upon us*." But Peter and the apostles answered, "We must obey God rather than men. The God of our fathers raised Jesus, whom you killed by hanging Him on a tree." (Acts 5:28–30 ESV)

As Christ warned and as the Jewish leaders feared, the blood of the righteous prophets and the guilt the Jewish leaders procured for themselves when they cried out to Pilate, "His blood be on us and on our children!" was visited with a horrible vengeance: *the destruction of Jerusalem.*

The fulfillment of Jesus's prophecy—the destruction of Jerusalem in A.D. 70 at the hands of the Roman army—was horrific. The details of the slaughter and suffering are beyond most imaginations. The temple was destroyed forever.

Note that the reckoning due for the blood of the prophets carried forward. Jesus declared that the punishment for the blood shed from Abel to Zechariah would be exacted on the generation He spoke to: the generation that would kill the God-Man, the perfect Prophet, Priest, and King—our Lord Jesus Christ.

The point of these passages for the purpose of this study is to show that this teaching about innocent blood, blood guilt, the reckoning for innocent bloodshed, etc., plays a key role in the life and words of Christ. *If someone loves Jesus, they should be repulsed by the shedding of innocent blood and terrified of the consequences that could come.*

But the destruction of Jerusalem that we will focus on now is not the destruction that happened in A.D. 70 at the hands of the Romans, but rather, the destruction of Jerusalem in 586 B.C. at the hands of the Babylonians. Let us return to that Jerusalem and to Solomon's Temple.

The First Temple: Built, Betrayed, and Destroyed

After Solomon finished building the temple and Almighty God gloriously filled it with His presence, God appeared to Solomon and gave him this promise and warning:

> I have heard your prayer and your plea, which you have made before Me. *I have consecrated this house that you have built, by putting My name there forever. My eyes and My heart will be there for all time.* And as for you, if you will walk

before Me, as David your father walked, with integrity of heart and uprightness, doing according to all that I have commanded you, and keeping My statutes and My rules, then I will establish your royal throne over Israel forever, as I promised David your father, saying, "You shall not lack a man on the throne of Israel." But if you turn aside from following Me, you or your children, and do not keep My commandments and My statutes that I have set before you, but go and serve other gods and worship them, then I will cut off Israel from the land that I have given them, *and the house that I have consecrated for My name I will cast out of My sight*, and Israel will become a proverb and a byword among all peoples. *And this house will become a heap of ruins.* Everyone passing by it will be astonished and will hiss, and they will say, *"Why has the LORD done thus to this land and to this house?"* Then they will say, "Because they abandoned the LORD their God who brought their fathers out of the land of Egypt and laid hold on other gods and worshiped them and served them. Therefore the LORD has brought all this disaster on them." (First Kings 9:3–9 ESV)

Sadly, as seen in the last chapter, King Solomon betrayed God and built pagan altars for his pagan wives, including an altar to Molech (also called Milcom), the false god to whom godless pagans sacrificed their children. As a punishment for Solomon's treachery, God divided the kingdom of Israel during the reign of his son Rehoboam.

The Northern Ten Tribes—or Israel, as they became known in Biblical literature—began under the reign of Jeroboam:

And the LORD was angry with Solomon, because his heart had turned away from the LORD, the God of Israel, who had appeared to him twice, and had commanded him concerning this thing, that he should not go after other gods; but he did not keep what the LORD commanded. Therefore the LORD said to Solomon, "Since this has been your mind and you have not kept My covenant and My statutes which I have commanded you, I will surely tear the kingdom from you and will give it to your servant. Yet for the sake of David your father I will not do it in your days, but I will tear it out of the hand of your son. However I will not tear away all the kingdom; but I will give one tribe to your son, for the sake of David My servant and for the sake of Jerusalem which I have chosen." (First Kings 11:9–13)

This judgment of God was directly connected to idolatry and the worship of the false god Milcom (aka Molech):

Thus says the LORD, the God of Israel, "Behold, I am about to tear the kingdom from the hand of Solomon...*because he has forsaken Me, and worshiped Ash'toreth the goddess of the Sido'nians, Chemosh the god of Moab, and Milcom the god of the Ammonites*, and has not walked in My ways, doing what is right in My sight and keeping My statutes and My ordinances, as David his father did." (First Kings 11:31–33)

The Southern Tribes, Judah and most of Benjamin, became known as Judah and continued to have a descendant of David on the throne until the destruction of Jerusalem by the Babylonians. (See the entire record of this division in First Kings chapters 11 and 12.)

These parallel kingdoms—the Northern Tribes and the Southern Tribes—Israel and Judah (all of them the descendants of Abraham, Isaac, and Jacob), both degenerated into idolatry, paganism, and child sacrifice. The Northern Ten Tribes survived until approximately 722 B.C., when under the reign of King Hoshea, they were defeated and displaced among the nations by the Assyrian army.

Note that the scattering of the Northern Kingdom was directly connected to child killing.

Then the king of Assyria invaded all the land and came to Samar'ia, and for three years he besieged it. In the ninth year of Hoshe'a the king of Assyria captured Samar'ia, and he carried the Israelites away to Assyria....

They forsook all the commandments of the LORD their God, and made for themselves molten images of two calves; and they made an Ashe'rah, and worshiped all the host of heaven, and served Ba'al. *And they burned their sons and their daughters as offerings, and used divination and sorcery, and sold themselves to do evil in the sight of the LORD, provoking Him to anger. Therefore the LORD was very angry with Israel, and removed them out of His sight; none was left but the tribe of Judah only.* (Second Kings 17:5–6, 16–18)

This dispersion of the Ten Tribes effectively ended the Northern Kingdom of Israel. God judged them into oblivion. They were scattered *and never restored.* (Historical note: The records of the lineage of the Northern Ten Tribes were obliterated—no record of the ancestry of those tribes exists. The few surviving Israelites intermarried with the pagan nations and became known as Samaritans. They were despised by the Jews of Christ's day and not considered true Israelites or Jews.)

For the sake of this narrative and teaching, the focus of this chapter will remain on the Southern Kingdom of Judah and her capital, Jerusalem—*the Bloody City.*

As generations passed after Solomon, idolatry and child killing grew in Judah. There were windows of time when the Jews would repent for their idolatry, but the trajectory was downward. They became more idolatrous, and more Jews committed the horrific crime of child killing.

Nearly three hundred years after Solomon, a twelve-year-old descendant of Solomon's—Manasseh, the son of King Hezekiah—ascended to the throne of Judah. He reigned in Jerusalem for fifty-five years. His reign was the vilest and most detestable in Israel's history.

This is what the Scripture says of Manasseh:

And he did what was *evil in the sight of the LORD, according to the abominable practices of the nations whom the LORD drove out before the people of Israel.* For he rebuilt the high places which Hezeki'ah his father had destroyed; and he erected altars for Ba'al, and made an Ashe'rah, as Ahab king of Israel had done, and worshiped all the host of heaven, and served them. *And he built altars in the house of the LORD,* of which the LORD had said, "In Jerusalem will I put My name." *And he built altars for all the host of heaven in the two courts of the house of the LORD. And he burned his son as an offering,* and practiced soothsaying and augury, and dealt with mediums and with wizards. He did much evil in the sight of the LORD, provoking Him to anger. *And the graven image of Ashe'rah that he had made he set in the house of which the LORD said to David and to Solomon his son,* "In this house, and in Jerusalem, which I have chosen out of all the tribes of Israel, I will put My name for ever; and I will not cause the feet of Israel to wander any more out of the land which I gave to their fathers, if only they will be careful to do according to all that I have commanded them, and according to all the law that My servant Moses commanded them." But they did not listen, and *Manas'seh seduced them to do more evil than the nations had done whom the LORD destroyed before the people of Israel.* (Second Kings 21:2–9)

It is almost unimaginable that a Jewish king, who possessed the Law of God, would sacrifice his children to demons and be so brazen as to put multiple pagan idols *inside* Solomon's Temple.

Manasseh also authorized ritual homosexual prostitution booths in Solomon's Temple (see Second Kings 23:7). The Scriptures specifically compare Manasseh to the pagan nations that lived in the promised land before the Jews, stating that he led Judah into more evil than the pagan nations.

Just as God condemned the Canaanites for killing their children, He *again* gave particular emphasis to the fact that child killing grew exponentially under Manasseh's wicked reign:

> Moreover Manas'seh *shed very much innocent blood, till he had filled Jerusalem from one end to another*, besides the sin which he made Judah to sin so that they did what was evil in the sight of the LORD. (Second Kings 21:16)

Manasseh killed his own son in the fire and literally built pagan altars to Molech and Baal throughout Jerusalem to be used for the grizzly massacre of untold numbers of babies. The flames would be kindled, the ritual words would be spoken, and then the child would be placed in the flames, while beating drums drowned out the screams of the dying baby. There are no words that can accurately describe this horror—the smell of burning flesh and blood, the charred corpses of innocent little babies—it was an unthinkable evil. This sin against Almighty God provoked His fury.

Shedding Innocent Blood Pollutes the Land

As with the commands given to Noah, the Law of God given to Moses shows the hideous nature of murder—the shedding of innocent blood:

> You shall not thus pollute the land in which you live; *for blood pollutes the land, and no expiation can be made for the land, for the blood that is shed in it, except by the blood of him who shed it.* (Numbers 35:33)

As seen earlier, God specifically revealed His hatred for child killing:

> When you come into the land which the LORD your God gives you, you shall not learn to follow the abominable practices of those nations. There *shall not be found among you any one who burns his son or his daughter as an offering. ... For whoever does these things is an abomination to the LORD; and*

because of these abominable practices the L<small>ORD</small> your God is driving them out before you. (Deuteronomy 18:9–12)

Yet God's chosen people rebelled against His commands, and many of them sacrificed their children. Others simply committed the sin of turning a blind eye to this crime, thus incurring God's judgment as delineated in Leviticus 20:4: "And if the people of the land do at all hide their eyes from that man, when he gives one of his children to Molech..." So, God sent His prophets to warn the people that they would reap the horrors due to them because of their idolatry in general and their murder of children in particular.

Jeremiah and Ezekiel repeatedly prophesied, echoing the threats in God's Law recorded by Moses, predicting the destruction of Jerusalem and Solomon's Temple because of idolatry coupled with the most hideous crime of all: *child killing.*

When considering these jarring words from Jeremiah, as well as pondering ancient Judah, the reader should *apply the prophet's words to the nation in which he or she lives* and the crimes against innocent blood that have been committed there:

Hear the word of the L<small>ORD</small>, O kings of Judah and inhabitants of Jerusalem. Thus says the L<small>ORD</small> of hosts, the God of Israel, Behold, I am bringing such evil upon this place that the ears of every one who hears of it will tingle. Because the people have forsaken Me, and have profaned this place by burning incense in it to other gods whom neither they nor their fathers nor the kings of Judah have known; *and because they have filled this place with the blood of innocents, and have built the high places of Ba'al to burn their sons in the fire as burnt offerings to Ba'al, which I did not command or decree, nor did it come into My mind;* therefore, behold, days are coming, says the L<small>ORD</small>, when this place shall no more be called To'pheth, or the valley of the son of Hinnom, but the valley of Slaughter. And in this place I will make void the plans of Judah and Jerusalem, and will cause their people to fall by the sword before their enemies, and by the hand of those who seek their life. *I will give their dead bodies for food to the birds of the air and to the beasts of the earth. And I will make this city a horror, a thing to be hissed at; every one who passes by it will be horrified and will hiss because of all its disasters.* (Jeremiah 19:3–8)

The wrath of God *against His people* for their crimes against innocent blood is palpable in this passage from Jeremiah:

This city has aroused My anger and wrath, from the day it was built to this day, so that I will remove it from My sight because of all the evil of the sons of Israel and the sons of Judah which they did to provoke Me to anger—their kings and their princes, their priests and their prophets, the men of Judah and the inhabitants of Jerusalem. They have turned to Me their back and not their face; and though I have taught them persistently they have not listened to receive instruction. *They set up their abominations in the house which is called by My name, to defile it. They built the high places of Ba'al in the valley of the son of Hinnom, to offer up their sons and daughters to Molech, though I did not command them, nor did it enter into My mind, that they should do this abomination,* to cause Judah to sin. (Jeremiah 32:31–35)

God rebuked His people—people who thought they could commit crimes of this magnitude but suffer no repercussions, simply because they went to the temple.

When reading the next passage, consider the millions of Christians who have killed their children, or the tens of millions who have done nothing to stop child killing—Christians who go to church regularly:

The word that came to Jeremiah from the LORD: "*Stand in the gate of the LORD's house,* and proclaim there this word, and say, Hear the word of the LORD, *all you men of Judah who enter these gates to worship the LORD.* Thus says the LORD of hosts, the God of Israel, Amend your ways and your doings, and I will let you dwell in this place. *Do not trust in these deceptive words: 'This is the temple of the LORD, the temple of the LORD, the temple of the LORD.'*

"For if you truly amend your ways and your doings, if you truly execute justice one with another, *if you do not oppress the alien, the fatherless or the widow, or shed innocent blood in this place*, and if you do not go after other gods to your own hurt, then I will let you dwell in this place, in the land that I gave of old to your fathers for ever.

"Behold, you trust in deceptive words to no avail. *Will you steal, murder, commit adultery, swear falsely, burn incense to Ba'al, and go after other gods that you have not known, and then come and stand before Me in this house, which is called by My name, and say, 'We are delivered!'—only to go on doing all these abominations?* Has this house, which is called by My name, become a den of robbers in your eyes? Behold, I Myself have seen it, says the LORD. Go now to My place that was in Shiloh, where I made My name dwell at first, and see what I did to it for the wickedness of My people Israel. And now, because you have done all these things, says the LORD, and when I spoke to you persistently you did not listen, and when I called you, you did not answer, therefore I will do to the house which is called by My name, and in which you trust, and to the place which I gave to you and to your fathers, as I did to Shiloh. And I will cast you out of My sight, as I cast out all your kinsmen, all the offspring of E'phraim." (Jeremiah 7:1–15)

"As I did to Shiloh, I will do to this temple." Shiloh was destroyed. God was warning His people that *He would destroy the temple that bore His name.*

Jeremiah preached his message in Jerusalem for thirty-seven years, until Jerusalem was sacked, the temple destroyed, the Ark of the Covenant lost forever, multitudes killed, and the scant survivors taken to Babylon. It took decades for His warnings to come true. God was patient—longsuffering. But there came a time when the Lord would no longer be patient—when His wrath emerged without remedy as He avenged the blood of the innocent.

The prophet Ezekiel preached his message from Babylon. He was a priest who was taken captive to Babylon before the final destruction of Jerusalem and the temple. He too thundered the wrath of God against the idolatry of the Jews, and especially against child killing:

> The LORD said to me: "Son of man…declare to them their abominable deeds. For they have committed adultery, *and blood is upon their hands; with their idols they have committed adultery; and they have even offered up to them for food the sons whom they had borne to Me.* Moreover this they have done to Me: they have defiled My sanctuary on the same day and profaned My sabbaths. *For when they had slaughtered their children in sacrifice to their idols, on the same day they came into My sanctuary to profane it.* And lo, this is what they did in My house." (Ezekiel 23:36–39)

It is hard to imagine that a Jewish couple would sacrifice their child—*murder* their child—and *then on the same day go to Solomon's Temple*, but they did. While their hands literally had the fresh blood of their babies on them, they lifted up those very hands in Solomon's Temple to pray. This defiled the temple and enraged God.

In that light, ponder how many Christians in recent decades have killed their children—or promoted and defended child killing, *or done little or nothing to stop child killing*—and have then gone to churches of every denomination Sunday after Sunday as if nothing were wrong—as if none of that mattered to God. Think of how many bumper stickers are seen on cars in church parking lots—Christians boldly and proudly declaring support for candidates who have pledged to defend and even promote the murder of children by abortion. Ponder the times that political proponents of child killing spoke in a church service, seeking votes. Consider the candidates who have a bishop or a priest or a pastor who is allegedly against killing babies yet in no way publicly rebukes or admonishes the candidate for his or her support of murder—but rather, embraces or endorses them or invites them to speak in church on a Sunday morning. Remember: these candidates' hands are covered with blood.

Both Ezekiel and Jeremiah invoke the imagery of God's people being a harlot who committed "spiritual adultery" with idols and slaughtered her children. Ezekiel's condemnation echoes Jeremiah and the Law of God:

> But you trusted in your beauty, and played the harlot because of your renown, and lavished your harlotries on any passer-by. You took some of your garments, and made for yourself gaily decked shrines, and on them played the harlot; the like has never been, nor ever shall be.... *And you took your sons and your daughters, whom you had borne to Me, and these you sacrificed to them to be devoured. Were your harlotries so small a matter that you slaughtered My children and delivered them up as an offering by fire to them?* (Ezekiel 16:15–16, 20–21)

Ezekiel prophesied the judgment of God on Judah because of their idolatry in general and the murder of their children in specific:

> Wherefore, O harlot, hear the word of the LORD: Thus says the Lord GOD, Because your shame was laid bare and your nakedness uncovered in your harlotries with your lovers, *and because of all your idols, and because of the blood of your children that you gave to them*, therefore, behold, I will gather all your lovers, with whom you took pleasure, all those you loved and all those you loathed; I will gather them against you from every side, and will uncover your nakedness to them, that they may see all your nakedness. *And I will judge you as*

women who break wedlock and shed blood are judged, and bring upon you the blood of wrath and jealousy. (Ezekiel 16:35–38)

Ezekiel prophesied that God would not have pity, because the land was full of blood:

Then He said to me, *"The guilt of the house of Israel and Judah is exceedingly great; the land is full of blood, and the city full of injustice*; for they say, 'The LORD has forsaken the land, and the LORD does not see.' As for Me, My eye will not spare, nor will I have pity, but I will requite their deeds upon their heads." (Ezekiel 9:9–10)

The Day of Reckoning... Slow in Coming

For those alive during the lifetimes of Jeremiah and Ezekiel who did not fear God or His punishments, the message of judgment from the prophets must have seemed repetitive, boring, and eventually, comical.

Picture a twelve-year-old boy walking into Solomon's Temple with his father, hearing Jeremiah preaching for the first time: "Woe to the bloody city! Amend your ways, or God will destroy this place!" It would have jarred and troubled any child of that age. And then picture the child's father consoling the boy, dismissing Jeremiah as a fool, and assuring the boy that Jeremiah's words were rubbish.

Then picture that same boy twenty-five years later, walking in as a grown man *with his own twelve-year-old-son*, hearing Jeremiah preach the same message: "Woe to the bloody city! Amend your ways, or God will destroy this place!"

The father could have turned to his son, saying, "That lunatic was here when I was your age! He's crazy. We are safe. This is God's House. We have nothing to fear."

But he did have something to fear. He mistook God's patience and repetition for God's approval and protection, or for Jeremiah being wrong. The terrifying judgments predicted by Jeremiah and Ezekiel would soon be upon that man and his son. Odds are, they died by the sword, famine, or the plague.

The Apostle Peter spoke of the judgment of God—both temporary and eternal—in his second epistle. He specifically wrote of "scoffers" who mocked the idea of God's coming judgment because it is slow in coming. Peter wrote:

> The Lord is not slow about His promise as some count slowness, but is forbearing toward you, not wishing that any should perish, but that all should reach repentance. (Second Peter 3:9)

But even though God is patient beyond human comprehension, there comes a time when His patience ceases, and His judgment is irrevocable. Mockers may mock God's messengers for a season without apparent repercussions, but without repentance, the reprieve is temporary, and the peace is fleeting.

Here is the epitaph of the fall of Jerusalem, the City of Blood:

> The LORD, the God of their fathers, sent persistently to them by His messengers, because He had compassion on His people and on His dwelling place; but they kept mocking the messengers of God, despising His words, and scoffing at His prophets, till the wrath of the LORD rose against His people, till there was no remedy. (Second Chronicles 36:15–16)

Sacred Scripture makes it clear that the horrific judgment from God, for which there was no remedy, came upon Judah and Jerusalem because they killed their children:

> Jehoi'akim was twenty-five years old when he began to reign, and he reigned eleven years in Jerusalem. His mother's name was Zebi'dah the daughter of Pedai'ah of Rumah. And he did what was evil in the sight of the LORD, according to all that his fathers had done.
>
> In his days Nebuchadnez'zar king of Babylon came up, and Jehoi'akim became his servant three years; then he

turned and rebelled against him. And the LORD sent against him bands of the Chalde'ans, and bands of the Syrians, and bands of the Moabites, and bands of the Ammonites, and sent them against Judah to destroy it, according to the word of the LORD which He spoke by His servants the prophets. *Surely this came upon Judah at the command of the LORD, to remove them out of His sight, for the sins of Manas'seh, according to all that he had done, and also for the innocent blood that he had shed; for he filled Jerusalem with innocent blood, and the LORD would not pardon.* (Second Kings 23:36–24:4)

The Lord would not pardon, because of the innocent blood crying from the ground for vengeance.

Before reviewing the last days of Judah and Jerusalem—the Bloody City—and considering the innocent blood shed in today's nation and cities, the danger they are in, and how they might be spared a fate like Jerusalem, let us ponder America's "Bloody City": New York, New York.

How Are the Mighty Fallen: New York, New York

America is a young country, and our cities are young. Rome is old; Athens is old; Jerusalem is old; even London and Paris are old by comparison to American cities.

But among America's cities are those that played an indispensable role in the settling of the American wilderness and the founding of the republic: Boston, Philadelphia, and New Amsterdam—now known as *New York*.

In the modern era, since World War II, New York has become one of the most influential and powerful cities in the world. This is the case because of finance and banking (Wall Street), culture (Broadway; the book, magazine, film, and TV industries, as well as the music industry), radio and telecommunications (ABC, CBS, NBC, and FOX), and the nation's most influential newspaper, the *New York Times*.

But New York City has also become America's *City of Blood. One in every ten babies killed in America is killed in NYC.* In some parts of NYC, there are more *murdered* babies than *live births.* New York City is literally the epicenter of child killing in all of North America.

Consider this: *Roe v. Wade* overturned the laws of all fifty states regarding child killing by abortion. It was a Supreme Court decision, not voted on or codified by state legislatures. So, in brazen and demonic support of child killing in the spirit of King Manasseh of ancient Jerusalem, on January 22, 2019, New York Governor Andrew Cuomo signed into law a bill passed by the New York State Legislature *that made it legal to kill babies up until the day of birth* AND EVEN AFTER THE DAY OF BIRTH. The legislators and activists who were present when he signed the bill *gave a standing ovation to cheer for this murderous atrocity.*

Governor Cuomo betrayed God. He betrayed innocent blood in true Judas fashion, and he betrayed the Catholic Church into which he was baptized and that he pretended to respect.

Just how strong is the commitment of these child killers to their murderous agenda? As a recent example, throughout the worst parts of the coronavirus pandemic in 2020 and 2021, while churches and businesses and restaurants and Broadway theaters were closed (and New York City Mayor de Blasio threatened to permanently close churches if they held services), Governor Cuomo and Mayor de Blasio ordered that all abortion clinics in New York City and New York State be allowed to remain open. Christians could not go to Easter Sunday services to celebrate the resurrection of Christ in New York City, but women could pay to have their babies torn from their wombs. This is an outrage.

Ponder this: between 1973 and the overturn of *Roe* that took place on June 24, 2022, the number of children killed in New York City *was almost equal to the entire population of New York City.* God has seen those murders. He has heard the cry of that blood.

By law, all ob-gyns in New York City are required to learn how to kill children. The blood of the innocent howls from the ground—from the sewers and garbage dumps—crying out to God for vengeance.

And He has heard that cry.

New York City is the epicenter of child killing, and as statistics show, *New York City was the epicenter of the coronavirus pandemic*. Death and economic woe swept through the city. Their economy plunged into a state of disaster, and violent crime rose a staggering 250 percent in 2021.

The death toll, the fear, and the economic crisis in New York City far surpassed the rest of the country. Is this random bad luck—chance? Or has God stretched out His hand with the first fruits of judgment because of the blood that is crying from the ground in the City of Blood?

Did New York City reap what it sowed?

The obvious answer is yes. Human folly alone could not have brought New York City to its knees. And as with ancient Jerusalem, God has many tools at His disposal to bring about catastrophe.

The fact that *Roe vs. Wade* has been overturned in America is a significant step in the right direction. It is comparable to the Allies taking Normandy Beach during WWII. Taking Normandy Beach was critical, but the goal was to get to Berlin and destroy the Nazis.

The goal in this epic war is to make it a crime to kill babies. In all fifty states in America, in all provinces in Canada, in all nations in Europe (and ultimately every nation in the world), it must be a crime to murder an unborn human being, from conception until death. That is the mission. Nothing other than the total protection of law for unborn humans is holy and just.

Having New York City remain the City of Blood, where women and girls can travel from around the world to murder their babies, is not victory. Christians in all nations have a duty to Christ to not stop fighting until all of "the least of Christ's brethren" have the protection and respect of law.

To that end, we must work to change the laws of North America and Europe and only vote for lawmakers who will promise to fully outlaw the murder of children. To do anything less is to betray Christ and betray innocent blood.

Have ye not read, that He who made man from the beginning, made them male and female? And He said:

For this cause shall a man leave father and mother, and shall cleave to his wife, and they two shall be in one flesh.

Matthew 19:4–5 DRB

You shall not lie with a male as with a woman; it is an abomination.

Leviticus 18:22

In a similar way, Sodom and Gomorrah and the surrounding towns gave themselves up to sexual immorality and perversion. They serve as an example of those who suffer the punishment of eternal fire.

Jude 1:7 NIV

12

LGBTQIA

The New Untouchables: "Above the Law"

Since the dawn of the Christian era, and under the Law of God given to Moses, it has been universally accepted in the Judeo-Christian world that sexual relations outside of marriage were sin. This included sexual relations between people of opposite genders and between people of the same gender.

Moreover, it was understood that not all sexual sins were of equal magnitude. I.e., two unmarried people of the opposite gender having sexual relations was considered sin, but it was not a capital offense. The remedy was marriage or a monetary punishment:

> If a man seduces a virgin who is not betrothed, and lies with her, he shall give the marriage present for her, and make her his wife. If her father utterly refuses to give her to him, he shall pay money equivalent to the marriage present for virgins. (Exodus 22:16–17)

However, in the Law of God, adultery, incest, homosexual acts, and sexual sins committed with animals were capital offenses. The death sentence for certain sexual sins was repeatedly called for in several passages of the Law of God. Here is one example:

If a man commits adultery with the wife of his neighbor, both the adulterer and the adulteress shall be put to death. The man who lies with his father's wife has uncovered his father's nakedness; both of them shall be put to death, their blood is upon them. If a man lies with his daughter-in-law, both of them shall be put to death; they have committed incest, their blood is upon them. If a man lies with a male as with a woman, both of them have committed an abomination; they shall be put to death, their blood is upon them. If a man takes a wife and her mother also, it is wickedness; they shall be burned with fire, both he and they, that there may be no wickedness among you. If a man lies with a beast, he shall be put to death; and you shall kill the beast. If a woman approaches any beast and lies with it, you shall kill the woman and the beast; they shall be put to death, their blood is upon them. (Leviticus 20:10–16)

Please note: this passage is NOT quoted here to call for the execution of individuals who have fallen into these sins, but rather to show the magnitude of certain sins. (Many Christian theologians and Church catechisms have explained why under the New Covenant, these sins remain serious sins but are no longer punishable by death.) That said, these sins are not to be downplayed or accepted as normal behavior.

Moreover, this chapter is not written to engender hatred toward any individuals and is certainly not written to promote violence against individuals or any group of people.

On the contrary, the Gospel calls Christians to "love their enemies." The Apostle Paul was once an adversary of the truth and an enemy of the Church. Yet he was forgiven for his murderous deeds against the innocent, and he became a servant of Christ and the most prolific author of the New Testament. As Paul stated:

Here is a trustworthy saying that deserves full acceptance: Christ Jesus came into the world to save sinners—of whom I am the worst. (First Timothy 1:15 NIV)

Compassion, Yes—Compromise, No

Our Lord Jesus scandalized the hyper-religious of His day by eating with sinners:

> And as He sat at table in his house, many tax collectors and sinners were sitting with Jesus and His disciples; for there were many who followed Him. And the scribes of the Pharisees, when they saw that He was eating with sinners and tax collectors, said to His disciples, "Why does He eat with tax collectors and sinners?" And when Jesus heard it, He said to them, "Those who are well have no need of a physician, but those who are sick; I came not to call the righteous, but sinners." (Mark 2:15–17)

But note: He never told them, "You're not sinners."

Christians should be motivated by compassion for individuals enslaved to a horrifying, self-destructive lifestyle, such as homosexual behavior or transgenderism. God knows the prayers, the anguish, and even the self-loathing that racks the hearts and minds of men and women struggling with their sexual identity and behavior. May God have mercy on them.

However, compassion is one thing; compromise is another. Where the Christian community has no right to compromise is in the matter of what is *right* and what is *wrong*. The crisis inside the Church and the Western formerly Christian nations is that of equivocation—compromise, and even surrender.

Beyond that, Christians have a duty to vigorously and publicly wage political, rhetorical, and spiritual war against the promoters and evangelists of the perverted sexual agenda that is cursing the horizon and seducing many young minds and bodies.

Not very long ago, it was believed and taught that certain sexual deeds were *always, objectively sinful*. Now, governments and certain clergy are proclaiming that those sexual deeds are *good* and *desirable, normal*, and a *"right."*

Until very recently, it was a universally accepted axiom that God's judgment came on Sodom and Gomorrah because of

sex between men and other sexual perversions (see Genesis 19).
From "Sodom" we derive the words *sodomy*—i.e., the deeds of
two or more men having sex with each other—and *sodomite*, the
men who do such things.

Moreover, the historic Christian Church has always held that
the sins of Sodom and Gomorrah are *sins that cry to God for
judgment.* Those sins are specifically referenced as *the reason God
destroyed the Canaanite nations.* God warns His people not to fall
into those evils:

> You shall not give any of your children to devote them
> by fire to Molech, and so profane the name of your God: I
> am the LORD. *You shall not lie with a male as with a woman;
> it is an abomination.* And you shall not lie with any beast and
> defile yourself with it, neither shall any woman give herself
> to a beast to lie with it: it is perversion.
>
> *Do not defile yourselves by any of these things,* for by all these
> the nations I am casting out before you defiled themselves;
> and the land became defiled, *so that I punished its iniquity,
> and the land vomited out its inhabitants.* But you shall keep My
> statutes and My ordinances and do none of these abomina-
> tions, either the native or the stranger who sojourns among
> you *(for all of these abominations the men of the land did, who
> were before you, so that the land became defiled); lest the land
> vomit you out, when you defile it, as it vomited out the nation that
> was before you.* (Leviticus 18:21–28)

This truth need not be belabored here. The point that must be
made regards the treachery of those who know these truths but
have betrayed them, denied them, and perverted them. Those
who promote these evils must be unflinchingly resisted. As the
Scripture says:

> Those who forsake the law praise the wicked,
> but those who keep the law *strive against them.*
> (Proverbs 28:4)

The crisis in the formerly Christian nations of the West, as well as inside many Christian denominations, is that a sin of this magnitude—what the Scripture calls "an abomination"—is now heralded as good and right and acceptable and laudable. Our nations are in a place that was unthinkable and unimaginable throughout human history—namely, that two people of the same gender can be "married." Even the pagan Greeks and Romans, among whom homosexual sins were common, did not stoop to calling those sexual acts the consummation of a marriage or dignify those relationships by calling them "marriages."

This rewriting and perverting of the Law of God regarding homosexual deeds—and now, so-called homosexual marriage—is a key reason why God's displeasure waxes hot against modern nations and His people.

In the book of Isaiah, God speaks through the prophet, condemning the treachery of calling something good that God says is evil. God warns of the punishment that is to follow:

> Woe to those who call evil good
> and good evil,
> who put darkness for light
> and light for darkness,
> who put bitter for sweet
> and sweet for bitter!
> Woe to those who are wise in their own eyes,
> and shrewd in their own sight!
> Woe to those who are heroes at drinking wine,
> and valiant men in mixing strong drink,
> who acquit the guilty for a bribe,
> and deprive the innocent of his right!
> Therefore, as the tongue of fire devours the stubble,
> and as dry grass sinks down in the flame,
> *so their root will be as rottenness,*
> *and their blossom go up like dust;*
> *for they have rejected the law of the LORD of hosts,*

and have despised the word of the Holy One of Israel.
Therefore the anger of the LORD was kindled against His
people,
and He stretched out His hand against them and
smote them,
and the mountains quaked;
and their corpses were as refuse
in the midst of the streets.
For all this His anger is not turned away
and His hand is stretched out still.
(Isaiah 5:20–25)

That atheists would scoff at the laws of God evokes little surprise. That communists and hedonists would deliberately violate
and undermine the sexual rules laid down by the Almighty is
to be expected.

However, to have Christian clergy, denominations, theologians, apologists, colleges, and think tanks embrace and endorse
the wave of sexual perversion that has swept across Western
nations is bewildering, frightening, and appalling. Rather than
resist this assault from hell, they have welcomed it, surrendered
to it, and become propagandists and advocates for sinful behaviors that invoke the judgment of God. The Prophet Jeremiah
cried out:

"Woe to the shepherds who destroy and scatter the sheep
of My pasture!" says the LORD....
Concerning the prophets:
My heart is broken within me,
all my bones shake;
I am like a drunken man,
like a man overcome by wine,
because of the LORD
and because of His holy words.
For the land is full of adulterers;
because of the curse the land mourns,

and the pastures of the wilderness are dried up.
Their course is evil,
and their might is not right.
"Both prophet and priest are ungodly;
even in My house I have found their wickedness,
says the LORD."...

Thus says the LORD of hosts: "Do not listen to the words of the prophets who prophesy to you, filling you with vain hopes; they speak visions of their own minds, not from the mouth of the LORD. They say continually to those who despise the word of the LORD, 'It shall be well with you'; and to every one who stubbornly follows his own heart, they say, 'No evil shall come upon you.'" (Jeremiah 23:1, 9–11, 16–17)

The Apostle Peter likewise wrote passionately of such traitors to the faith:

But these, as natural brute beasts, made to be taken and destroyed, speak evil of the things that they understand not; and shall utterly perish in their own corruption;

And shall receive the reward of unrighteousness, as they that count it pleasure to riot in the day time. Spots they are and blemishes, sporting themselves with their own deceivings while they feast with you;

Having eyes full of adultery, and that cannot cease from sin; beguiling unstable souls: an heart they have exercised with covetous practices; cursed children:

Which have forsaken the right way, and are gone astray, following the way of Balaam the son of Bosor, who loved the wages of unrighteousness;

But was rebuked for his iniquity: the dumb ass speaking with man's voice forbad the madness of the prophet.

These are wells without water, clouds that are carried with a tempest; to whom the mist of darkness is reserved for ever.

For when they speak great swelling words of vanity, they allure through the lusts of the flesh, through much wantonness, those that were clean escaped from them who live in error.

While they promise them liberty, they themselves are the servants of corruption: for of whom a man is overcome, of the same is he brought in bondage.

For if after they have escaped the pollutions of the world through the knowledge of the Lord and Saviour Jesus Christ, they are again entangled therein, and overcome, the latter end is worse with them than the beginning.

For it had been better for them not to have known the way of righteousness, than, after they have known it, to turn from the holy commandment delivered unto them.

But it is happened unto them according to the true proverb, The dog is turned to his own vomit again; and the sow that was washed to her wallowing in the mire. (Second Peter 2:12–22 KJV)

It is tragic that hundreds of thousands of young and old are trapped in sinful, self-destructive behaviors. But to have clergy and theologians of all streams speaking "great swelling words of vanity," alluring "through the lusts of the flesh" and promising enslaved souls "liberty" is a betrayal of those embracing these sins and a betrayal of God Himself.

Follow this example: A man may cohabit with a woman who is not his wife; he may declare his love for her; he may have sex with her; he may have children by her. But the day that he says, "God made me this way," or, "What I am doing is not sin in the eyes of God or man," he has not only disobeyed the laws of heaven, *he has sought to overturn them.*

To go further, to ask government officials to pass laws declaring that the cohabitation of that man and woman is the same thing as marriage, and then have theologians lining up behind the government to validate these laws and behaviors, reveals a corruption of the government *and* the Church. And worse yet, the duplicity and corruption of the *clergy* may endanger the souls of those *living in defiant sin* and endanger the souls of all who see and hear of this "new morality" and are seduced into debauchery by advocates for evil and their governmental and ecclesial partners.

This reprobate behavior from many Christian clergy is precisely what St. Paul discussed in Romans chapter 1. Consider again this passage in Romans 1 in regard to Christian clergy who knew God, but claiming to be wise, became fools and degenerated into sexual perversion:

> *For although they knew God they did not honor Him as God* or give thanks to Him, but they became futile in their thinking and their senseless minds were darkened. *Claiming to be wise, they became fools. ...*

> Therefore God gave them up in the lusts of their hearts to impurity, to the dishonoring of their bodies among themselves, because *they exchanged the truth about God for a lie. ...*

> For this reason God gave them up to dishonorable passions. Their women exchanged natural relations for unnatural, and the men likewise gave up natural relations with women and were consumed with passion for one another, men committing shameless acts with men and receiving in their own persons the due penalty for their error.

> *And since they did not see fit to acknowledge God, God gave them up to a base [reprobate] mind* and to improper conduct.... *Though they know God's decree* that those who do such things deserve to die, they not only do them but approve those who practice them. (Romans 1:21–32)

Wrestling with the Scriptures

Verses against sexual immorality are profuse in the Scriptures. Yet, a degenerate breed of theologians from virtually every strain of Christianity, starting with Catholic bishops and priests and continuing to Episcopalians, Lutherans, Methodists, Baptists, and more, is making *intricate* yet *false arguments*, claiming that Scripture does not condemn same-gender sex and that people should be able to marry someone of the same gender.

St. Peter wrote of those who thus pervert the truth and lead others into "the error of lawless men":

> So also our beloved brother Paul wrote to you according to the wisdom given him, speaking of this as he does in all his letters. There are some things in them hard to understand, *which the ignorant and unstable twist to their own destruction, as they do the other Scriptures.* You therefore, beloved, knowing this beforehand, *beware lest you be carried away with the error of lawless men and lose your own stability.* (Second Peter 3:15–17)

The prophet Jeremiah contended with false teachers in his day as well:

> Thus says the Lord of hosts: *"Do not listen to the words of the prophets* who prophesy to you, filling you with vain hopes; they speak visions of their own minds, *not from the mouth of the Lord. They say continually to those who despise the word of the Lord, 'It shall be well with you'; and to every one who stubbornly follows his own heart, they say, 'No evil shall come upon you.'"*
> *For who among them has stood in the council of the Lord*
> *to perceive and to hear His word,*
> *or who has given heed to His word and listened? ...*
> "But if they had stood in My council,
> *then they would have proclaimed My words to My people,*
> *and they would have turned them from their evil way,*
> *and from the evil of their doings."*
> (Jeremiah 23:16–18, 22)

The Apostle Paul likewise spoke of false teachers, saying they were imitators of Satan:

> *For such men are false apostles, deceitful workmen, disguising themselves as apostles of Christ.* And no wonder, *for*

even Satan disguises himself as an angel of light. So it is not strange if his servants also disguise themselves as servants of righteousness. Their end will correspond to their deeds. (Second Corinthians 11:13–15)

Those "Traditional Family Values"— But Whose Tradition?

In recent decades, many political activists in the so-called "religious right" in America have made it their political mission to uphold Christian ethics, but without Christianity, without mentioning Christ, and certainly without mentioning the Ten Commandments and the Law of God. Instead, they speak of "traditional values."

The effort to reform America based on "traditional values" has failed because it is *based on nothing*—nothing except the preferences and traditions of certain individuals or groups. The person who says, "Thus saith the Lord," or, "This is what God commands and what He forbids," is speaking from the perspective of eternal, unchanging truth. The person who says, "This is what I think," or, "We want 'traditional values'," has no greater claim to truth and justice than the most articulate humanist or the most debauched and rank pagan.

After all, there are many traditional values. For example, *the Canaanites also had traditions and values*—traditions that led to God bringing cataclysmic judgment against them. Jesus said:

> *"And why do you transgress the commandment of God for the sake of your tradition?* For God commanded, 'Honor your father and your mother,' and, 'He who speaks evil of father or mother, let him surely die.' But you say, 'If any one tells his father or his mother, What you would have gained from me is given to God, he need not honor his father.' So, *for the sake of your tradition, you have made void the word of God.* You hypocrites! Well did Isaiah prophesy of you, when he said:

> "'This people honors Me with their lips,
> but their heart is far from Me;
> in vain do they worship Me,
> *teaching as doctrines the precepts of men.*'"
> (Matthew 15:3–9)

False teachings abound on what the lesson of Sodom is and why God destroyed them. Some false teachers say it was pride. Others say it was rape. Others say it was a lack of hospitality. And still others say that it was cult prostitution.

And then they echo the antinomian lie: "Jesus never mentioned homosexuality." Of course, they deliberately ignore the fact that Jesus confirmed the destruction of Sodom as the judgment of God (see Luke 17:29) and the fact that God the Son was present for that destruction.

These false prophets tell us: "Homosexuals have been with us since the dawn of time." Well, so have murderers. So have thieves. So have adulterers. The presence of people addicted to or committing certain sins does not mean that it is not sin *or that it is normal.*

And now these false shepherds are performing same-sex marriages in their churches. They have breached a wall that has never been breached in the history of the human race. Not in the worst days of pagan Greece or pagan Rome, both of which are known for sexual debauchery and same-gender immorality, did they stoop to saying two people of the same gender could be married. As Jude declares, this endorsement of sin may cost those men and women their eternal souls.

Nicer than Jesus

Sadly, many Christians don't believe in same-gender marriage, but they don't want to say anything controversial or unkind. In effect, they want to be nicer than Jesus. Jesus fashioned a whip; He drove malefactors from the temple of God.

Jesus did not tell the woman taken in adultery that she was a respectable sex worker and that nothing she was doing was immoral. He told her, "Go, and do not sin again."

Jesus did not tell her, "You can't help whom you love. You can't help it if he is married to another woman. You are just following the desires God put in you."

A misguided, twisted compassion for people trapped in a sinful, self-destructive lifestyle has blunted people's wisdom and poisoned their love. In a misguided effort to tell them, "We love you," they have betrayed God and His Word as well as *the person thus trapped. It is not in their temporal or eternal interest to be trapped in a sin and for that sin to be legitimized.*

Allow one key point of logic: if there is no God who created us and gave us His Laws; if we are simply the chance arrangement of molecules; if there is no heaven and no hell and no fixed unchanging standards of behavior—i.e., the Ten Commandments—then truly, *anything goes.*

The very words *good* and *evil* cease to have meaning. *Good* can be the latest court ruling, the latest fad, a majority vote, the barrel of a gun, winning an argument, a spellbinding orator, or overwhelming force. *Evil* can change like the wind. *Evil* can be the opposite of the current "good." Hence, the new "good" of transgenderism is resisted by the "evil people" who believe in the foolish, oppressive notion of God and the Bible.

Perhaps the only notion more troubling than this—the total absence of God-ordained absolutes—is when clergy who say they believe in the Triune God reject His commands and seek to redefine *good* and *evil* according to the schemes of their hearts or the pollutants of the day. The current rush of Christian clergy to twist Bible passages and tell struggling people that sinful, disordered behavior is not sinful is part of the rush toward divine judgment.

As Isaiah said:

To the law and to the testimony: if they speak not according to this word, it is because there is no light in them. (Isaiah 8:20 KJV)

And Jeremiah:

I have seen also in the prophets of Jerusalem an horrible thing: they commit adultery, and walk in lies: they strengthen also the hands of evildoers, that none doth return from his wickedness; they are all of them unto Me as Sodom, and the inhabitants thereof as Gomorrah. (Jeremiah 23:14 KJV)

Another Attack from Hell: Genital Mutilation

Words fail to express the contempt and rage deserved by the "drag queen" and "transgender" movements.

Satan hates children. He wants to destroy them. If they escape death by abortion, he wants them sexually molested or abused or abandoned. Failing that, he wants young peoples' innocence marred. He wants them delving into drugs, pornography, sexual immorality. He comes to "steal, kill, and destroy."

The latest demonic assault defies all that is good—namely, the lie that a child (or an adult) can mutilate their genitals chemically or surgically and change genders.

This is a lie from the bowels of hell.

It is a scientific fact that a man cannot have a baby, and a woman does not have a penis. To assert otherwise is to defy God's created order and to defy science and logic. "Male and female He created them."

The headlines of the news are beyond belief: "Former Man Identifies as Woman; Sentenced to 30 Years in Prison; Impregnates Two Female Prisoners." "Female Athlete [formerly a male] Wins All Races, Sets New Records." "Man Gets Pregnant."

The efforts of celebrities, activists, and politicians to herald this brave new sexual world all work to advance this tragic "gender dysphoria." Their goal is to legitimize and normalize a spiritual and mental disease and ultimately recruit young people into this private hell.

Comic book "heroes" are "coming out" as lesbian, homosexual, bisexual, and transgender. Millions of young people are reading these comics and then exploring on the Internet the "meanings" and "lifestyles" in discussion.

For the children unfortunate enough to have parents who let them take drugs that mutilate their internal sexual chemistry, many of them, when they reach an age where they think, "I want to be the gender I was when I was born," find that the chemicals they have taken have lifelong ramifications. Many of them will be sterile—never able to have children of their own.

For those who choose to have "doctors" (in league with the satanic) surgically mutilate them, the damage is irreversible.

The suicide rate among these poor souls in the coming decades will be horrifying.

One of the aspects of this recent onslaught that is truly terrifying is the silence of so many Christian clergy. Those called to be "watchmen on the wall" crying out against evils of this magnitude are eerily silent.

Isaiah had these words of condemnation for these useless shepherds:

His watchmen are blind,
they are all without knowledge;
they are all dumb dogs,
they cannot bark;
dreaming, lying down,
loving to slumber.
The dogs have a mighty appetite;
they never have enough.
The shepherds also have no understanding;
they have all turned to their own way,
each to his own gain, one and all.
"Come," they say, "let us get wine,

let us fill ourselves with strong drink;
and tomorrow will be like this day,
great beyond measure." (Isaiah 56:10–12)

What good is a watchman on the wall *that is blind*? What good is a watchdog *that does not bark*?

So many clergy have taken the path of least resistance, or no resistance at all. They have a mighty appetite—they seek gain—but they are useless in the mighty battles that are destroying formerly Christian nations and useless as shepherds to protect young lambs from the wolves.

The suddenness of this onslaught is bewildering, the ruthlessness of the proponents of this evil to silence and crush all opposition is unnerving, and the willingness of millions of people—leaders in every field—and huge businesses to get swept away in this madness is terrifying.

It signifies the danger the formerly Christian nations are in. To be handed over to this madness without significant opposition does not bode well when considering whether Christians will give God a reason to show mercy. Will Christians bring forth "fruits of repentance" for their silence and inaction?

Be not deceived. God is not mocked.

The mission of Christian leaders and laymen should be to resist and condemn these evils in spite of any ridicule they may face, or other ramifications, to protect their children and grandchildren from the paths of death and to restore a Scriptural definition and cultural norm of human sexuality and behavior to the laws and cultures of their respective nations.

If they do not resist these debauched plans in one nation after another, it will become a crime to oppose this sexual perversion and insanity. The force of law will be used to sustain these evils and to crush those who hold to the eternal truths of Sacred Scripture. Then, the severe chastening of a nation will be inevitable.

Righteousness belongs to the Lord our God, but confusion of face to us and our fathers, as at this day. All those calamities with which the Lord threatened us have come upon us.

Baruch 2:6–7

Therefore He [God] brought up against them [Judah] the king of the Chalde'ans, who slew their young men with the sword in the house of their sanctuary, and had no compassion on young man or virgin, old man or aged; He gave them all into his hand. And all the vessels of the house of God, great and small, and the treasures of the house of the LORD, and the treasures of the king and of his princes, all these he brought to Babylon. And they burned the house of God, and broke down the wall of Jerusalem, and burned all its palaces with fire, and destroyed all its precious vessels. He took into exile in Babylon those who had escaped from the sword, and they became servants to him and to his sons until the establishment of the kingdom of Persia, to fulfil the word of the LORD by the mouth of Jeremiah.

Second Chronicles 36:17–21

The LORD could no longer bear your evil doings and the abominations which you committed; therefore your land has become a desolation and a waste and a curse, without inhabitant, as it is this day.

Jeremiah 44:22

13

THE END OF THE WORLD
AS THEY KNEW IT

The demise of Jerusalem happened in stages. God told Moses in His Law what would happen if His people killed their children. God told Solomon what would happen to God's temple if the Israelites rebelled against Him. Jeremiah, Ezekiel, and other prophets warned Israel that the promises and warnings of God through Moses and to Solomon were coming and were imminent.

The warnings were consistent. When the judgment came, it was *progressive*. It came in stages.

After Manasseh's death, his son, Amon, another evil king, reigned for two years and was then assassinated. The assassins were executed, and his eight-year-old son, Josiah, was put on the throne of Judah. Josiah was a righteous, godly boy and king. The Bible says of him:

> Before him there was no king like him, who turned to the LORD with all his heart and with all his soul and with all his might, according to all the law of Moses; nor did any like him arise after him. (Second Kings 23:25)

Jeremiah began preaching in the thirteenth year of Josiah's reign and preached to the Jews in Jerusalem for forty years, through the reigns of five kings up to the destruction of Jerusalem in 586 B.C.

In the eighteenth year of his reign, when Josiah was twenty-six years old, after Jeremiah had been preaching for five years, Josiah ordered the temple to be repaired. The temple repairs had nothing to do with the idols and other abominations taking place there. This was simply a decree to repair ailing walls and pillars, etc.

While Josiah was a good and righteous king in his devotion to God, he had done nothing to stop the evils practiced inside the temple, or the hideous crime of child killing. It is not known if he personally heard Jeremiah preach up until that point.

Josiah's decree to repair the temple had a very different outcome from the one he originally pictured.

One can question how Josiah could be considered good yet let the idolatry continue in the temple. The reason is that up until the eighteenth year of his reign, *he had never actually heard or read the Law of God.*

God required that every king of Israel copy the five books of the Law, or the Pentateuch, as it is known—Genesis, Exodus, Leviticus, Numbers, and Deuteronomy—*with his own hand*:

> And when he [the king] sits on the throne of his kingdom, he shall write for himself in a book a copy of this law, from that which is in charge of the Levitical priests; and it shall be with him, and he shall read in it all the days of his life, that he may learn to fear the LORD his God, by keeping all the words of this law and these statutes, and doing them; that his heart may not be lifted up above his brethren, and that he may not turn aside from the commandment, either to the right hand or to the left; so that he may continue long in his kingdom, he and his children, in Israel. (Deuteronomy 17:18–20)

Josiah had never done this. Clearly, the evils of his father, Manasseh, and the overall corruption of the Davidic line of kings had become so severe that even a "good king" like Josiah was bereft of the Law of God—that is, until they found the book of the Law during the temple renovations.

King Josiah gave a command to Shaphan, his secretary, regarding the costs of the repairs:

> "Go up to Hilki'ah the high priest, that he may reckon the amount of the money which has been brought into the house of the LORD, which the keepers of the threshold have collected from the people; and let it be given into the hand of the workmen who have the oversight of the house of the LORD; and let them give it to the workmen who are at the house of the LORD, repairing the house, that is, to the carpenters, and to the builders, and to the masons, as well as for buying timber and quarried stone to repair the house."…

The work was commenced. In God's mercy and Providence, they found a copy of the Sacred Scriptures. What began as a building project ended with the fear of God:

> And Hilki'ah the high priest said to Shaphan the secretary, "I have found the book of the law in the house of the LORD." And Hilki'ah gave the book to Shaphan, and he read it.… Then Shaphan the secretary told the king, "Hilki'ah the priest has given me a book." And Shaphan read it before the king.
>
> And when the king heard the words of the book of the law, he rent [tore] his clothes.

The impact of God's holy Law on Josiah was immediate and profound. The righteous fear of the Lord gripped his soul:

> And the king commanded Hilki'ah the priest, and Ahi'kam the son of Shaphan, and Achbor the son of Micai'ah, and Shaphan the secretary, and Asai'ah the king's servant, saying, *"Go, inquire of the LORD for me, and for the people, and for all Judah, concerning the words of this book that has been*

found; for great is the wrath of the LORD that is kindled against us, because our fathers have not obeyed the words of this book, to do according to all that is written concerning us."

He sent his men to talk with the prophetess Hulda. She boldly stated:

Tell the man who sent you to me, Thus says the LORD, Behold, I will bring evil upon this place and upon its inhabitants, all the words of the book which the king of Judah has read.

Because they have forsaken Me and have burned incense to other gods, that they might provoke Me to anger with all the work of their hands, therefore My wrath will be kindled against this place, and it will not be quenched.

But Hulda also consoled and encouraged Josiah with these words from God:

But as to the king of Judah,…regarding the words which you have heard, because your heart was penitent, and you humbled yourself before the LORD, when you heard how I spoke against this place, and against its inhabitants, that they should become a desolation and a curse, and you have rent your clothes and wept before Me, I also have heard you, says the LORD…. And you shall be gathered to your grave in peace, and your eyes shall not see all the evil which I will bring upon this place. (Second Kings 22:4–20)

King Josiah was encouraged and emboldened by the words of the prophetess. While he knew from her words that a severe chastening was coming, he also knew from the words of the Law he had read that God would show mercy to His people if they would repent. He knew that the coming judgment could take many forms and reach many levels. He could look to the Northern Tribes and see that Israel had been completely obliterated by the judgment of God. *Israel was gone, never to be restored.* He did not want that for Judah.

So he set his face like flint, and he began the work of a reformer. He possessed a zeal for righteous reform that has never been equaled in Biblical history, and perhaps the history of the world.

He moved swiftly, methodically, and without the permission or approval of his enemies, or the enemies of God. First, he wanted all the elders, priests, and people to understand what he was doing *and why*:

> Then the king sent, and all the elders of Judah and Jerusalem were gathered to him. And the king went up to the house of the LORD, and with him all the men of Judah and all the inhabitants of Jerusalem, and the priests and the prophets, all the people, both small and great; and he read in their hearing all the words of the book of the covenant which had been found in the house of the LORD. And the king stood by the pillar and made a covenant before the LORD, to walk after the LORD and to keep His commandments and His testimonies and His statutes, with all his heart and all his soul, to perform the words of this covenant that were written in this book; and all the people joined in the covenant. (Second Kings 23:1–3)

King Josiah stood at Solomon's Temple and read the book of the Law to the multitude present—*with his own voice*—and then committed to God in the presence of all those witnesses that he would obey and uphold the words of the covenant. He invited the people to join him in that covenant. Whether sincerely or in pretense, they did.

Josiah read the Scriptures that this present work is analyzing—passages that condemned idolatry; passages that warned the people of God that they must *never kill their children*; passages condemning sexual crimes. He read the threats of what would happen if the Israelites disobeyed the voice of the Lord. God would hurl them out of the land just as He had hurled out the Canaanites before them. He read passages that commanded that child sacrifice be stopped and that pagan idolatry was to be obliterated from Judah.

This dramatic scene—King Josiah reading the Law of God—set the stage for what came next. Josiah went on a righteous crusade to purge Judah of the crimes that had provoked God's wrath and therefore threatened their survival:

> And the king commanded Hilki'ah, the high priest, and the priests of the second order, and the keepers of the threshold, to bring out of the temple of the LORD all the vessels made for Ba'al, for Ashe'rah, and for all the host of heaven; he burned them outside Jerusalem in the fields of the Kidron, and carried their ashes to Bethel. (Second Kings 23:4)

He physically destroyed the accouterments that were used in pagan worship. He showed them no respect. He did not offer them to anyone. He did not put them in a museum. He destroyed them. Then he turned his eyes on the Aaronic priests who had betrayed God:

> And he deposed the idolatrous priests whom the kings of Judah had ordained to burn incense in the high places at the cities of Judah and round about Jerusalem; those also who burned incense to Ba'al, to the sun, and the moon, and the constellations, and all the host of the heavens. (Second Kings 23:5)

Those priests were no longer allowed to serve in the temple. Having destroyed the vessels of false gods and removed the priests of the false gods, he now moved to destroy the idols themselves. Every pagan idol and altar that was in Solomon's Temple he destroyed. He burned them in fire and scattered the ashes on graves or in brooks:

> And he brought out the Ashe'rah from the house of the LORD, outside Jerusalem, to the brook Kidron, and burned it

at the brook Kidron, and beat it to dust and cast the dust of it upon the graves of the common people. (Second Kings 23:6)

Josiah then purged the temple of homosexual prostitution:

And he broke down the houses of the male cult prostitutes which were in the house of the LORD, where the women wove hangings for the Ashe'rah. (Second Kings 23:7)

Then he made his move against the child killers. He defiled Topheth, the prime location for child sacrifice, and he was the first and only king to destroy the pagan idols built by Solomon that began Judah's descent into hell:

And he defiled To'pheth, which is in the valley of the sons of Hinnom, that no one might burn his son or his daughter as an offering to Molech.... And the king defiled the high places that were east of Jerusalem, to the south of the mount of corruption, *which Solomon the king of Israel had built* for Ash'toreth the abomination of the Sido'nians, and for Chemosh the abomination of Moab, and for Milcom the abomination of the Ammonites. And he broke in pieces the pillars, and cut down the Ashe'rim, and filled their places with the bones of men. (Second Kings 23:10, 13–14)

Josiah performed many other reforms, including executing the pagan priests of the high places on their pagan altars—priests who were involved in child sacrifice. He burned human bones on the altars as a deterrent against future crimes against God:

And all the shrines also of the high places that were in the cities of Samar'ia, which kings of Israel had made, provoking the LORD to anger, Josi'ah removed; he did to them according to all that he had done at Bethel. And he slew all the priests of the high places who were there, upon the altars, and burned the bones of men upon them. Then he returned to Jerusalem....

Moreover Josi'ah put away the mediums and the wizards and the teraphim and the idols and all the abominations that were seen in the land of Judah and in Jerusalem, that he might establish the words of the law which were written in the book that Hilki'ah the priest found in the house of the LORD. (Second Kings 23:19–20, 24)

Never before in the history of Israel had an Israelite king undertaken such righteous reform—purging the temple, destroying idols, and ending the public practice of child killing. Scripture says of Josiah:

Before him there was no king like him, who turned to the LORD with all his heart and with all his soul and with all his might, according to all the law of Moses; nor did any like him arise after him. (Second Kings 23:25)

These reforms, by any standard, are amazing. But sadly, it was not enough because of the sins of Manasseh—i.e., the shedding of innocent blood. What happened next demonstrates how heinous the shedding of innocent blood is to God. After Josiah's heroic efforts, the Scriptures record:

Still the LORD did not turn from the fierceness of His great wrath, by which His anger was kindled against Judah, *because of all the provocations with which Manas'seh had provoked Him*. And the LORD said, "I will remove Judah also out of My sight, as I have removed Israel, and I will cast off this city which I have chosen, Jerusalem, and the house of which I said, My name shall be there." (Second Kings 23:26–27)

Josiah reigned for thirty-one years in Jerusalem. His reforms held *publicly* for a little over a decade. But evildoers—starting with his sons—were waiting in the wings to return to child killing and paganism with vigor once Josiah was dead.

Josiah should have lived and reigned for a long time, but tragically, he was cut down in a battle with Egypt when he was thirty-nine years old—a battle that he should not have been in.

Immediately after his death, idolatry and child killing were reinstituted publicly in Judah through each of Josiah's offspring. They were Jehoahaz (reigned three months), Jehoiakim (reigned eleven years), Jehoi'achin (reigned three months), and finally, Zedekiah (reigned eleven years). Regarding the first three kings, God gave this condemning overview of their reign: "And he did what was evil in the sight of the LORD, according to all that his fathers had done." With Zedekiah, the fourth king after Josiah, God said: "And he did what was evil in the sight of the LORD, according to all that Jehoi'akim had done" (see Second Kings 23:32, 37, 24:9, 19).

These evils continued through the reign of all four kings that succeeded Josiah, until the final fall of Jerusalem and the destruction of the temple during the reign of Zedekiah.

It is worth noting again: the severity of the horrors that fell on Judah and Jerusalem could have been mitigated—some even avoided—*if the Jews had but continued to repent of their idolatry and child killing.* God told His people through Jeremiah:

> Behold, like the clay in the potter's hand, so are you in My hand, O house of Israel. If at any time I declare concerning a nation or a kingdom, that I will pluck up and break down and destroy it, and *if that nation, concerning which I have spoken, turns from its evil, I will repent of the evil that I intended to do to it.* (Jeremiah 18:6–8)

Surely if Josiah's reforms had held, things would have gone differently. Yes, some type of reckoning had to happen because of the innocent blood that cried for vengeance. But if all the threats from God through Jeremiah and Ezekiel and other prophets are looked at in aggregate, we see that to the very end God kept offering the Jews a chance to mitigate the level of destruction that was coming, but they hardened their hearts and refused to repent.

For example, King Zedekiah met with Jeremiah secretly before Jerusalem was destroyed. Jerusalem was under siege, surrounded by Babylonian armies. Even then, God offered mercy in the midst of judgment:

> King Zedeki'ah sent for Jeremiah the prophet and received him at the third entrance of the temple of the LORD....
>
> Then Jeremiah said to Zedeki'ah, "Thus says the LORD, the God of hosts, the God of Israel, If you will surrender to the princes of the king of Babylon, then your life shall be spared, *and this city shall not be burned with fire, and you and your house shall live. But if you do not surrender to the princes of the king of Babylon, then this city shall be given into the hand of the Chalde'ans, and they shall burn it with fire, and you shall not escape from their hand....* Obey now the voice of the LORD in what I say to you, and it shall be well with you, and your life shall be spared. But if you refuse to surrender, this is the vision which the LORD has shown to me....
>
> "All your wives and your sons shall be led out to the Chalde'ans, and you yourself shall not escape from their hand, but shall be seized by the king of Babylon; and this city shall be burned with fire." (Jeremiah 38:14–23)

The final fate of Jerusalem was in Zedekiah's hands. All he had to do, even at that late hour, was accept God's offer of a mitigated sentence by surrendering to Nebuchadnezzar. Sadly, Zedekiah hardened his heart. He "did what was evil in the sight of the LORD.... For because of the anger of the LORD it came to the point in Jerusalem and Judah that He cast them out from His presence" (Second Kings 24:19–20).

The Babylonians were masters of sieges. They had time, patience, and an army to wreak havoc once the city surrendered or fell. The fruit of Zedekiah's repeated rebellion was about to ripen.

Jerusalem was literally starved to death. The king and his officials were the last to have food. When they ran out of provisions, King Zedekiah, his guard, and his family made a desperate attempt to save their own lives and abandon their countrymen. In the dark of night, they opened the gate near the king's palace and rushed out on horseback. Due to the surprise factor and the cover of night, they were able to break through the Babylonian line, but it did not matter. The Babylonians pursued them and overtook them on the plains of Jericho.

Zedekiah's disobedience and rejection of God's offer of mercy brought a bloody end to him and his family:

> They slew the sons of Zedeki'ah before his eyes, and put out the eyes of Zedeki'ah, and bound him in fetters, and took him to Babylon. (Second Kings 25:7)

His sons were literally butchered in front of him one by one. All pleas for mercy went unheard. All protestations of sorrow and regret were ignored. His sons were slain. That was the last thing he saw in this life before his eyes were cut out.

It is frightening to ponder how many times individuals, families, and nations missed the opportunity for the mercy of God because they rejected His offers of mercy but preferred rather to remain in the pattern of disobeying Him.

Before the final destruction of Jerusalem, a number of Jews surrendered to Nebuchadnezzar and were taken captive to Babylon.

Very few Jews—some twenty thousand or so, depending on various records—survived as the result of several deportations of Jews from Judah to Babylon that occurred during the short reigns of Josiah's heirs, before Jerusalem was wiped out. The first large deportation actually helped the Jews maintain certain aspects of their culture and heritage. The king, Jehoiachin, and his mother and wives were deported to Babylon after they peacefully surrendered. Some ten thousand Jews, including court officials, priests, artisans, and craftsmen, were taken hostage to Babylon with them, where they survived—many as slaves.

The prophets Ezekiel and Daniel were likely in this first deportation. Both Ezekiel and Daniel exercised their prophetic ministries while in captivity in Babylon. The experience of these surviving Jews is known as the "Babylonian captivity."

But the vast majority of the Jewish people died horrific deaths by the sword, famine, and plague. In the torments of starvation, they committed cannibalism, eating their dead children and neighbors. Wild animals and birds ate their unburied bodies. Men were brutally killed, pregnant women were ripped open, and young women were ravaged.

It was terror and heartache of the highest order, all in fulfillment of the judgment of God because of the shedding of innocent blood—*the blood of children*—that cried from the ground for vengeance, as well as the accursed idolatry and sexual crimes that had become commonplace.

The full Scriptural record of the destruction of the temple and the burning of Jerusalem is found in Second Kings chapters 23–25 and Second Chronicles chapters 35 and 36. Several chapters in the book of Jeremiah give an intimate and terrifying view of the end, as do passages of Baruch, Ezekiel, Lamentations, and Nehemiah.

Second Chronicles gives this overview of the final fall of Jerusalem and the burning of the temple:

> The LORD, the God of their fathers, sent persistently to them by His messengers, because He had compassion on His people and on His dwelling place; but they kept mocking the messengers of God, despising His words, and scoffing at His prophets, *till the wrath of the LORD rose against His people, till there was no remedy.*

Therefore He brought up against them the king of the Chalde'ans, who slew their young men with the sword in the house of their sanctuary, and had no compassion on young man or virgin, old man or aged; He gave them all into his hand. And all the vessels of the house of God, great and small, and the treasures of the house of the LORD, and the treasures of the king and of his princes, all these he brought to Babylon. And they burned the house of God, and broke down the wall of Jerusalem, and burned all its palaces with fire, and destroyed all its precious vessels. He took into exile in Babylon those who had escaped from the sword, and they became servants to him and to his sons until the establishment of the kingdom of Persia, to fulfil the word of the LORD by the mouth of Jeremiah, until the land had enjoyed its sabbaths. All the days that it lay desolate it kept sabbath, to fulfil seventy years. (Second Chronicles 36:15–21)

Jeremiah preached his warnings of disaster and punishment till the end. When Jerusalem fell, he did not rejoice. He grieved. The book of Lamentations records the heart-wrenching lament of Jeremiah when all his words came true.

The following passage emotionally captures the anguish that the Jews experienced:

The Lord has destroyed without mercy
all the habitations of Jacob;
in His wrath He has broken down
the strongholds of the daughter of Judah;
He has brought down to the ground in dishonor
the kingdom and its rulers.
He has cut down in fierce anger
all the might of Israel,
He has withdrawn from them His right hand
in the face of the enemy;

He has burned like a flaming fire in Jacob,
consuming all around.
He has bent His bow like an enemy,
with His right hand set like a foe;
and He has slain all the pride of our eyes
in the tent of the daughter of Zion;
He has poured out His fury like fire.
The Lord has become like an enemy,
He has destroyed Israel;
He has destroyed all its palaces,
laid in ruins its strongholds;
and He has multiplied in the daughter of Judah
mourning and lamentation.
He has broken down His booth like that of a garden,
laid in ruins the place of His appointed feasts;
the LORD has brought to an end in Zion
appointed feast and sabbath,
and in His fierce indignation has spurned
king and priest.
The Lord has scorned His altar,
disowned His sanctuary;
He has delivered into the hand of the enemy
the walls of her palaces;
a clamor was raised in the house of the LORD
as on the day of an appointed feast.
The LORD determined to lay in ruins
the wall of the daughter of Zion;
He marked it off by the line;
He restrained not His hand from destroying;
He caused rampart and wall to lament,
they languish together.
Her gates have sunk into the ground;
He has ruined and broken her bars;
her king and princes are among the nations;

the law is no more,
and her prophets obtain
no vision from the LORD.
The elders of the daughter of Zion
sit on the ground in silence;
they have cast dust on their heads
and put on sackcloth;
the maidens of Jerusalem
have bowed their heads to the ground.
My eyes are spent with weeping;
my soul is in tumult;
my heart is poured out in grief
because of the destruction of the daughter of my people,
because infants and babes faint
in the streets of the city.…
Happier were the victims of the sword
than the victims of hunger,
who pined away, stricken
by want of the fruits of the field.
The hands of compassionate women
have boiled their own children;
they became their food
in the destruction of the daughter of my people.
(Lamentations 2:2–11, 4:9–10)

The fate of Jerusalem stands as a warning to all nations and should give genuine dread to any nation that sheds innocent blood and commits other crimes that cry to God for vengeance. *God will avenge blood. God will carry out the judgments He has declared. God is not mocked.*

Let the reader pause and consider the danger America, Canada, and European nations are in King Solomon wrote Sacred Scripture. God appeared to him. God warned him to obey His Law, yet it was Solomon who built the first altar to Molech in Judah and thereby gave child killing a foothold in Israel. That crime against God and man ultimately led to the Northern Tribes' total annihilation and the destruction of Judah, Jerusalem, and the temple.

Thomas Jefferson wrote the Declaration of Independence. He was a vestryman at his church. He knew his Bible, yet he owned slaves and helped slavery become established in our nation. That crime against God and man ultimately led to the Civil War.

The Supreme Court justices in the United States swore an oath on the Bible—an oath to God to uphold the laws of the United States. Yet, in 1973, they betrayed their oath and gave legal status for child killing in *Roe vs. Wade*. After nearly fifty years, *Roe* was overturned, but the blood of tens of millions of children cries from the ground, and child killing continues unabated in the most populated states. Overturning *Roe* was a significant step toward justice for unborn babies, but much more must be done if America is to avert judgment.

Likewise, Canada and the Western democracies of Europe are similarly stained with innocent blood. Moreover, they have shown an unholy, brazen contempt for the covenant of marriage, elevating abominable sexual sins to the legal level of marriage under their national laws. Some nations are diving headlong into the lie that a child can change their gender by mutilating their genitals chemically or surgically. These "sins that cry to heaven" will be avenged.

The fate of each nation, and the length and severity of the coming judgments on all these nations, will depend on the actions taken to end the slaughter of the innocents and the return to God's norms concerning sex and human sexuality.

Let us remember the words of Thomas Jefferson, the author of America's Declaration of Independence—with fear:

I tremble for my country when I reflect that God is just: that His justice cannot sleep for ever: that considering numbers, nature and natural means only, a revolution of the wheel of fortune, an exchange of situation, is among possible events: *that it may become probable by supernatural interference!*[1]

---

1. Thomas Jefferson, *Notes on the State of Virginia*, Query XVIII. Manners (1871), Online Library of Liberty, oll.libertyfund.org/title/jefferson-the-works-vol-4-notes-on-virginia-ii-correspondence-1782-1786#lf0054-04_head_010.

For the eyes of the Lord are upon the righteous,
and His ears are open to their prayer.
But the face of the Lord is against those that do evil.

First Peter 3:12

If one turns away his ear from hearing the law,
even his prayer is an abomination.

Proverbs 28:9

Therefore, thus says the LORD, Behold, I am bringing evil upon them
which they cannot escape; though they cry to Me, I will not listen to
them.... Therefore do not pray for this people, or lift up a cry or prayer
on their behalf, for I will not listen when they call to Me in the time
of their trouble.

Jeremiah 11:11, 14

For you know that afterward, when he wanted to inherit the blessing,
he was rejected, for he found no place for repentance, though he sought
it diligently with tears.

Hebrews 12:17 NKJV

14

WHEN GOD WON'T HEAR PRAYER

When the Lord Jesus taught His disciples to pray, according to the Gospel of Luke, after teaching them the Lord's Prayer, He said this:

> Which of you who has a friend will go to him at midnight and say to him, "Friend, lend me three loaves; for a friend of mine has arrived on a journey, and I have nothing to set before him"; and he will answer from within, "Do not bother me; the door is now shut, and my children are with me in bed; I cannot get up and give you anything"? I tell you, though he will not get up and give him anything because he is his friend, yet because of his importunity he will rise and give him whatever he needs. And I tell you, Ask, and it will be given you; seek, and you will find; knock, and it will be opened to you. For every one who asks receives, and he who seeks finds, and to him who knocks it will be opened. What father among you, if his son asks for a fish, will instead of a fish give him a serpent; or if he asks for an egg, will give him a scorpion? If you then, who are evil, know how to give good gifts to your children, how much more will the heavenly Father give the Holy Spirit to those who ask Him! (Luke 11:5–13)

This passage arms Christians with hope and encourages them to *persevere in prayer.* This is the calling of the believer.

However, the Scriptures also teach that there are times during moments of God's judgment when He will *not* hear prayers regarding the welfare of a nation. He will hear prayers for individuals but not for the nation. This teaching from Scripture is real and abundant. When God unleashes His judgments on a nation, there are times when no prayers will avert the judgment that is falling.

As alluded to above, a clear distinction exists between prayers for individual forgiveness, salvation, and even personal protection vs. prayers to God that He will avert judgment on a given nation.

"Whosoever shall call upon the name of the Lord shall be saved." When God's judgment is poured out on a people, He will not turn His back on those who cry out to Him for mercy on their souls. Even the murderer on death row is offered hope by the priest that the blood of Jesus can wash his sins away.

Personal forgiveness, redemption, and the promise of eternal life are at the heart of the Gospel. Nothing in this chapter—or this entire work for that matter—should be construed as meaning that God will not hear the prayer of the repentant sinner. As David wrote:

> Blessed is he whose transgression is forgiven,
> whose sin is covered.
> Blessed is the man to whom the LORD imputes
> no iniquity....
> I acknowledged my sin to Thee,
> and I did not hide my iniquity;
> I said, "I will confess my transgressions to the LORD";
> then Thou didst forgive the guilt of my sin.
> (Psalm 32:1–2, 5)

These are joyous words to the heart of any penitent sinner.

When a Nation Falls, Individuals May Be Spared

Consider the prophets Daniel, Ezekiel, and Jeremiah. Remember Baruch and the Hebrew children of the book of Daniel. God protected all of them as He was pouring out judgment on Judah.

The four Hebrew children who were taken to Babylon were Daniel, Hanani'ah, Mish'a-el, and Azari'ah—the Babylonian names imposed on them were Belteshaz'zar, Shadrach, Meshach, and Abed'nego.

They were hostages, elite slaves whose task was to serve the king after they had been trained for three years. The Babylonian captivity, as it is known, *was the judgment of God*. Even though these four were righteous, they endured the long trip through the desert as captives. They never saw their homeland again. Yet their lives were spared, even in the judgment of captivity.

In the fear of God, those four young men insisted that they not eat the unclean food of the palace but, instead, be served vegetables and water. Their request was granted, their lives were spared, and they flourished.

Three of the young men would later find themselves facing death for refusing to bow before the idol of the king (see Daniel chapters 2 and 3). They were thrown into a fiery furnace to be killed, yet they miraculously survived.

Daniel, the fourth youth, was used by the Lord repeatedly as a prophet and advisor in Babylon for decades. He too escaped death in the lion's den after he was sentenced to die for refusing to pray only to the king (see Daniel chapter 6).

Consider Ezekiel the prophet. He was a young priest, also taken hostage to Babylon, who prophesied God's Word for decades in Babylon. He escaped all plots against him.

Remember Baruch, Jeremiah's personal scribe. God told him:

The word that Jeremiah the prophet spoke to Baruch the son of Neri'ah, when he wrote these words in a book at the dictation of Jeremiah, in the fourth year of Jehoi'akim the son of Josi'ah, king of Judah: "Thus says the LORD, the God of Israel, to you, O Baruch: You said, 'Woe is me! for the LORD has added sorrow to my pain; I am weary with my groaning, and I find no rest.' Thus shall you say to him, Thus says the LORD: Behold, what I have built I am breaking down, and what I have planted I am plucking up—that is, the whole land. And do you seek great things for yourself? Seek them not; for behold, I am bringing evil upon all flesh, says the LORD; but I will give you your life as a prize of war in all places to which you may go." (Jeremiah 45:1–5)

We don't know what "great things" Baruch was seeking for himself or what he was asking of God in prayer. Nevertheless, his life was spared when God's judgment was poured out on Judah.

And finally, consider the Prophet Jeremiah. His life was frequently in danger, yet he remained faithful to proclaim God's Word until the fall of Jerusalem. He was among the hostages when a Babylonian official found him and gave him his liberty. He chose to remain in Jerusalem with a handful of survivors and ultimately went to Egypt with the Jews who fled punishment for the assassination of a Babylonian official. It appears he died there in peace.

These examples and many others in the Old and New Testaments teach that in the midst of God's outpoured judgment, He will protect those He means to protect. We can have hope that in the midst of the coming hardships and judgment, God will care for those who are seeking Him, His mercy, and His righteousness, as He cared for Daniel, Ezekiel, Jeremiah, Baruch, and the three Hebrew children.

And for those who die in the service of the Lord God, faithful to the Lord even in the midst of His judgment: "Precious in the sight of the LORD is the death of His saints" (Psalm 116:15).

Christians have the promise of God that gives eternal perspective:

We are afflicted in every way, but not crushed; perplexed, but not driven to despair; persecuted, but not forsaken; struck down, but not destroyed; always carrying in the body the death of Jesus, so that the life of Jesus may also be manifested in our bodies. For while we live we are always being given up to death for Jesus' sake, so that the life of Jesus may be manifested in our mortal flesh....

For this slight momentary affliction is preparing for us an eternal weight of glory beyond all comparison, because we look not to the things that are seen but to the things that are unseen; for the things that are seen are transient, but the things that are unseen are eternal. (Second Corinthians 4:8–11, 17–18)

The Old and New Testaments are full of Scriptures that encourage believers to draw near to the throne of grace to receive help from the Almighty in a time of need.

However, many of the promises of God are conditional. The breadth and depth of the promises in Scripture that God *hears* prayer cannot nullify the Scriptural cases that, in some circumstances, *God will NOT hear certain prayers.*

Jeremiah

Jeremiah chapter 7 is the record of Jeremiah standing at the temple of the Lord, telling the people of God that God is going to destroy the temple as He destroyed Shiloh (Jeremiah 7:14–15). Jeremiah was obedient to God to deliver the message, but it must have caused him great distress. He prayed fervently for his fellow Jews. In response to his prayers, God said to Jeremiah:

As for you, *do not pray for this people, or lift up cry or prayer for them*, and *do not intercede with Me, for I do not hear you.* (Jeremiah 7:16)

The rest of the chapter is the record of why God would not hear Jeremiah's prayers, ending with the prediction of the bloody punishment the Jews would endure—punishment that Jeremiah could not avert with his prayers:

> For the sons of Judah have done evil in My sight, says the LORD; *they have set their abominations in the house which is called by My name, to defile it. And they have built the high place of To'pheth, which is in the valley of the son of Hinnom, to burn their sons and their daughters in the fire; which I did not command, nor did it come into My mind.* Therefore, behold, the days are coming, says the LORD, when it will no more be called To'pheth, or the valley of the son of Hinnom, but the valley of Slaughter: for they will bury in To'pheth, because there is no room elsewhere. And the dead bodies of this people will be food for the birds of the air, and for the beasts of the earth; and none will frighten them away. And I will make to cease from the cities of Judah and from the streets of Jerusalem the voice of mirth and the voice of gladness, the voice of the bridegroom and the voice of the bride; for the land shall become a waste. (Jeremiah 7:30–34)

Jeremiah knew the Scriptures. He knew that God threatened His people with judgment during the lives of Moses and Samuel. He also knew that when Moses and Samuel interceded for God's people, God turned away His anger and spared His people from His judgments. Perhaps God was answering the questions or prayers of Jeremiah's heart when He told Jeremiah:

> Then the LORD said to me, *"Though Moses and Samuel stood before Me, yet My heart would not turn toward this people.* Send them out of My sight, and let them go! And when they ask you, 'Where shall we go?' you shall say to them, 'Thus says the LORD:
>
> "'Those who are for pestilence, to pestilence,
> and those who are for the sword, to the sword;
> those who are for famine, to famine,
> and those who are for captivity, to captivity.'

"I will appoint over them four kinds of destroyers, says the LORD: the sword to slay, the dogs to tear, and the birds of the air and the beasts of the earth to devour and destroy." (Jeremiah 15:1–3)

God then again told Jeremiah why He was bringing these gruesome judgments and why He would not hear Jeremiah's prayers for Judah. *It was because of idolatry and child killing*:

And I will make them a horror to all the kingdoms of the earth because of what Manas'seh the son of Hezeki'ah, king of Judah, did in Jerusalem. (Jeremiah 15:4)

As shown, the haunting, most damning sin of Manasseh was child killing:

Moreover Manas'seh shed very much innocent blood, till he had filled Jerusalem from one end to another, besides the sin which he made Judah to sin so that they did what was evil in the sight of the LORD. (Second Kings 21:16)

The LORD...sent them [the Babylonians] against Judah to destroy it, according to the word of the LORD which He spoke by His servants the prophets. Surely this came upon Judah at the command of the LORD, to remove them out of His sight, for the sins of Manas'seh, according to all that he had done, and also for the innocent blood that he had shed; for he filled Jerusalem with innocent blood, and the LORD would not pardon. (Second Kings 24:2–4)

And lest anyone argue that the "innocent blood" being spoken of was *not* that of children, the Scripture again and again makes that connection crystal clear:

They sacrificed *their sons
and their daughters* to the demons;
*they poured out innocent blood,
the blood of their sons and daughters,*

whom they sacrificed to the idols of Canaan;
and the land was polluted with blood....
Then the anger of the LORD was kindled against His
people.
and He abhorred His heritage;
He gave them into the hand of the nations,
so that those who hated them ruled over them.
Their enemies oppressed them,
and they were brought into subjection under their power.
(Psalm 106:37–42)

Ezekiel

Ezekiel, hundreds of miles away, was praying for his brethren.
Like God did with Jeremiah, He declared He would *not hear
prayer* because of idolatry and child killing:

> He said to me, "Have you seen this, son of man? Is it a
> trivial matter for the people of Judah to do the detestable
> things they are doing here? *Must they also fill the land with
> violence and continually arouse My anger?... Therefore I will
> deal with them in anger; I will not look on them with pity or spare
> them. Although they shout in My ears, I will not listen to them."*
> (Ezekiel 8:17–18 NIV)

> Wherefore say to the house of Israel, Thus says the Lord
> GOD: Will you defile yourselves after the manner of your
> fathers and go astray after their detestable things? When
> you offer your gifts and *sacrifice your sons by fire*, you defile
> yourselves with all your idols to this day. *And shall I be
> inquired of by you, O house of Israel? As I live, says the Lord
> GOD, I will not be inquired of by you.* (Ezekiel 20:30–31)

Ezekiel also picked up the theme of righteous men interceding
with God for His mercy on His rebellious people. Again, God
said He would not spare the land because of righteous men
interceding:

The word of the LORD came to me: "Son of man, if a country sins against Me by being unfaithful and I stretch out My hand against it to cut off its food supply and send famine upon it and kill its people and their animals, *even if these three men—Noah, Daniel and Job—were in it, they could save only themselves by their righteousness, declares the Sovereign* LORD....

"Or if I send a plague into that land and pour out My wrath on it through bloodshed, killing its people and their animals, as surely as I live, declares the Sovereign LORD, *even if Noah, Daniel and Job were in it, they could save neither son nor daughter. They would save only themselves by their righteousness.* (Ezekiel 14:12–14, 19–20 NIV)

The purpose of focusing on these passages of the Scriptures is to prove to the reader *the severity with which God hates child killing*—a hatred so fierce that He tells His people that He will abandon them because they abandoned the babies. He will not hear their cries because they stopped their ears and refused to hear the cry of babies—*the cry of innocent blood.*

Tragically, there are Christian clergy and laymen who believe that child killing—abortion, as it is deceitfully called—is not such a grave matter and that it is just "one issue among many." They are woefully, demonically deceived and often deceive others. *There will be a dreadful recompense given for this bloodshed in North America and Europe.*

Isaiah

The Prophet Isaiah is consistent with Jeremiah and Ezekiel in stating that God will not hear the prayers of His people *when they have blood on their hands*—that is, when innocent blood is being shed *and God's people are complicit because they do not stop it.*

Behold, the LORD's hand is not shortened, that it cannot save,

or His ear dull, that it cannot hear;
but your iniquities have made a separation
between you and your God,
and your sins have hid His face from you
so that He does not hear.
For your hands are defiled with blood
and your fingers with iniquity;
your lips have spoken lies,
your tongue mutters wickedness....
Their works are works of iniquity,
and deeds of violence are in their hands.
Their feet run to evil,
and they make haste to shed innocent blood.
(Isaiah 59:1–3, 6–7)

Isaiah chapter 1 makes a chilling connection between *unanswered prayers* and *innocent blood*. In this passage, we see God condemning holy religious rituals—*rituals instituted by Him*—because His people were not defending the innocent. God said:

When you come to appear before Me,
who requires of you
this trampling of My courts?
Bring no more vain offerings;
incense is an abomination to Me.
New moon and sabbath and the calling of assemblies—
I cannot endure iniquity and solemn assembly.
Your new moons and your appointed feasts
My soul hates;
they have become a burden to Me,
I am weary of bearing them. (Isaiah 1:12–14)

Coming to the courts of the Lord, the offerings, the incense, the appointed feasts, and of course the Sabbath, *all of these activities and duties were instituted by God Himself*. God was rebuking them for doing what He commanded, because His people were not obeying "the weightier matters of the law" (see Matthew 23:23).

The words that God said through Isaiah would have been confusing and infuriating to the Jews. They would have caused offense because the Jews were doing the things that God had commanded them to do.

Then God again declared that He would not hear prayers, and He told them why:

When you spread forth your hands,
I will hide My eyes from you;
even though you make many prayers,
I will not listen;
your hands are full of blood. (Isaiah 1:15)

Only the willfully blind would not see that the shedding of innocent blood is abhorrent to God. Only the stubborn hearted would refuse to see that God wants child killing ended, and that He has promised to *not* hear prayers in certain circumstances, in times and situations that are directly connected to shedding innocent blood.

The following verses from Isaiah are critical to understanding what God desires as "fruits of repentance." He calls His people to repent of sins they are committing (the sins of *commission*), and He calls them to repent of what they are *not* doing, *but they should be doing* (the sins of *omission*).

Wash yourselves; make yourselves clean;
remove the evil of your doings
from before My eyes;
cease to do evil,
learn to do good;
seek justice,
correct oppression;
defend the fatherless,
plead for the widow. (Isaiah 1:16–17)

This Scripture shows *specific actions God commands His people to do*—actions most of His people *then, and now, have failed to do.*

Hence, God demands: *"learn to do good!"* What *good* does God want His people to *learn* and to *do*? What is the repentance He is looking for? His demands are very specific:

Seek justice,
correct oppression;
defend the fatherless,
plead for the widow.

In many areas of North America and Europe, *justice* is wanting, and *oppression* exists. Christians should be the first to *seek justice* and *correct oppression.*

However, *can there be any crime committed in these nations today that is more detestable to God than the killing of innocent babies?*

God demands that His people *"defend the fatherless."* Who is more fatherless than a child scheduled to die, with her mother's determination and often her father's consent?

The overarching evil of these times—the sin that is crying out to God for judgment and hurling nations to perdition—is the shedding of innocent blood—the murder of tens of millions of innocent children by abortion.

From heaven's point of view—from the view of the holy angels that see us—one can hardly picture a more heinous crime against God and man than reaching into the womb of a pregnant mother to murder an innocent human being made in the image of God. Jesus said: "Whatever you did for one of the least of these brothers and sisters of Mine, you did for Me."

If the nations of Europe and North America are going to survive without becoming despotic, murderous states—if they are going to be restored to justice and righteousness—God's people will have to repent of the negligence and callousness regarding the murder of babies that brought these nations under God's judgment. If God has mercy and hears the prayers for restoration, it will be because His people—perhaps just a remnant—defended His babies and brought the "legal killing" of children to an end.

It is critical to remember that *after* the Jews were so severely punished—Jerusalem and the surrounding cities destroyed, Solomon's Temple destroyed, perhaps millions of Jews killed by the sword, famine, and the plague—this judgment produced "fruits of righteousness."

Namely, the Jews *stopped killing their children*, and they *stopped idolatry*.

At the end of the seventy-year Babylonian captivity, when the years predicted by the Prophet Jeremiah were fulfilled, the Prophet Daniel was still alive—though an old man—having served God through decades of tumult. Daniel prayed this sublime prayer for mercy and restoration, and this time, *God heard his prayer.* But note: it was *after* all the punishment God foretold had been fulfilled that the chastenings produced fruits of repentance:

> In the first year of Darius the son of Ahasu-e'rus, by birth a Mede, who became king over the realm of the Chalde'ans—in the first year of his reign, I, Daniel, perceived in the books the number of years which, according to the word of the LORD to Jeremiah the prophet, must pass before the end of the desolations of Jerusalem, namely, seventy years.
>
> Then I turned my face to the Lord God, seeking Him by prayer and supplications with fasting and sackcloth and ashes. I prayed to the LORD my God and made confession, saying, "O Lord, the great and terrible God, who keeps covenant and steadfast love with those who love Him and keep His commandments, *we have sinned and done wrong and acted wickedly and rebelled, turning aside from Thy commandments and ordinances; we have not listened to Thy servants the prophets, who spoke in Thy name to our kings, our princes, and our fathers, and to all the people of the land.* To Thee, O Lord, belongs righteousness, but to us confusion of face, as at this day, to the men of Judah, to the inhabitants of Jerusalem, and to all Israel, those that are near and those that are far away, in all the lands to which Thou hast driven them, because of

the treachery which they have committed against Thee. To us, O Lord, belongs confusion of face, to our kings, to our princes, and to our fathers, because we have sinned against Thee. To the Lord our God belong mercy and forgiveness; because we have rebelled against Him, and have not obeyed the voice of the LORD our God by following His laws, which He set before us by His servants the prophets. *All Israel has transgressed Thy law and turned aside, refusing to obey Thy voice. And the curse and oath which are written in the law of Moses the servant of God have been poured out upon us, because we have sinned against Him.* He has confirmed His words, which He spoke against us and against our rulers who ruled us, by bringing upon us a great calamity; for under the whole heaven there has not been done the like of what has been done against Jerusalem. *As it is written in the law of Moses, all this calamity has come upon us, yet we have not entreated the favor of the LORD our God, turning from our iniquities and giving heed to Thy truth.* Therefore the LORD has kept ready the calamity and has brought it upon us; for the LORD our God is righteous in all the works which He has done, and we have not obeyed His voice. And now, O Lord our God, who didst bring Thy people out of the land of Egypt with a mighty hand, and hast made Thee a name, as at this day, we have sinned, we have done wickedly. O Lord, according to all Thy righteous acts, let Thy anger and Thy wrath turn away from Thy city Jerusalem, Thy holy hill; because for our sins, and for the iniquities of our fathers, Jerusalem and Thy people have become a byword among all who are round about us. Now therefore, O our God, hearken to the prayer of Thy servant and to his supplications, and for Thy own sake, O Lord, cause Thy face to shine upon Thy sanctuary, which is desolate. O my God, incline Thy ear and hear; open Thy eyes and behold our desolations, and the city which is called by Thy name; for we do not present our supplications before Thee on the ground of our righteousness, but on the ground of Thy great mercy. O LORD, hear; O LORD, forgive; O LORD, give heed and act; delay not, for Thy own sake, O my God, because Thy city and Thy people are called by Thy name." (Daniel 9:1–19)

God heard this prayer, and Judah was soon restored and the temple rebuilt under the edict of Cyrus. But the beauty, power, and efficacy of this prayer came forth many decades after we heard God saying to Jeremiah and Ezekiel that *He would not hear the prayers of His prophets nor the prayers of His people to avert the judgments that are referred to in Daniel's beautiful prayer.* Israel had much hardship and suffering to pass through before God would have mercy and restore them, because of the innocent blood crying from the ground.

When the Jews returned from Babylon and rebuilt the temple and the city, never again did they descend into the evil of idolatry. Never again did they offer their children as sacrifices to demons and pagan gods. They "learned to do good."

Imagine

Imagine God sending a prophet to the great churches of today, saying: "What is the multitude of your services? I'm weary of singing and preaching and liturgy—your hands are covered with blood. Seek justice, correct oppression, rescue babies." Consider the convulsions that will continue if true repentance does not come. Picture the restoration and blessing of God if the Church and the nations do repent.

If Christians refuse to repent, continuing in their apathy and their collaboration with abominable evils—if the killing of children and the LGBTQ agenda continue apace—the Church in various nations will have a dreadful season of recompense to face. For, as the Scripture says, *judgment begins at the house of God.*

This work now turns to the specific "fruits of repentance" God looks for in His people—fruits He seeks in all ages—namely, the end of legalized child killing, the restoration of the legal definition of marriage, and the total rejection of the perverse practice of genital mutilation and gender swapping, also known as "transvestism."

Thus says the LORD of hosts: "Do not listen to the words of the prophets who prophesy to you, filling you with vain hopes; they speak visions of their own minds, not from the mouth of the LORD. They say continually to those who despise the word of the LORD, 'It shall be well with you'; and to every one who stubbornly follows his own heart, they say, 'No evil shall come upon you.'"

Jeremiah 23:16–17

*Your prophets have seen for you
false and deceptive visions;
they have not exposed your iniquity
to restore your fortunes,
but have seen for you oracles
false and misleading.*

Lamentations 2:14

*An astonishing and horrible thing
Has been committed in the land:
The prophets prophesy falsely,
And the priests rule by their own power;
And My people love to have it so.
But what will you do in the end?*

Jeremiah 5:30–31 NKJV

Woe to you, when all men speak well of you, for so their fathers did to the false prophets.

Luke 6:26

But a hireling, he who is not the shepherd, one who does not own the sheep, sees the wolf coming and leaves the sheep and flees; and the wolf catches the sheep and scatters them. The hireling flees because he is a hireling and does not care about the sheep.

John 10:12–13 NKJV

15

FALSE PROPHETS AND WORTHLESS SHEPHERDS

His watchmen are blind,
they are all without knowledge;
THEY ARE ALL DUMB DOGS,
THEY CANNOT BARK;
dreaming, lying down,
loving to slumber.
The dogs have a mighty appetite;
they never have enough.
THE SHEPHERDS ALSO HAVE NO UNDERSTANDING;
THEY HAVE ALL TURNED TO THEIR OWN WAY,
EACH TO HIS OWN GAIN, ONE AND ALL.

Isaiah 56:10–11

"FOR FROM THE LEAST TO THE GREATEST OF THEM,
EVERY ONE IS GREEDY FOR UNJUST GAIN;
AND FROM PROPHET TO PRIEST,
EVERY ONE DEALS FALSELY.
They have healed the wound of My people lightly,
saying, 'Peace, peace,'
when there is no peace.

WERE THEY ASHAMED WHEN THEY COMMITTED ABOMINATION?
NO, THEY WERE NOT AT ALL ASHAMED;
THEY DID NOT KNOW HOW TO BLUSH.
Therefore they shall fall among those who fall;
at the time that I punish them, they shall be overthrown,"
says the LORD.

Jeremiah 6:13–15

The Apostle Paul exhorted Timothy in his duty as a spokesman for God. Note the range of hardships Paul said he would face:

> I charge you in the presence of God and of Christ Jesus who is to judge the living and the dead, and by His appearing and His kingdom: preach the word, be urgent in season and out of season, convince, rebuke, and exhort, be unfailing in patience and in teaching. For the time is coming when people will not endure sound teaching, but having itching ears they will accumulate for themselves teachers to suit their own likings, and will turn away from listening to the truth and wander into myths. As for you, always be steady, endure suffering, do the work of an evangelist, fulfill your ministry. (Second Timothy 4:1–5)

Preaching, being urgent, convincing, rebuking, exhorting, suffering, and dealing with people who have "itching ears" and *who want to be lied to*, "to suit their own likings"—that is what awaited Timothy, and that is what awaits anyone who dares to proclaim "the whole counsel of God."

Sadly, men and women of this caliber and understanding are in woefully short supply. The suffocating lack of these valiant spokesmen for God is part of why nations are being seduced by sirens of evil.

Sadly, men and women are present in droves inside the Church who speak words of delusion and false comfort—words that do nothing to call people to sorrow and the fruits of repentance for their sins and the sins of the nation. Christian civilization is dying in the West, in part because of the tragic lack of courageous men and women who speak the truth of God without equivocation, who fear not the face of man, but rather fear God and speak all that He has commanded. The Apostle James wrote:

> Draw near to God and He will draw near to you. Cleanse your hands, you sinners, and purify your hearts, you men of double mind. *Be wretched and mourn and weep. Let your laughter be turned to mourning and your joy to dejection.* Humble yourselves before the Lord and He will exalt you. (James 4:8–10)

This is a key passage regarding repentance and restoration, but one would be hard pressed to hear sermons from this text in any Christian-denomination pulpit or radio or TV show. It is far more popular to tell "itching ears" that God has called them to prosperity and peace.

Who Speaks for God?

The Scriptures speak a good deal about false teachers and false prophets. Perhaps the most famous line in the Scriptures about false prophets comes from the Lord Jesus Himself in His Sermon on the Mount:

> Beware of false prophets, who come to you in sheep's clothing but inwardly are ravenous wolves. You will know them by their fruits. Are grapes gathered from thorns, or figs from thistles? So, every sound tree bears good fruit, but the bad tree bears evil fruit. A sound tree cannot bear evil fruit, nor can a bad tree bear good fruit. Every tree that does not bear good fruit is cut down and thrown into the fire. Thus you will know them by their fruits. (Matthew 7:15–20)

Jesus warned His disciples:

> For false messiahs and false prophets will appear and per-
> form great signs and wonders to deceive, if possible, even
> the elect. (Matthew 24:24 NIV)

Peter warned the Church:

> But there were also false prophets among the people,
> just as there will be false teachers among you. They will
> secretly introduce destructive heresies, even denying the
> sovereign Lord who bought them—bringing swift destruc-
> tion on themselves. Many will follow their depraved
> conduct and will bring the way of truth into disrepute.
> (Second Peter 2:1–2 NIV)

Paul also warned Christians of false apostles:

> For such people are false apostles, deceitful workers, mas-
> querading as apostles of Christ. *And no wonder, for Satan
> himself masquerades as an angel of light.* It is not surprising,
> then, if his servants also masquerade as servants of righ-
> teousness. Their end will be what their actions deserve.
> (Second Corinthians 11:13–15 NIV)

Beautiful Robes, False Prophets, and Murder

The slaying of children in ancient Israel was a *religious rite*—an
act of worship. The priest would wear special garments and utter
solemn prayers before the child was slain. But no matter how
religious the ceremony appeared—no matter how many prayers
were said—*the act of killing the child was murder—an abomination
to God that provoked His rage.*

Likewise today, Protestant churches are littered with clergymen and women who declare that aborting a baby is *not* murder,
but *healthcare* and a *right*. These wolves in sheep's clothing are
following in the path of the priests of Molech. They are false
prophets and liars and must be passionately resisted.

In many Catholic dioceses, the bishops and many priests are of little use in combating what is arguably the greatest evil in the world. They will occasionally pay lip service to the pro-life cause, but little more.

Worse yet, in many Protestant seminaries, clergy are taught that abortion is a permissible, ethical choice. This poisonous lie has taken deep root in mainline Protestant denominations.

This is an outrage against God, a betrayal of His Law, and an assault on Christ Himself. Jesus said: *"Whatever you do to the least of these My brethren, you do to Me."*

Any clergymen or women who tell a pregnant woman it is ethically permissible with God to kill her baby—no matter how sanctimonious they sound, no matter how merciful they appear, no matter what Bible verses they quote and twist—those clergy are accessories to murder *and servants of hell for their part in the murder of a child of God.*

Multitudes of clergy remain silent on the shedding of inno-cent blood. Many of them fear offending or hurting the feelings of people who participated in killing a child. Others might fear causing a decrease in financial offerings. In such an hour, the "prophets" who proclaim "peace, peace" are a special offence to God:

"For from the least to the greatest of them,
every one is greedy for unjust gain;
and from prophet to priest,
every one deals falsely.
They have healed the wound of My people lightly,
saying, 'Peace, peace,'
when there is no peace.
Were they ashamed when they committed abomination?
No, they were not at all ashamed;
they did not know how to blush.
Therefore they shall fall among those who fall;

at the time that I punish them, they shall be overthrown," says the LORD. (Jeremiah 6:13–15)

Dueling Prophets

While Judah was killing her children and God was warning them that He would bring the Babylonians in judgment against Judah, Jerusalem, and the temple, the false prophets were preaching exactly what the Jews did *not* need to hear: *that everything was going to be fine.*

The book of Jeremiah gives us a stark record of the struggle between the *true prophetic voice* and the *false prophetic voice.* Jeremiah was instructed by God to make a yoke, like one would use on an ox to pull a plow, and to wear the yoke while he prophesied to Judah and King Zedekiah of Judah:

> "Make yourself thongs and yoke-bars, and put them on your neck.... "'Now I [God] have given all these lands into the hand of Nebuchadnez'zar, the king of Babylon, My servant, and I have given him also the beasts of the field to serve him. All the nations shall serve him and his son and his grandson....
>
> ""'But if any nation or kingdom will not serve this Nebuchadnez'zar king of Babylon, and put its neck under the yoke of the king of Babylon, I will punish that nation with the sword, with famine, and with pestilence, says the LORD, until I have consumed it by his hand. So do not listen to your prophets, your diviners, your dreamers, your soothsayers, or your sorcerers, who are saying to you, 'You shall not serve the king of Babylon.' *For it is a lie which they are prophesying to you, with the result that you will be removed far from your land, and I will drive you out, and you will perish.'"'...*
>
> To Zedeki'ah king of Judah I spoke in like manner: "Bring your necks under the yoke of the king of Babylon, and serve him and his people, and live. Why will you and your people die by the sword, by famine, and by pestilence,

as the LORD has spoken concerning any nation which will not serve the king of Babylon? *Do not listen to the words of the prophets who are saying to you, 'You shall not serve the king of Babylon,' for it is a lie which they are prophesying to you. I have not sent them, says the LORD, but they are prophesying falsely in My name, with the result that I will drive you out and you will perish, you and the prophets who are prophesying to you."* (Jeremiah 27:2, 6–15)

An arrogant and foolish "prophet" named Hananiah took it upon himself to contradict Jeremiah and proceeded to break the yoke that God told Jeremiah to wear. He then prophesied to all who were standing in the temple:

In that same year, at the beginning of the reign of Zedeki'ah king of Judah, in the fifth month of the fourth year, Hanani'ah the son of Azzur, the prophet from Gib'eon, spoke to me in the house of the LORD, in the presence of the priests and all the people, saying, "Thus says the LORD of hosts, the God of Israel: I have broken the yoke of the king of Babylon. Within two years I will bring back to this place all the vessels of the LORD's house, which Nebuchadnez'zar king of Babylon took away from this place and carried to Babylon. I will also bring back to this place Jeconi'ah the son of Jehoi'akim, king of Judah, and all the exiles from Judah who went to Babylon, says the LORD, for I will break the yoke of the king of Babylon."…

Then the prophet Hanani'ah took the yoke-bars from the neck of Jeremiah the prophet, and broke them. And Hanani'ah spoke in the presence of all the people, saying, "Thus says the LORD: Even so will I break the yoke of Nebuchadnez'zar king of Babylon from the neck of all the nations within two years." But Jeremiah the prophet went his way.

Hanani'ah may have been a compelling, inspiring preacher. He may have been a true patriot who loved Judah with all his heart. One can imagine him taking the yoke off Jeremiah's shoulders with great drama, beckoning the crowd to watch as he broke the yoke that God told Jeremiah to make. Maybe his listeners cheered and yelled, "Amen!" and clapped as the yoke was splintered.

But he was wrong, and no matter how excited or inspired or hopeful his preaching made the Jews feel, *he was a false prophet.*

Hanani'ah was dead within a year, and *most of his hearers were cut down by the famine, disease, or the sword.*

> Sometime after the prophet Hanani'ah had broken the yoke-bars from off the neck of Jeremiah the prophet, the word of the LORD came to Jeremiah: "Go, tell Hanani'ah, 'Thus says the LORD: You have broken wooden bars, but I will make in their place bars of iron. For thus says the LORD of hosts, the God of Israel: I have put upon the neck of all these nations an iron yoke of servitude to Nebuchadnez'zar king of Babylon, and they shall serve him, for I have given to him even the beasts of the field.'" *And Jeremiah the prophet said to the prophet Hanani'ah, "Listen, Hanani'ah, the LORD has not sent you, and you have made this people trust in a lie. Therefore thus says the LORD: 'Behold, I will remove you from the face of the earth. This very year you shall die, because you have uttered rebellion against the LORD.'"*
>
> *In that same year, in the seventh month, the prophet Hanani'ah died.* (Jeremiah 28:1–4, 10–17)

This passage serves as an ominous warning: those prophets, priests, pastors, preachers, televangelists, and teachers who ignore the danger Western nations are in, or who actually tell Christians they are not in danger of God's judgment, are putting God's people *in greater danger* by their negligence and falsehoods.

Jeremiah was in anguish over the fact that the Jews were getting two completely opposite messages:

Then I said: "Ah, Lord GOD, behold, the prophets say to them, 'You shall not see the sword, nor shall you have famine, but I will give you assured peace in this place.'" And the LORD said to me: "*The prophets are prophesying lies in My name; I did not send them, nor did I command them or speak to them. They are prophesying to you a lying vision, worthless divination, and the deceit of their own minds.* Therefore thus says the LORD concerning the prophets who prophesy in My name although I did not send them, and who say, 'Sword and famine shall not come on this land': By sword and famine those prophets shall be consumed. And the people to whom they prophesy shall be cast out in the streets of Jerusalem, victims of famine and sword, with none to bury them—them, their wives, their sons, and their daughters. For I will pour out their wickedness upon them. (Jeremiah 14:13–16)

Jeremiah recorded the words of God regarding the false prophets. The Lord declares what may be the darkest element of false teachers and preachers: they do not turn people from their sin:

In the prophets of Samar'ia
I saw an unsavory thing:
they prophesied by Ba'al
and led My people Israel astray.
But in the prophets of Jerusalem
I have seen a horrible thing:
they commit adultery and walk in lies;
they strengthen the hands of evildoers,
so that no one turns from his wickedness;
all of them have become like Sodom to Me,
and its inhabitants like Gomor'rah (Jeremiah 23:13–14)

Thus says the LORD of hosts: "*Do not listen to the words of the prophets who prophesy to you, filling you with vain hopes; they speak visions of their own minds, not from the mouth of the*

LORD. They say continually to those who despise the word of the LORD, 'It shall be well with you'; and to every one who stubbornly follows his own heart, they say, 'No evil shall come upon you.'" (Jeremiah 23:16–17)

I did not send the prophets,
yet they ran;
I did not speak to them,
yet they prophesied.
But if they had stood in My council,
then they would have proclaimed My words to My people,
and they would have turned them from their evil way,
and from the evil of their doings. (Jeremiah 23:21–22)

False prophets need not only be religious. They can be secular, political, and even educational. For example, one can turn on the evening news and watch a liberal or socialist say: "We are going to save the country," or "We are going to save the planet," followed by the sentiment, "No harm will come to you."

Likewise, one can turn on the news and watch a conservative or a constitutionalist say, "We just need to get government back in the hands of people like us. And then, no harm will come to you."

What they share in common and how they are both false prophets is that they *do not confront, deal with, or even mention the sins that cry to God for vengeance.*

In most Western nations, there are political parties, leaders, and spokespeople in the media to which Christians and conservatives tend to gravitate. Overall, those Christians and conservatives find the echo of Judeo-Christian values, "family values," conservative economic policies, and conservative policies on crime, immigration, and fuel.

The political parties, leaders, and media personalities that champion the shedding of innocent blood, or who revel in the sexual debaucheries outlined in Romans chapter 1 that plague the nations, are bold as lions. They herald lies and sins without fear, with brazen faces.

Conversely, the political parties, leaders, and spokespeople that supposedly hold to Judeo-Christian values, even those that are allegedly against the sins that cry for vengeance, rarely if ever mention those sins. One can watch hours of television in Western nations, or listen to hours of conservative radio, and never hear that the shedding of innocent blood brings a curse on a nation or that the sexual crimes of Sodom and Gomorrah, or the sexual perversion of the Canaanite nations that caused their demise, will likewise bring divine judgment on nations today.

Both Left and Right, liberal and conservative, pagan and Christian will promise solutions to the chastisements that befall nations, but they will not identify and root out the causes of those chastisements—the sins that cry to God for vengeance.

Political parties and leaders insist they can fix drought, famine, plagues, violence, fear, economic calamity, terrorism, military threats—i.e., the chastisements of God—without calling for repentance and the end of the crimes that have brought drought, famine, plagues, violence, fear, economic calamity, terrorism, and military threats.

Pagan and Christian alike promise to fix the "problems," ignoring or denying that these "problems" are in fact divine judgments—judgments that can only be fixed by ending the legalization of "sins that cry to God for vengeance."

If those sins—those crimes against God and man—are not dealt with, harm will come, no matter who is in charge. Yes, *harm will come.*

A true prophet turns people away from sin. Conversely, false prophets *don't turn people away from sin*—whether sins of *commission* or sins of *omission*.

The false prophets and counselors to the kings and people of Jeremiah's day perished from famine, plague, or Nebuchadnezzar's hand because they ignored or lied about what God had said. But worse, they denied their hearers the opportunity to repent and be saved from the horrors that were coming *because they did not tell them the truth.*

Ezekiel, prophesying during the same period from captivity in Babylon, cried out:

> The word of the LORD came to me: "Son of man, prophesy against the prophets of Israel, prophesy and say to those who prophesy out of their own minds: 'Hear the word of the LORD!' Thus says the Lord GOD, *Woe to the foolish prophets who follow their own spirit, and have seen nothing!* Your prophets have been like foxes among ruins, O Israel. You have not gone up into the breaches, or built up a wall for the house of Israel, that it might stand in battle in the day of the LORD. *They have spoken falsehood and divined a lie; they say, 'Says the LORD,' when the LORD has not sent them, and yet they expect Him to fulfil their word.*" (Ezekiel 13:1–6)

In the following passage, God makes the direct connection between corruption in the political leaders—the "princes who are shedding blood"—and *the corrupting influence of the priests and prophets who do not confront the princes*, the political leaders of the day. It is heart wrenching to consider how many politicians in office today support child killing and are bolstered and supported in their sin by a clergyman, a political commentator, or *by the silence of both*:

> And the word of the LORD came to me: "Son of man, say to her, You are a land that is not cleansed, or rained upon in the day of indignation. *Her princes in the midst of her are like a roaring lion tearing the prey; they have devoured human lives*; they have taken treasure and precious things; they have made many widows in the midst of her. *Her priests have done violence to My law and have profaned My holy things; they have made no distinction between the holy and the common, neither have they taught the difference between the unclean and the clean*, and they have disregarded My sabbaths, so that I

am profaned among them. *Her princes in the midst of her are like wolves tearing the prey, shedding blood,* destroying lives to get dishonest gain. *And her prophets have daubed for them with whitewash,* seeing false visions and divining lies for them, saying, 'Thus says the Lord GOD,' when the LORD has not spoken." (Ezekiel 22:23–28)

These false prophets rightly deserve to be held in derision. But perhaps just as bad—or worse—are those who suspect or believe that danger is coming *but issue forth no warnings*.

The Sin of Silence

Perhaps the most damning sin of a nation's shepherds—coming from pulpits, radio and TV shows, books, blogs, websites, and other forms of communication—is *silence*. Tens of thousands of Christian clergy, speakers, and writers from multiple denominations do not speak what they know to be true because of *fear*.

Catholic priests fear being silenced by their bishop or moved to a parish on the edge of oblivion if they dare to speak the truth about child killing, or if they speak of the sacrament of marriage being solely between a man and a woman.

Independent evangelical pastors fear being voted out of the pulpit by boards, trustees, or congregations if they dare to speak the truth about innocent blood crying from the ground.

Mainline-denomination clergy (who still hold to orthodoxy) fear being defrocked, suspended, or moved to a tiny church if they speak out with the boldness of Jeremiah against the murder of children and go against the liberal tide that has corrupted their entire denomination.

And yet others who have no fear of a bishop or a board punishing them also refuse to tell the truth for any number of reasons, most of which boil down to a love of money, fear, a false sense of compassion, and *an unholy love of self*.

This silence—these *sins of omission*—is crippling the nations of North America and Europe and paving the way for divine judgment.

One of the ancient congregational confessions of sin says in part:

> I confess to almighty God
> and to you, my brothers and sisters,
> that I have greatly sinned
> in my thoughts and in my words,
> in what I have done
> *and in what I have failed to do.*

This phrase *"and in what I have failed to do"* hearkens to the book of James, where James said:

> Whoever knows what is right to do *and fails to do it*, for him it is sin. (James 4:17)

Our Lord Jesus made this statement:

> And that servant who knew his master's will, but did not make ready or act according to his will, shall receive a severe beating. (Luke 12:47)

In addition to the Scriptural teaching on the sin of omission, the Scriptures also condemn the *sin of silence*. God rebukes the shepherds and watchmen who *sin by silence*:

> His [God's] watchmen are blind,
> they are all without knowledge;
> they are all dumb dogs,
> they cannot bark;
> dreaming, lying down,
> loving to slumber. (Isaiah 56:10)

The NASB translates this verse this way:

> His watchmen are blind,
> All of them know nothing.
> All of them are mute dogs unable to bark,
> Dreamers lying down, who love to slumber.

What good is a blind watchman? What use is a watchdog that does not bark a warning?

God warned Ezekiel of the grave sin of silence at the beginning of his prophetic ministry. God threatened Ezekiel with having to account for the blood of the wicked if he failed to warn them:

> Son of man, all My words that I shall speak to you receive in your heart, and hear with your ears. And go, get you to the exiles, to your people, and say to them, "Thus says the Lord GOD"; whether they hear or refuse to hear....
>
> Son of man, I have made you a watchman for the house of Israel; whenever you hear a word from My mouth, you shall give them warning from Me. If I say to the wicked, "You shall surely die," and you give him no warning, nor speak to warn the wicked from his wicked way, in order to save his life, that wicked man shall die in his iniquity; but his blood I will require at your hand. But if you warn the wicked, and he does not turn from his wickedness, or from his wicked way, he shall die in his iniquity; but you will have saved your life. (Ezekiel 3:10–11, 17–19)

Years later in his ministry, God again warned Ezekiel not to commit *the sin of silence*:

> *But if the watchman sees the sword coming and does not blow the trumpet, so that the people are not warned, and the sword comes, and takes any one of them; that man is taken away in his iniquity, but his blood I will require at the watchman's hand.*
>
> *So you, son of man, I have made a watchman for the house of Israel; whenever you hear a word from My mouth, you shall give them warning from Me.* If I say to the wicked, O wicked man, you shall surely die, *and you do not speak to warn the wicked to turn from his way, that wicked man shall die in his iniquity, but his blood I will require at your hand.* But if you warn the wicked to turn from his way, and he does not turn from his

way; he shall die in his iniquity, *but you will have saved your life*. (Ezekiel 33:6–9)

It is not uncommon to desire to remain silent in the face of hostility. But the Lord Jesus gave this exhortation to all who follow Him:

Do not think that I have come to bring peace on earth; I have not come to bring peace, but a sword. For I have come to set a man against his father, and a daughter against her mother, and a daughter-in-law against her mother-in-law; and a man's foes will be those of his own household. He who loves father or mother more than Me is not worthy of Me; and he who loves son or daughter more than Me is not worthy of Me; *and he who does not take his cross and follow Me is not worthy of Me. He who finds his life will lose it, and he who loses his life for My sake will find it.* (Matthew 10:34–39)

Christian clergy, laymen, and media personalities must speak the truth out of the love and fear of God, and because of a love for and a fear for individuals and the nations of the earth.

Jeremiah and Ezekiel had to contend with lying prophets who spoke in God's name, saying, "Jerusalem will not be destroyed." God rebuked these worthless shepherds: "'Woe to the shepherds who destroy and scatter the sheep of My pasture!' says the LORD.... 'From the least to the greatest of them, every one is greedy for unjust gain.... They have healed the wound of My people lightly, saying, "Peace, peace," when there is no peace'" (see Jeremiah 23, 6).

One glaring example of this treachery from clergy—accompanied by a deafening silence—is the vast majority of Roman Catholic bishops in North America and Europe. Many of them, individually or collectively, will wax eloquent regarding immigration; they will talk about health care for the poor; they will discuss the rights of workers; they will criticize various government policies that impinge on their freedoms or rights; now a number of them are speaking out in defense of sexual perversions that the Church clearly says are disordered or sinful.

But consider how few actually ever do or say anything bold and forthright regarding the murder of babies. Think how few have ever been on their local news shows, saying, "Abortion is murder."

In America, remember how little was said by bishops when *Roe vs. Wade* was overturned. In Canada, consider how few ever give a public condemnation of murder. In Europe, how many bishops have made public, bold stands against the slayers of unborn babies?

The collective magnitude of what Catholic bishops have failed to do is staggering. Why this treachery? Perhaps they don't know or don't believe the teachings of the Scriptures and the Catholic Church. That is unlikely.

More likely, it's about money and the praise of men.

For example, the Catholic Church in the United States has received multiple billions of dollars from the American federal government for its programs. Much of this money comes from politicians who support the murder of babies by abortion. The bishop's hand is out and open—his mouth is shut regarding innocent blood.

Some bishops say they're afraid of losing their tax-exempt status. If a clergyman refuses to preach the truth in order to receive the financial benefits of tax exemption, the argument can be made that his silence is bought. "A bribe blinds the eyes" (Deuteronomy 16:19).

Consider so many prophets of the Old Testament. The spokesmen for God did not hide behind a tax shelter, nor did they pretend to not see the sins that the kings were committing. They confronted kings and princes *by name, and often to their faces* for their sins. Here are a few examples from dozens found in Sacred Scripture:

Samuel the prophet confronted King Saul for his rebellion and told him the kingdom was taken from him and given to David.

After King David had taken Bathsheba and had her husband killed, the prophet Nathan rebuked King David to his face: "You are the man!" and then pronounced judgment on him—the sword would never leave his house.

Ahijah prophesied that because of the sins of Solomon (marrying pagan women, worshiping idols, and building an altar for child sacrifice), the kingdom of Israel would be divided and the Northern Ten Tribes would be given to Jeroboam.

Ahijah later prophesied the destruction of Jeroboam's family and dynasty because Jeroboam had led the Northern Ten Tribes into idolatry.

Elijah rebuked King Ahab to his face and prophesied that dogs would eat his wife, Jezebel's dead body, which they did.

John the Baptist, who came "in the spirit and power of" Elijah and was the greatest man who ever lived besides Jesus, rebuked King Herod to his face: "[Herod!] It is not lawful for you to have your brother's wife!"

Sadly, the number of Catholic bishops that will call out "kings and princes" (i.e., political leaders) by name for the grotesque sin of child murder is pitifully small.

One American bishop, explaining why he did not confront political leaders as John the Baptist and others clearly did, told this author plainly that *John the Baptist did not have to worry about real estate, money, and making mortgage payments.* He feared that if he spoke the truth about the president of the United States or other political candidates and officeholders, it could cause economic hardship on him and his diocese.

This financial justification is the defining sin of the *hireling.* Jesus said that the hireling flees when he sees the wolf coming *because he is a hireling.* The true shepherd lays down his life for the sheep. Speaking like Nathan or John the Baptist or Jeremiah is part of the duty of the bishop, as quoted from St. Paul in the beginning of this chapter.

The crowning heartbreak of this treachery is that most Catholic bishops in North America and Europe will serve Holy Communion to the political child killers, putting the Holy Sacrament into hands that are covered with blood. These bishops know that abortion is murder, and they know who the proponents of murder are. Yet they equivocate and excuse and give specious arguments for why they should not "politicize" communion. This cowardice emboldens the evildoers and scandalizes the faithful.

And when a faithful bishop has the courage and integrity to withhold communion from a known proponent of child killing, he is criticized and ostracized by his "brother bishops." Many of them will tell the sin-serving politician, "You can have Communion in my diocese." It is horrifying.

Many protestant leaders and evangelical TV and radio stars are sadly cut from the same nonconfrontational "hireling" cloth. They can reach millions in their pulpits and hundreds of millions through their broadcasts, yet when it comes to calling out the sin of child killing or so-called homosexual marriage, they are eerily silent.

Likewise, the great media personalities of the day that are silent about sins that cry for vengeance commit the same act of betrayal and treachery: silence.

Accessories to Murder—Voting for Death

Most Christian leaders of all denominations do not solemnly warn their flocks: "If you vote for so-and-so, and they promote the murder of innocent babies, you are an accessory to their crimes against children. You have blood on your hands."

The logic of this "sermon" is unimpeachable:

If you vote for candidate X, who has promised you that he will use his power to continue the holocaust of children, you share in the guilt of the babies that will be slaughtered. It does not matter if you have other issues on which you agree with him or her. If you agreed with him on everything except he wanted to own slaves, would you vote for him? If you agreed on everything except she wanted to put Jews in concentration camps, would you vote for her?

If you put your personal political preferences ahead of the lives of the innocent, how are you any different from the great tyrants of history and those who helped them in their crimes?

Simple, direct words of this nature delivered by clergy in pulpits, writings, and on their multitude of communication platforms would speedily lead to the end of legalized child killing in many nations.

The result of the silence and gross negligence from Catholic and Protestant clergy is that a majority of Roman Catholic parishioners vote for child killers in the United States, and one-third of evangelicals do the same. The numbers are similar, and even worse, in other Western nations.

It is at once heartbreaking and sobering to know that *the one major political party in America that promotes murder, sodomy, and the transvestite agenda* would collapse without the treachery of the Catholic and evangelical votes.

Said again—for emphasis—this evildoing political party, candidates, and their entire wicked agenda would be swept away if not for the treachery against God and babies committed by Catholic and evangelical voters.

False Equations from False Prophets

Many Catholic theologians, using the Catholic catechism and Scripture—and Protestant theologians using the Scriptures—teach that there are four or five sins that cry out to God.

The five are:

1. Shedding innocent blood
2. The sins of Sodom
3. Slavery

4. The treatment of the "stranger," orphans, and widows
5. Withholding wages from the wage earner

Some of these betrayers of babies have gone on to say that all of these sins are *equal*, or that numbers 3 through 5 are so critical that Christians could knowingly vote for child killers and "LGBTQ, etc.," candidates—because of their positions on the treatment or mistreatment of immigrants and the desire for "economic justice" (whatever that means in an election cycle).

This argument proves false on two counts. First, none of sins 2 through 5 is equal to murder. Murder stands alone as a sin in the Scriptures for reasons we have already discussed (consider Cain and Abel, God's command to Noah, Deuteronomy 21:1–9; Leviticus 20:1–5, etc.).

Second, even considering the horrifying nature of slavery, slavery is in no way as barbaric as child killing. Sound logic proves this point:

- A slave can run away; a child cannot run anywhere.
- A slave can beg for mercy; a child cannot beg for anything.
- A slave can defend himself with force; a child cannot defend himself.
- Slaves can unite and fight for their freedom; babies are isolated and cannot unite for anything.
- Slaves can articulate the injustices they suffer and can make cogent arguments; a baby can do none of these things.
- A slave can run, hide, fight, cry for help, beg for mercy, appeal for justice; all a child can do is die, unless he or she is one of the few hundred every year who survive a "late-term abortion."

Concerning wages and the treatment of immigrants, this argument also proves false. When one looks at all human history regarding the treatment of the poor and immigrants, consider the treatment of immigrants in North America and Europe. What nations in the last two hundred years have provided greater opportunities and freedoms to immigrants who reached their shores than Western democracies, formerly known as "Christendom"? None. Has China? Russia? Africa? No.

If the facts are studied, the entire argument these Catholic advocates make is ludicrous. Furthermore, unborn children who are killed are brutally ripped apart, limb from limb, or burned to death with a saline solution, or shot in the heart with a needle full of poison—*by the millions.* Those pastors, "theologians," and clergy of all types who claim that the issue of immigration is equal to or greater than child killing are deceived and deceiving others.

Judgment Begins at the House of God, with the Elders

This silence and betrayal of the Church will not go unpunished. As the Apostle Peter wrote: "For the time is, that judgment should begin at the house of God" (First Peter 4:17 DRB). This warning from Peter is an allusion to a passage of the Scriptures that most Christians are not familiar with: the judgment of God on Solomon's Temple that was predicted in Ezekiel chapter 9. But as Peter hints in his passage, this judgment was not merely on a building—it was on the men and women—the individuals—who had betrayed God.

Please read this passage from Ezekiel slowly. Note in this vision the men (angels?) with weapons, and one man with an inkhorn. Note who is judged and why. And note especially who is spared:

> Then He cried in my ears with a loud voice, saying, "Cause those who are in charge of the city to draw near, each man with his destroying weapon in his hand." Behold, six men came from the way of the upper gate, which lies toward the north, *every man with his slaughter weapon in his hand.* One man in the middle of them was clothed in linen, *with a writer's inkhorn by his side.* They went in, and stood beside the bronze altar [at Solomon's Temple].
>
> The glory of the God of Israel went up from the cherub, whereupon it was, to the threshold of the house; and He

called to the man clothed in linen, who had the writer's inkhorn by his side. Yahweh said to him, "Go through the middle of the city, through the middle of Jerusalem, and *set a mark on the foreheads of the men THAT SIGH AND THAT CRY OVER ALL THE ABOMINATIONS THAT ARE DONE WITHIN IT.*

To the others He said in my hearing, "*Go through the city after him, and strike. Don't let your eye spare, neither have pity. Kill utterly the old man, the young man, the virgin, little children and women; BUT DON'T COME NEAR ANY MAN ON WHOM IS THE MARK. BEGIN AT MY SANCTUARY.* [I.e., judgment begins at the house of God.]

Then they began at the old men who were before the house.

He said to them, "Defile the house, and fill the courts with the slain. Go out!"

They went out, and struck in the city. While they were killing, and I was left, I fell on my face, and cried, and said, "Ah Lord Yahweh! Will You destroy all the residue of Israel in Your pouring out of Your wrath on Jerusalem?"

Then He said to me, "*The iniquity of the house of Israel and Judah is exceedingly great, and the land is full of blood, and the city full of perversion* [i.e., child killing and sexual perversion]; for they say, 'Yahweh has forsaken the land, and Yahweh doesn't see.' As for Me also, *My eye won't spare, neither will I have pity, but I will bring their way on their head.*"

Behold, the man clothed in linen, who had the inkhorn by his side, reported the matter, saying, "I have done as You have commanded me." (Ezekiel 9:1–11 WEB)

Judgment began *at the house of God*, WITH THE ELDERS. If this passage holds true in the woes that will come upon America, our churches, our Christian high schools and colleges, and our cowardly, silent church leaders will be the first to experience the judgment of God.

Persecution, judgment, and hardship are coming, and not "from the devil." They are the chastisement of God on Christian leaders, pastors, priests, etc., who have betrayed God by their silence and *who have not sighed and cried for the abominations that are happening in this nation.*

Sins and Crimes, and When the Twain Shall Meet

Yes, child killing and homosexual acts took place when those sins were still crimes. And sadly, they will continue to happen after they are made crimes again. It is against the law to steal, to hold a slave, to rape, and to murder born humans. But those sins/crimes are still committed in our nation even though they are against the law. The reason that the judgment of God comes is because certain sins/crimes that cry to God for judgment are codified and *protected by law* rather than being *against the law*.

Moreover, the level of the crime goes up or down exponentially based on what the law says is legal or illegal. I.e., when it was *legal* to own slaves, many slaves were held. When it became *illegal* to own slaves, very few slaves were held.

When child killing is made illegal again and it becomes a crime for mothers and abortionists to conspire to kill children, the number of children slaughtered will drop significantly because most people will obey the law.

As long as the feel-good, false prophets of our day continue to give succor and legitimacy to evildoers in government and provide a numbing salve to their guilty consciences, nations will continue down paths of iniquity and destruction.

Therefore, as the Holy Spirit says,
"Today, when you hear His voice,
do not harden your hearts as in the rebellion.

Hebrews 3:7–8

"Yes, they made their hearts like flint, refusing to hear the law and the words which the LORD *of hosts had sent by His Spirit through the former prophets. Thus great wrath came from the* LORD *of hosts. Therefore it happened, that just as He proclaimed and they would not hear, so they called out and I would not listen," says the* LORD *of hosts. "But I scattered them with a whirlwind among all the nations which they had not known. Thus the land became desolate after them, so that no one passed through or returned; for they made the pleasant land desolate."*

Zechariah 7:12–14 NKJV

Truly I tell you, whatever you did not do for one of the least of these, you did not do for Me.

Matthew 25:45 NIV

Hate evil, and love good,
and establish justice in the gate;
it may be that the LORD, *the God of hosts,*
will be gracious to the remnant of Joseph. . . .
Take away from Me the noise of your songs;
to the melody of your harps I will not listen.
But let justice roll down like waters,
and righteousness like an everflowing stream.

Amos 5:15, 23–24

16

Fruits of Repentance:
Spiritual, Physical, and Legal

To avert God's chastening hand and to help restore a nation to health and righteousness, God's people must bring forth "fruits of repentance." What does that fruit look like?

The Spiritual Fruits of Repentance

"Hardness of heart" is rampant in the Christian community. Most Christians have lived comfortably beside the murder of babies and the sexual pollution of Western nations for so long, they have grown calloused. Many—or even most—are no longer scandalized and outraged. *They are indifferent.*

Ezekiel recorded that God would spare people "who sigh and groan" over the abominations that were committed in Jerusalem.

> And the LORD said to him, "Go through the city, through Jerusalem, and put a mark upon the foreheads of the men *who sigh and groan over all the abominations that are committed in it.*" And to the others He said in my hearing, "Pass through the city after him, *and smite; your eye shall not spare, and you shall show no pity; slay old men outright, young men and maidens, little children and women, but touch no one upon whom is the mark.* And begin at My sanctuary." So they began with the elders who were before the house. (Ezekiel 9:4–6)

Saint Peter wrote that Lot was spared in part because his soul was tormented. He said that God turned...

the cities of Sodom and Gomorrah into ashes, condemned them to destruction, making them an example to those who afterward would live ungodly; and delivered righteous Lot, who was oppressed by the filthy conduct of the wicked (for that righteous man, dwelling among them, *tormented his righteous soul from day to day by seeing and hearing their lawless deeds*)—then the Lord knows how to deliver the godly out of temptations and to reserve the unjust under punishment for the day of judgment. (Second Peter 2:6–9 NKJV)

The Christian community must beg God for mercy and confess before the Almighty that "we have sinned, in what we have done and *what we have failed to do*. We have not sighed, grieved, and groaned. We have not been tormented as Lot was. We have not fought for Your justice in the way that was our duty to do."

The Prophet Daniel provides a passionate example of confessing the sins that brought judgment and begging God for mercy. This prayer was given at the end of the seventy years of the Babylonian captivity, prior to the Jews being restored to Judah, at which time they rebuilt Jerusalem, the wall, and Solomon's Temple:

Then I set my face toward the Lord God to make request by prayer and supplications, with fasting, sackcloth, and ashes. And I prayed to the LORD my God, and made confession, and said, "O Lord, great and awesome God, who keeps His covenant and mercy with those who love Him, and with those who keep His commandments, we have sinned and committed iniquity, we have done wickedly and rebelled, even by departing from Your precepts and Your judgments. Neither have we heeded Your servants the prophets, who spoke in Your name *to our kings and our princes, to our fathers and all the people of the land....*

"As it is written in the Law of Moses, all this disaster has come upon us; yet we have not made our prayer before the LORD our God, that we might turn from our iniquities and understand Your truth. Therefore the LORD has kept the disaster in mind, and brought it upon us; for the LORD our God is righteous in all the works which He does, though we have not obeyed His voice. And now, O Lord our God, who brought Your people out of the land of Egypt with a mighty hand, and made Yourself a name, as it is this day—we have sinned, we have done wickedly!

"O Lord, according to all Your righteousness, I pray, let Your anger and Your fury be turned away from Your city Jerusalem, Your holy mountain; because for our sins, and for the iniquities of our fathers, Jerusalem and Your people are a reproach to all those around us. Now therefore, our God, hear the prayer of Your servant, and his supplications, and for the Lord's sake cause Your face to shine on Your sanctuary, which is desolate. O my God, incline Your ear and hear; open Your eyes and see our desolations, and the city which is called by Your name; for we do not present our supplications before You because of our righteous deeds, but because of Your great mercies. O Lord, hear! O Lord, forgive! O Lord, listen and act! Do not delay for Your own sake, my God, for Your city and Your people are called by Your name." (Daniel 9:3–6, 13–19 NKJV)

This prayer shows grief, remorse, and perhaps most importantly, *honesty before God.*

If Western nations are going to be restored, *public prayers of this magnitude—prayers focusing on the sins of the nation and the justice of God—must be prayed.*

In short, *the participation in evil, the arrogance, the indifference, and the hardness of heart among God's people regarding the sins that cry to heaven for vengeance must be truly faced, confessed, and dealt with.*

Daniel's prayer was the beginning of the end of the judgment, but not the end. The Jews had suffered horrendous bloodshed, death, famine, plague, the loss of their homes, the destruction of the temple, and so much more that the average person today cannot imagine, much less comprehend. Daniel's prayer was prayed at the end of seventy years of judgment.

The chastened Jews would still have to cross the desert and return to Judah—to the destruction and the waste—and begin the arduous work of rebuilding Jerusalem, rebuilding the wall around Jerusalem, and rebuilding the temple.

The Physical Fruits of Repentance

Usually with repentance prayers comes *the duty to change*. The word *repentance* in Greek is deep in meaning. It means *to turn*, to *have sorrow and regret*, to *have a change of mind*, and to *have a change of deeds*. Other common definitions of repentance include "making amends," "setting things right," "making restitution," "changing your ways," and "reparation."

Part of repentance—the reparation or "repairing the damage done"—that must be *exhibited in the physical realm* is to do what one can to save babies from murder and to work to make it a crime (as it was for centuries) to kill in-utero humans. (More on this in a moment.)

Simply put, in the story of "the Good Samaritan," the priest and the Levite sinned by passing by on the other side of the road and leaving the beaten man to die in the ditch.

Again, *the priest and the Levite sinned* when they "passed by on the other side." They failed to love their neighbor as themselves.

Likewise today, Christians have sinned by leaving human babies to die in the "ditch" of abortuaries. The Christian community *knows exactly where babies are dying*. They know who is killing these children. And like the Jews of thousands of years ago, they look the other way while the slaughter continues.

This can be very personal. Millions of babies have been killed, and women marred for life, while a Christian *stood by and did little or nothing—said little or nothing*. No frantic, life-and-death intervention was attempted—no loving, desperate help was offered. The imminent death of a child was faced with indifference: "It's not my problem," or worse, "I'll support you in whatever decision you make."

If a mass murderer were hovering with a sword over a child's head, deciding if the child will live or die, would the appropriate Christian response be to say to the murderer, "I'll support you in whatever decision you make"?

Christians have an obligation, when it is possible, to intervene with courage and passion and determination on behalf of babies in danger. *They have the duty to circumvent normal niceties because they are faced with a life-and-death situation.*

Christians are called to ponder—to truly think: *"What would I want someone to do if I were about to be murdered?"*

Christians are called to "rescue strangers," to go to these abortuaries and speak up for these children, to attempt to rescue them by holding a sign, to beg the mother not to kill her baby, or to take any number of other effective actions. "Love your neighbor as yourself" means doing for your neighbor whose life is in jeopardy *what you would want done for you if your life were in jeopardy*.

Not everyone lives in an area where children are killed by abortion. Also, there are Christians who have severe health issues or are at the end of their lives with limited mobility. For those, the physical repentance is more limited, or different.

But those exceptions aside, virtually everyone who reads these words in a nation that kills children, or a nation that allows so-called "homosexual marriage," has the ability to have their *voice heard in the public square*. If nothing else, they have the ability to confront these evils and speak against these crimes against God.

The reason that most Christians look the other way, as did the priest and Levite who left the man to die in the ditch, is because of the *love of self* and the *fear of losing something*. Christians need to repent of this self-love and unholy fear, and the repentance must be of a *spiritual*, *physical*, and *governmental* nature. (More on governmental in a moment.)

The Apostle John made clear the heavenly distinction between the words of Christians and the *deeds* of Christians:

> But if any one has the world's goods and sees his brother in need, yet closes his heart against him, how does God's love abide in him? Little children, let us not love in *word or speech* but in *deed and in truth*. (First John 3:17–18)

Words are important, but as the popular saying declares, "actions speak louder than words." John also wrote:

> If someone says, "I love God," and hates his brother, he is a liar; for *he who does not love his brother whom he has seen, how can he love God whom he has not seen?* And this commandment we have from Him: that *he who loves God must love his brother also*. (First John 4:20–21 NKJV)

A Christian can say the words of a prayer of repentance but have no *true repentance* of *motive* and *action*. As Isaiah said, "This people honors Me with their lips, but their heart is far from Me."

Most Christians would say, "I am against abortion," or "I am pro-life." But these words may only reflect a dull sentiment, not a burning conviction. The proof of the Christian's commitment will be in *actions* or *lack of actions*.

For example, the Apostle James wrote: "If a brother or sister is ill-clad and in lack of daily food, and *one of you says to them*, 'Go in peace, be warmed and filled,' without giving them the things needed for the body, what does it profit?"

Hence, applied to this crisis, if *corresponding actions* are not connected to the words, "I am against abortion," what good is it?

Words are important, but they are usually not enough, especially against an epic abomination—a literal holocaust—of this magnitude. The duty of the Christian is to "love your neighbor as yourself." These words mean a love that serves, helps, sacrifices, and takes risks.

There are some sins in the world that are spiritual, or internal. For example, jealousy, or even covetousness, can be at work in the heart of a human with no corresponding outward action. Jealousy is a *sin*, but if not acted on in any way, the impact is solely on the one harboring the sin. It is a sin but not a *crime*.

But other sins, such as the act of murder, are simultaneously spiritual, physical, and legal. I.e., hatred has filled someone's heart, they have committed the action of taking someone's life, and now they must face the consequence of committing murder in a court of law.

The Legal and Political Fruits of Repentance

Perhaps the arena of Christian communities where repentance for the sins of commission and omission for the mass slaughter of innocent babies, and other sins that cry to the heavens, is most critical is the legal/political realm.

The final "fruit of repentance" that must be brought forth in Christian nations is that *it must become a crime to kill a human being from conception till birth.*

For clarity and emphasis, child killing—abortion, as it is euphemistically called—*must be a crime under the governmental laws in the nation where one lives.*

If aborting an innocent human being in the womb is murder—which it is—there must be laws prohibiting those murders. If the laws are not changed, judgment will come.

Why? *It is a matter of justice.*

In Leviticus chapter 20, God demanded that the Israelites prosecute and punish the man who offered his children to Molech:

Any man of the people of Israel, or of the strangers that sojourn in Israel, who gives any of his children to Molech shall be put to death; the people of the land shall stone him with stones. (Leviticus 20:2)

This is a juridical, or legal, judgment. It was "against the law" to kill their children, and if anyone did, they were to be prosecuted and executed.

However, if the Israelites did not enforce the law, God made clear He would bring judgment on those who killed their children *and* those who did not stop them:

> And if the people of the land do at all hide their eyes from that man, when he gives one of his children to Molech, and do not put him to death, then I will set My face against that man and against his family, and will cut them off from among their people, him and all who follow him in playing the harlot after Molech. (Leviticus 20:4–5)

The Law as Teacher and Deterrent

One of the main purposes of law is to deter criminal deeds (such as murdering babies) using the fear of punishment. St. Paul wrote:

> For rulers are not a terror to good conduct, but to bad. Would you have no fear of him who is in authority? Then do what is good, and you will receive his approval, for he is God's servant for your good. But if you do wrong, be afraid, for he does not bear the sword in vain; he is the servant of God to execute His wrath on the wrongdoer. (Romans 13:3–4)

"If you do wrong, be afraid." One of the main purposes God established criminal laws, and established government officials to enforce those laws—and punish those who break them—is to *deter criminal acts through the fear of punishment*. Said differently, some people will obey the law because they fear the consequences if they break the law.

Ponder how different Israel's history would have been if the first few people who offered their children to Molech were arrested, prosecuted, and executed speedily. Sadly, many people today would commit murder, theft, or other crimes were it not for the fear of being caught and being punished.

The inverse is also true: if a criminal fears no punishment, they have no deterrent against committing crime.

For example, at one point in certain cities in the United States and Europe, government authorities responsible to enforce the laws announced or made clear that they would not prosecute crimes of theft and robbery that were under certain dollar amounts. The fruit of this was that thieves walked straight into certain stores and boldly walked out carrying items (stealing the items, more precisely) that added up to less than the declared monetary threshold. *Without the fear of punishment, no deterrent existed to keep certain thieves from stealing.*

Clearly stated: *the nations of former Christendom must restore the laws that make it a criminal act to murder a human being from conception until death.*

Personal Repentance: "Did I Give Him the Power?"

Laws in nations—i.e., laws against drunk driving, theft, rape, or murder—are intended to be based on the laws of God, yet they have been codified and implemented by men in the political sphere. I.e., murder, perjury, theft, and rape are all criminal acts in the Law of Moses, and they are all criminal acts in the laws of Western nations. It is the intent of God that man's laws be based on His laws.

Without exception, the laws of Western nations are made by "lawmakers," "politicians," "members of parliament," "members of congress," etc., who are elected by the voters of those nations.

Judges, police departments, and law-enforcement officials are either elected directly by voters or are hired or appointed by those with the power given to them by those elected by the voters. In other words, Western nations are not functional dictatorships. The laws of Western nations primarily reflect the voting patterns of the electorate. (More will be said about rogue, tyrannical judges and those who obey them.)

Hence, the slaughter of innocents in Western nations is sustained by those in political power, and those in political power are sustained by the votes of their citizens.

Tragically stated: *the murder of human beings from conception until death is sustained largely by voters who are Christians.*

To be clear: the statistics show those *confessing* Christianity, or those who have had a *Trinitarian baptism*, vary widely in various European and North American nations.

At the time of this book's first printing, roughly 75 percent of Americans claim some form of Christianity, 64 percent of French, 55 percent of Germans, and barely 50 percent of English. That said, without the vote of Christians, those who promote the murder of children could not sustain their grip on power.

Or said positively, if the Christian community in every Western democracy repented of voting for child killers, the child killers would be swept out of power, and the legalized killing of babies would grind to a halt. The tragic fact is that the hands of Christian voters are stained with the blood of innocent babies: Well does Isaiah say:

> When you spread forth your hands,
> I will hide My eyes from you;
> even though you make many prayers,
> I will not listen;
> *your hands are full of blood.*
> Wash yourselves; make yourselves clean;
> remove the evil of your doings
> from before My eyes;
> *cease to do evil,*
> *learn to do good;*
> *seek justice,*
> *correct oppression;*
> *defend the fatherless,*
> *plead for the widow.* (Isaiah 1:15–17)

Obeying the framework of repentance we find in Isaiah chapter 1 would look something like this:

"Cease to do evil": Stop voting for those who have declared their support for child murder.

"Learn to do good": Put the lives of innocent babies ahead of your own interests. Be like the good Samaritan, not the priest and the Levite.

"Seek justice": Actively work for justice in the law for innocent babies. Learn how politics works and use politics and the law to obtain justice.

"Correct oppression": Again, a function of law. Babies are oppressed—repair this "breach in the wall."

"Defend the fatherless": With your voice, your vote, your time, your sacrifices.

"Plead for the widow": Fight the movement toward euthanasia in Western nations.

This is not hard to understand. This is also not hyperbole. Child killing is sustained in Western nations in part because of the treachery of Christian voters.

In America, at the time of this book's first printing, *over 50 percent of Roman Catholics voted for candidates that actively promote the murder of children in the last five general elections. Likewise, over one-third of professing evangelicals cast a vote for those who steadfastly promote the murder of babies.*

To Illustrate the Point

Whoever says to the guilty, "You are innocent,"
will be cursed by peoples and denounced by nations.
But it will go well with those who convict the guilty,
and rich blessing will come on them.
(Proverbs 24:24–25 NIV)

For those who need an illustration to prove this point or who can use one to help confront and convert their fellow Christians, here are two examples:

Imagine someone asks for a ride in an automobile and tells the driver, "I need a ride to get food for my ailing neighbor. Then I need to go to the pharmacy to pick up a medical prescription for my mother. Then I need to drop off some used items at Salvation Army for the poor. Then I need to go to the bank, where I will rob the bank and shoot the bank employees."

If the driver says to this person, "I will take you to these destinations," that person is culpable before God and a criminal court because he or she knew the intent of the person seeking the ride.

It would do no good to say, "*I did not agree with the robbery and murder*," or "I am strongly opposed to bank robbery and murder, but I gave him a ride because of the other things he was doing—I agree with those things." The person who drove the car would still be an accessory to murder.

When a Christian votes for someone who promotes murder and same-gender marriage, or transgenderism, they are "giving a ride" to a politician to get to the seat of power, and they share in the guilt of what that politician does when he gets there.

One more illustration shows how Christians *must remain true to eternal ethics, not blown in the wind* by what is politically acceptable at any given moment:

If there were a candidate who had political and policy opinions on every current political issue in an election cycle except that he wanted to *reinstate slavery*—owning black people as chattel property—could a Christian ethically vote for that politician by saying, "I don't agree with his position on slavery, but I'm voting for him because of the other issues we agree on"?

Or if a candidate held great positions on every current political issue in an election cycle, except that he wanted to gas Jews to death in concentration camps, could a Christian ethically vote for that politician by saying, "I don't agree with his position on killing Jews, but I'm voting for him because of the issues we agree on"?

One would hope that most Christians would say, "That politician's position on slavery, or killing Jews, makes him unfit for office, and I cannot ethically vote for him. I will not be part of his agenda to own slaves or kill Jews."

But if they *did* vote for him and he was able to own slaves or kill Jews, *the Christians who voted for him would be accessories to his crimes* because they helped him attain power, knowing what he intended to do.

This is precisely how the sins of commission and omission in the Christian voting block in every Western nation have led to the murder of hundreds of millions of babies, the desecration of the meaning of marriage, and the legitimization of the abomination of "transgenderism." And this is precisely where the fruits of repentance are most keenly needed.

For example, in the ethical comparison between killing babies and slavery, one must remember that *killing babies is worse*. The ethical comparison between killing babies and killing Jews shows at best that they are equal crimes—at worst, the case can be made that *killing babies is worse because of the helplessness of the children*. As shown earlier regarding slaves, Jews can run, hide, fight, cry for help, beg for mercy, appeal for justice, etc. Babies can do none of these things. They are completely reliant on the very people who have often betrayed them: Christian voters.

Roe Overturned, Homosexual "Marriage" Made Legal: The Fruit of the Vote

In the American system of government, Supreme Court justices obtain a lifetime seat in the Supreme Court once they have been nominated by the president and confirmed by the Senate. They are beyond the reach of voters, and they have no term limit. Many Supreme Court justices have served for decades.

Those who vote in America for president must remember that their vote for president will also impact the Supreme Court and hence all of the major issues facing America for decades.

Sadly, for multiple generations in America, the most perverse and evil changes in American law and jurisprudence were handed down by the Supreme Court. (And more sadly, American presidents and Congress did not oppose rulings that were tyrannical—but that is a subject for another book.)

Specifically, slavery as a "right"; the flood of pornography; prayer, Scripture reading and the display of the Ten Commandments being outlawed in public (government) schools and buildings; child killing by abortion; so-called "homosexual marriage"—all these were forced on America by the Supreme Court, without firing a shot.

So, when a Christian votes for a president, they must know and either oppose or embrace the political philosophy of that presidential candidate. They must cast their vote in large part knowing what kind of federal judges the president will nominate.

By the grace of God, and the three appointments made by then-President Trump, the demonic decision *Roe vs. Wade* was finally overturned.

The battle to end child killing in America is nowhere near complete (at the time of the first printing of this book). Whether true victory is had in all fifty states will depend on whether or not Christians truly repent of their part in sustaining the holocaust of children.

The End of the Matter and the End of the Killing

As long as Christians continue to betray God and babies with their votes, the holocaust in America will not come to an end. The same is true in Canada and the nations of Western Europe. Until there is genuine repentance in the Christian community on this huge point, babies will continue to be fed to the wolves.

Christian leaders of all stripes—clergy, teachers, TV and radio personalities, businessmen—have a duty before God and man to use their positions of authority and influence to call Christians to repentance, urging them to vote for candidates who support the lives of the innocent.

The hour is long past for Christian leaders and Christian laymen to boldly declare:

> If you vote for [insert name here], knowing that he promotes child killing, so-called homosexual marriage, and the perverse crime against children of transgenderism, you have betrayed Jesus Christ and the laws of God with your vote. You must repent of serving those who hate God with your vote, and rather, use your vote to turn our nation from the "sins that cry to God for vengeance."

Those Christian leaders who refuse to urge Christians to vote against those who promote murder, whether they are motivated by fear, a lust for power, personal perversion and treachery, a false sense of mercy, party loyalty, greed for money from government programs—whatever—they are no longer fit to serve in the Christian community.

They are the false prophets, the cowardly clergy, the corrupt bishops and priests, the dogs who do not bark, the watchmen who do not see. They are, by their silence and corruption, a corrosive force inside the Body of Christ, eating away at her valor and mission—wolves in sheep's clothing, collaborators with the merchants of death, hirelings to be devoutly ignored.

Let each reader, inside the nation and the station in which he finds himself, weigh how best to "bring forth the fruits of repentance" in the spiritual, physical, and political realms so that the innocent will be protected, holy sexual ethics will be restored in the public square, and the nations of the West will be restored to truth and justice.

If the Christian community awakens from its slumber and repents of the sins that have perpetrated this holocaust and advanced perversions, our nations can be restored and the judgments of God mitigated or averted.

If not—if the Christians of the Western democracies continue in their rebellion against God, content in their hardness of heart, following the cowardly path of "the priest and the Levite," voting for baby killers and the servants of Sodom—the judgments forewarned in God's holy Law shall be poured out according to His timeline in each nation, as seems best to Him.

The nations that have rejected the Lordship of Christ shall drink of the cup of His indignation, staggering on into heartache—fear, drought, economic hardship, disease, famine, and the sword—in whatever way the Almighty chooses to unsheathe them.

And none shall be able to say: "Why have these dreadful things come upon us? We do not deserve this."

If the nations continue to reject the wisdom and fear of God, they shall reap the fruit of their ways:

Because I have called and you refused to listen,
have stretched out My hand and no one has heeded,
and you have ignored all My counsel
and would have none of My reproof,
I also will laugh at your calamity;
I will mock when panic strikes you,
when panic strikes you like a storm,
and your calamity comes like a whirlwind,
when distress and anguish come upon you.
Then they will call upon Me, but I will not answer;
they will seek Me diligently but will not find Me.
Because they hated knowledge
and did not choose the fear of the LORD,
would have none of My counsel,
and despised all My reproof,
therefore they shall eat the fruit of their way
and be sated with their own devices.
For the simple are killed by their turning away,
and the complacence of fools destroys them;

but he who listens to Me will dwell secure
and will be at ease, without dread of evil.
(Proverbs 1:24–33)

*I am no prophet, nor a prophet's son; but I am a herdsman, and a dresser of sycamore trees, and the L*ORD *took me from following the flock, and the L*ORD *said to me, "Go, prophesy to My people Israel."*

Amos 7:14–15

*And I said: "Woe is me! For I am lost; for I am a man of unclean lips, and I dwell in the midst of a people of unclean lips; for my eyes have seen the King, the L*ORD *of hosts!"*

Then flew one of the seraphim to me, having in his hand a burning coal which he had taken with tongs from the altar. And he touched my mouth, and said: "Behold, this has touched your lips; your guilt is taken away, and your sin forgiven." And I heard the voice of the Lord saying, "Whom shall I send, and who will go for Us?" Then I said, "Here am I! Send me." And He said, "Go, and say to this people…"

Isaiah 6:5–9

Blessed are they that suffer persecution for justice' sake: for theirs is the kingdom of heaven.

Blessed are ye when they shall revile you, and persecute you, and speak all that is evil against you, untruly, for My sake:

Be glad and rejoice, for your reward is very great in heaven. For so they persecuted the prophets that were before you.

Matthew 5:10–12 DRB

And they demolished the pillar of Ba'al, and demolished the house of Ba'al, and made it a latrine to this day.

Thus Jehu wiped out Ba'al from Israel.

Second Kings 10:27–28

*Now therefore thus shall you say to My servant David, "Thus says the L*ORD *of hosts, I took you from the pasture, from following the sheep, that you should be prince over My people Israel."*

First Chronicles 17:7

Epilogue One

You, the reader, have persevered to get to this point in our study of divine judgment. Now that you have the Scriptural foundation for this critical message, I would like to shift the focus slightly. Allow me to speak, not as an anonymous author, but as myself, Randall Terry—*to you*.

My goal for Christians in any Western nation is that they be able to read this book—in 2025, or 2042, or even the year 2092—and apply the principles and axioms of the Scriptures referenced in this work to the world in which they live.

In short, I want you, the reader, to be able to see your own nation and your own time in this study on the laws and judgments delineated in Sacred Scripture. It is my hope that your life is altered—redirected—for the purposes of Almighty God, in whatever nation and era you find yourself.

Western nations—*including yours*—are desperate for men and women who will unflinchingly proclaim the truth and fight for what is right in God's eyes in every arena—especially the arts, communications, commerce, education, the judiciary, and politics.

You may recognize that God is trying to get the attention of your nation. You may have nodded your head at points as you read this book. You may have sighed and grieved. A holy fear may have gripped your heart upon reading certain Scriptures.

You may have wept for yourself, your family, or your country and begged God for mercy. If this work is even remotely accurate in its application of Sacred Scriptures to the nations of today, *many nations are in grave danger.* A dreadful reckoning is coming. The only way out of that danger is for nations to bring forth "fruits of repentance" that are required and acceptable to Almighty God and that will mitigate His visitation of judgment. The sins that cry for vengeance—legalized in our nations—must be made illegal again.

That said, the *warning* of judgment, the *call* to repentance, and the *hope* and *promise* of mercy all require *words—words delivered by messengers.*

If you believe the warnings and threats of the Scriptures apply to today—if you see the chaos in your nation as a self-evident sign of God's chastening hand—are you willing to declare it to those around you? Will you be God's messenger?

When Isaiah saw Almighty God on His throne, he recorded the scene:

> And I heard the voice of the Lord saying, "Whom shall I send, and who will go for Us?"

Hearing God ask the question is somewhat perplexing to me. But it again affirms the fact that God uses people—*frail human beings*—as His messengers.

Will We Respond Like Isaiah?

"And I heard the voice of the Lord saying, 'Whom shall I send, and who will go for Us?'" Isaiah responded: "Here am I! Send me." And God said, "Go, and say to this people..." Isaiah offered himself for the job. He chose to offer his services as a messenger.

Will you offer yourself to be a messenger for God? You do in fact have a choice in the matter—it's called *free will.*

Free will is a precious and sometimes frightening gift to humans from the hand of God. God can (and sometimes does) intervene in human affairs as He sees fit. He has the freedom—as the sovereign Lord of the universe—to do whatever He wants, whenever He wants. But nevertheless, He has given humanity free will.

We choose to obey; we choose to disobey.

We choose to be clear and unflinching; we choose to equivocate and dissemble.

We choose to speak; we choose to be silent.

The questions you should ask yourself are these: If you agree with the message of this book, are you willing to declare this message in your circle of friends, family, associates, and acquaintances? Are you willing to share these concepts at your church? With your pastor?

If you are a political officeholder, or part of the judiciary, or a candidate for some post, are you willing to make these truths a key part of your public agenda?

If you are a clergyman, a teacher, or a broadcaster and you believe the general theme of this work, are you willing to declare this message to your parish, or congregants, or members, or your listening audience?

Let us go one step further. Are you willing to say words and take actions that will get this message heard beyond the circles in which you currently travel?

These are doable actions you can take to get this message out to hundreds, thousands, and sometimes millions of people. But first, *you have to be willing*. You have to say with Isaiah: "Here am I! Send me."

Ask yourself: "Could I prophesy God's truth about innocent blood, holy marriage, the "sins that cry to God," the perils of the judgment we face, and the call to repentance?"

You may say, yes! If so, God bless you and give you courage and strength for the path ahead of you.

Or you may come up with reasons why *you are not able to take on this mission*—excuses why "I'm not the one for this job."

You would not be alone if you said, "I am not able to do this." In fact, you would be among a long line of Biblical heroes. Think of Moses, Saul, Elijah, Isaiah, Jonah, Jeremiah, and others.

When God called Moses, Moses protested. Moses had a litany of excuses. His excuses even made God angry at one point:

> But Moses said to God, "*Who am I that I should go to Pharaoh*, and bring the sons of Israel out of Egypt?"...
>
> But Moses said to the LORD, "Oh, my Lord, *I am not eloquent*, either heretofore or since Thou hast spoken to Thy servant; but *I am slow of speech and of tongue.... Oh, my Lord, send, I pray, some other person." Then the anger of the LORD was kindled against Moses.* (Exodus 3:11, 4:10, 13–14)

When God called Gideon, Gideon had a similar reaction to that of Moses:

> And the LORD turned to him and said, "Go in this might of yours and deliver Israel from the hand of Mid'ian; do not I send you?" And he said to Him, "Pray, Lord, how can I deliver Israel? Behold, my clan is the weakest in Manas'seh, and I am the least in my family." (Judges 6:14–15)

When the prophet Samuel told Saul that he was the desire of all Israel (Saul was soon to be anointed king), Saul responded:

> Am I not a Benjaminite, from the least of the tribes of Israel? And is not my family the humblest of all the families of the tribe of Benjamin? Why then have you spoken to me in this way? (First Samuel 9:21)

Before Isaiah offered himself to God ("Here am I! Send me"), he said:

> Woe is me! For I am lost; for I am a man of unclean lips, and I dwell in the midst of a people of unclean lips; for my eyes have seen the King, the LORD of hosts! (Isaiah 6:5)

After Elijah had a spectacular victory against the prophets of Baal, he fled for fear of Jezebel:

> Ahab told Jez'ebel all that Eli'jah had done, and how he had slain all the prophets with the sword. Then Jez'ebel sent a messenger to Eli'jah, saying, "So may the gods do to me and more also, if I do not make your life as the life of one of them by this time tomorrow." Then he was afraid, and he arose and went for his life, and came to Beer-sheba, which belongs to Judah, and left his servant there.
>
> But he himself went a day's journey into the wilderness, and came and sat down under a broom tree; and he asked that he might die, saying, "It is enough; now, O Lord, take away my life; for I am no better than my fathers." (First Kings 19:1–4)

When God called Jonah, Jonah immediately ran in the other direction:

> Now the word of the Lord came to Jonah the son of Amit'tai, saying, "Arise, go to Nin'eveh, that great city, and cry against it; for their wickedness has come up before Me." But Jonah rose to flee to Tarshish from the presence of the Lord. He went down to Joppa and found a ship going to Tarshish; so he paid the fare, and went on board, to go with them to Tarshish, away from the presence of the Lord. (Jonah 1:1–3)

When God called Jeremiah, Jeremiah responded with his own set of concerns:

> Then I said, "Ah, Lord God! Behold, I do not know how to speak, for I am only a youth." (Jeremiah 1:6)

Perhaps you, like these great heroes mentioned above, have objections and excuses. God had a response to encourage each of these heroes of the faith. Likewise, for every objection and excuse you might have, *God has an answer*. Look at the answers

God gave to each of these messengers. In response to Moses, God said:

> "Who has made man's mouth? Who makes him dumb, or deaf, or seeing, or blind? Is it not I, the LORD? Now therefore go, and I will be with your mouth and teach you what you shall speak."...
>
> *Then the anger of the LORD was kindled against Moses* and He said, "Is there not Aaron, your brother, the Levite? I know that he can speak well; and behold, he is coming out to meet you, and when he sees you he will be glad in his heart. And you shall speak to him and put the words in his mouth; and I will be with your mouth and with his mouth, and will teach you what you shall do." (Exodus 4:11–12, 14–15)

With Samuel and Saul, Samuel anointed Saul with oil and spoke to him of the Lord's intentions:

> Then Samuel took a vial of oil and poured it on his head, and kissed him and said, "Has not the LORD anointed you to be prince over His people Israel? And you shall reign over the people of the LORD and you will save them from the hand of their enemies round about.... Then the Spirit of the LORD will come mightily upon you, and you shall prophesy with them and be turned into another man." (First Samuel 10:1, 6)

To inspire obedience in Jonah, God sent a mammoth, living "taxi" at sea:

> And the LORD appointed a great fish to swallow up Jonah; and Jonah was in the belly of the fish three days and three nights. Then Jonah prayed to the LORD his God from the belly of the fish.... And the LORD spoke to the fish, and it vomited out Jonah upon the dry land. (Jonah 1:17–2:1, 10)

To Jeremiah's claim he was too young to be a messenger of God, God replied:

"Do not say, 'I am only a youth';
for to all to whom I send you you shall go,
and whatever I command you you shall speak.
Be not afraid of them,
for I am with you to deliver you, says the LORD."

Then the LORD put forth His hand and touched my mouth; and the LORD said to me,

"Behold, I have put My words in your mouth.
See, I have set you this day over nations
and over kingdoms,
to pluck up and to break down,
to destroy and to overthrow,
to build and to plant...

"But you, gird up your loins; arise, and say to them everything that I command you. Do not be dismayed by them, lest I dismay you before them. And I, behold, I make you this day a fortified city, an iron pillar, and bronze walls, against the whole land, against the kings of Judah, its princes, its priests, and the people of the land. They will fight against you; but they shall not prevail against you, for I am with you, says the LORD, to deliver you." (Jeremiah 1:7–10, 17–19)

To reassure Gideon, God said:

And the LORD said to him, "But I will be with you, and you shall smite the Mid'ianites as one man." (Judges 6:16)

To further bolster his confidence, God gave Gideon the signs of the fleece:

Then Gideon said to God, "If Thou wilt deliver Israel by my hand, as Thou hast said, behold, I am laying a fleece of wool on the threshing floor; if there is dew on the fleece alone, and it is dry on all the ground, then I shall know that Thou wilt deliver Israel by my hand, as Thou hast said." And it was so. When he rose early next morning and squeezed the fleece, he wrung enough dew from the fleece to fill a bowl with water. Then Gideon said to God, "Let not Thy anger burn against me, let me speak but this once; pray, let me make trial only this once with the fleece; pray, let it be dry only on the fleece, and on all the ground let there be dew." And God did so that night; for it was dry on the fleece only, and on all the ground there was dew. (Judges 6:36–40)

For Isaiah, God cleansed his lips:

Then flew one of the seraphim to me, having in his hand a burning coal which he had taken with tongs from the altar. And he touched my mouth, and said: "Behold, this has touched your lips; your guilt is taken away, and your sin forgiven." And I heard the voice of the Lord saying, "Whom shall I send, and who will go for Us?" Then I said, "Here am I! Send me." And He said, "Go, and say to this people…" (Isaiah 6:6–9)

Some might think they are too young or too old, too weak, or not smart enough. They, like Amos, might say, "I am not a prophet." Or, in more modern terms: "I'm not called to the ministry." Or, "I'm not called to preach." Or, "I don't have that apostolate."

You might believe you are *too sinful* to speak God's laws to anyone. You may be troubled by sinful words or deeds in your past that haunt your memories or sins that you struggle with to this very day. You may believe that you are not worthy to speak God's Word in a public forum.

If you are shackled by guilt or remorse, I urge you to consider King David and the Apostle Peter. King David committed adultery and murder, yet God forgave him and continued to use him to write Sacred Scripture, including the two most beautiful psalms of repentance in the Bible: Psalm 51 and Psalm 32.

Likewise, the Apostle Peter denied the Lord three times—once with cursing and swearing—yet our Lord Jesus restored him, appointed him the first pastor of His Church, and used him to write two books in the New Testament.

These two towering men, with the gritty details of their sins and failures and inspiring tales of their redemption and restoration, should give us all hope and assurance. Remember: *both David and Peter were commissioned by God to write Sacred Scripture AFTER their failures.*

Most other saints and heroes of the faith (heroes from both the Bible and Church history) had faults—faults large and small, yet God used them to proclaim His Word and accomplish His will. And when you recognize that you are a *sinner* in the present tense, take comfort in the command of Jesus that we forgive those who sin against us "seventy times seven" times a day. If God requires that we forgive those who sin against us frequently, we can have confidence that He will forgive us as we continue to struggle against our besetting sins.

Whatever reason you may have to believe that you cannot proclaim God's truth at some level, it's likely that it is an excuse that someone else has tried to use. God has an answer to your objection—if you will hear it.

One other point: if you're worried that you have a big ego, and yet in your heart you want to herald God's Word, you should not be overly concerned—if you truly herald the truth like Jeremiah did, you will have your ego squeezed out of you by the winepress of contempt and hatred that comes upon you.

Count the Cost:
"Blessed are those who are persecuted..."

This leads to what is perhaps a far more critical discussion: *the cost of speaking out.* We must all ask: are we willing to declare the truth in the face of adversity and hostility?

If God said to you, "Go stand on the street corner and proclaim My Word to all who pass by," would you do it? If God called you to say, "Abortion is murder," and "It is a sin to vote for a pro-choice candidate," would you do it?

If God called you to declare that "marriage can only be between a man and a woman," or that "our nation is under judgment because of the sins that cry out to heaven," would you say it?

Likewise, if God called you to run for school board, or your state assembly or state senate, or for state or federal judge, or for the U.S. House or U.S. Senate—or even the presidency—would you do it?

Yes, or no?

Many ways exist for you to proclaim God's Word boldly, such as letters to the editor in your local newspaper or favorite online news outlet. You might call in to live radio talk shows where you can declare the justice and judgments of God. You can hold events in public where local news outlets might interview you and give you the chance to tell all viewers that the shedding of innocent blood is a sin that cries to God for vengeance and will bring divine judgment on the nation.

You can use one or more of the dozens of platforms in "cyber space" to herald this message. You can literally be heard around your nation—around the world—in a moment's time with concise words, images, or videos.

"The fear of man lays a snare."
"The righteous are bold as a lion."

It is my belief that a cowardly man looking for a way to justify his retreat from battle coined the phrase, "Wisdom is the better part of valor." It is often used to give solace to those who will *not* fight for what is right or *not* say what is true because they are afraid of ridicule or defeat.

The Christian world is in a fight for the soul of Christian civilization, and the Christians, the Church, the Trinitarian denominations of all kinds, and our shared Judeo-Christian values (at the time of the first printing) are losing terribly. We are ripe for divine judgment.

If our nations are to be redeemed, forgiven, and restored, part of the path to restoration will require bold men and women who proclaim God's laws and judgments—men and women who follow the path of Jeremiah and Ezekiel and the other prophets.

This will require a price to be paid on the part of anyone who says, "Here am I! Send me."

Jesus promised that those who do what is right for His sake will be met with persecution and hostility:

> Blessed are those who are persecuted for righteousness' sake, for theirs is the kingdom of heaven.
>
> Blessed are you when men revile you and persecute you and utter all kinds of evil against you falsely on My account. Rejoice and be glad, for your reward is great in heaven, for so men persecuted the prophets who were before you. (Matthew 5:10–12)

Note that "your reward is great in heaven"—i.e., often there is *little reward on earth*. Also note that Jesus compares you ("Blessed are *you*") to the *prophets*. It is a great honor to be compared to the prophets of the Old Testament. If you say what needs to be said and do what needs to be done, you will be persecuted. But, *like the prophets we have studied in this book, you will have a great reward in heaven*.

I close this epilogue on a personal note. I have been privileged to be used by God as a herald of His truth to multiple nations.

Four and a half decades ago I had a "sense" that burned in my soul that God would use me to proclaim His truth to America. I was in my late teens. When I was in my twenties, I knew that I would lead thousands of people in social and political battles against the murder of children. I knew it—I "saw" it in my heart before any of it unfolded before my eyes.

Slowly, steadily, small steps at a time, I was faithful to do the next thing in front of me—with many failings, I assure you. I spoke to those I could speak to. I took the opportunities I saw in front of me. When I failed, I asked God's help and *kept going forward*. When I got knocked down, by God's grace, I got back up and *kept going forward*. When I sinned, I begged God's forgiveness and *kept going forward*.

I remembered David. I remembered Peter. I looked to great men like Winston Churchill for inspiration.

Over time, I found men and women of like vision. We became a "band of happy warriors" on a mission to proclaim the truth and end the murder of children in America.

By God's grace, I led the largest peaceful civil-disobedience movement in American history. We had over seventy thousand arrests from 1987 to 1994 in Operation Rescue for peacefully blocking the houses of death (abortion mills) in the United States. Jails were filled. The media coverage was astronomical.

We saved tens of thousands of babies—babies now grown who have children of their own.

By God's grace, I proclaimed the truth—"If you believe abortion is murder, act like it's murder! God will avenge this innocent blood!"—to *tens of millions of people* via secular news outlets in America. But beyond the shores of America, I was able to preach a warning of the coming judgment because of the blood of babies crying from the ground, across the globe in multiple nations and languages via hundreds of television, radio, and newspaper outlets. Operation Rescue became an international phenomenon.

But sadly, we did not prevail. The baby-killing attorney general of the United States stated that it was her priority to stop Operation Rescue. We endured a flurry of state and federal lawsuits. The federal government passed a law making it a federal crime to block the entrance of abortion mills. Those two factors effectively broke the back of the large-scale disobedience movement. Many of us went to jail for months, and some spent years in jail for peaceful protest.

I lost my home to the attorneys of Planned Parenthood and the National Organization for Women.

Child killing continued for decades and continues to this very day in most of America. Likewise, child killing is entrenched in most formerly Christian nations of the West. Fortunately, *Roe vs. Wade*—the Supreme Court decision that unleashed child sacrifice on America—has been overturned. At the time of the first printing, the battle is joined in earnest to make child killing a crime once again in the United States.

Ultimately, our mission—our duty in America—is to make it a crime in all fifty states via some type of federal legislation or constitutional amendment to kill an unborn baby from conception until birth.

The mission and duty to criminalize child killing is the same in all nations. The end of this chapter of human history has not yet been written. The Christian community in some nations may still bring forth fruits of repentance, end the slaughter of babies, and restore a true definition of marriage.

In some nations, the bulk of the Christian community may continue being silent and inactive while their nations continue down the path of destruction, reaping what they have sown as they plummet deeper into hell.

It Has Been a Privilege

I confess to Almighty God and to you, my brothers and sisters, that on many occasions I felt the exhilaration of being used by God to reach millions. And at other times, I felt the despair and anguish of a man who has failed. And on many occasions, I felt the bitter sting of one who is abandoned. It has been a difficult path, but nevertheless, it has been a privilege to serve God in this way.

However, *I believe I was not God's first choice for this mission.*

I could be wrong, but I believe God asked other men and women to do what I set out to do, but they declined His offer. They told Him no.

I told Him yes. I said, "Here am I! Send me."

With all my frailties and fears, all my heartaches and broken dreams, with all my lost friendships and alienation from friends and family, He sent me—He used me—to reach millions and millions of people with His truth. He worked through me to rescue thousands of children from death.

I tell you this in this moment of honesty to encourage *you—in whatever decade and in whatever nation you find yourself.*

I don't know the will of God for your life. But this I know: *We do not have to have a special call from God to love our neighbor as ourselves.* It is the *duty* of all Christians to love our neighbor as ourselves.

When Jesus explained what it meant to love our neighbor as ourselves, He told the story of the Good Samaritan, who saved the half-dead man that lay bleeding and dying in the ditch between Jerusalem and Jericho. The good Samaritan risked his health, his life, and his reputation and sacrificed his time and money to keep the man from dying and get him to safety.

The priest and the Levite passed the man in the ditch and left him to die. Maybe they thought they were too spiritual. Maybe they were afraid. Maybe they did not want to get dirty. Maybe they lied to themselves and told themselves, "I am not called to a 'ditch ministry'."

Whatever the reason, they failed. *They passed by on the other side, leaving the man to die.* They failed to love their neighbor as God commands us to do.

The picture Christ painted for us is this: a fellow human is in danger of death. We have the capacity to try and save his life. Doing so will cost us time, effort, and money, and we'll get dirty in the process. It will be a sacrifice to save that person's life. And we will have to take risks.

But Jesus said it is a *commandment* to love our neighbor. It is not a suggestion.

You Are Already Called to Do *Something*

You are already called to defend innocent blood, *because you are commanded to love your neighbor as yourself*. Babies are dying in "the ditch" of the abortion holocaust. You are called to help save them, because you are called to love your neighbor as yourself.

In whatever nation you find yourself, in whatever decade, if your nation is committing sins that cry to God for vengeance, it is in great danger.

What will you do to rescue your nation from divine judgment?

Pray for strength and courage. Take whatever steps you can. Ask God to use you beyond your natural strengths and gifts. Be faithful in little opportunities, and greater opportunities will present themselves.

Pray the prayer of Isaiah: "Here am I! Send me!" and see how God uses you in His purposes.

If at any time I declare concerning a nation or a kingdom, that I will pluck up and break down and destroy it, and if that nation, concerning which I have spoken, turns from its evil, I will repent of the evil that I intended to do to it. And if at any time I declare concerning a nation or a kingdom that I will build and plant it, and if it does evil in My sight, not listening to My voice, then I will repent of the good which I had intended to do to it. Now, therefore, say to the men of Judah and the inhabitants of Jerusalem: "Thus says the LORD, Behold, I am shaping evil against you and devising a plan against you. Return, every one from his evil way, and amend your ways and your doings."

Jeremiah 18:7–11

Epilogue Two

How Bad Will It Get in North America and Europe?
When Will All These Things Take Place?

How bad will things get for Western nations under the judgment of God? And when will it end?

We don't know.

Someone could read this book in 2032, in the third year of a seven-year drought, with food shortages and out-of-control inflation.

Someone could read it in 2029, or 2039, the week after a nuclear strike from China or Pakistan or Russia. The chaos that would follow such an event is beyond the scope of any human experience. It would dwarf Hiroshima and Nagasaki.

Someone could read this in 2042, after the political territory of the United States has been forever altered because the nation disintegrated into factional fighting, and various governors and state legislators refused to submit to federal tyranny.

Someone could read this in 2027, the year Europe experiences another wave of Muslim terrorist attacks, setting off internal crises not seen in centuries.

We could see a 78 percent drop in the stock market in 2025 and economic chaos such as has never been seen before.

A series of natural catastrophes in 2029 could leave hundreds of thousands dead, or homeless and destitute.

We could see major cities in North America or Europe melt down into veritable war zones, outside of the stability of "law and order."

How bad will things get for North America or Europe under divine judgment?

When reading in the Scriptures about the destruction of Jerusalem and God's holy temple, it should be remembered that the first time God warned of such a judgment was in the lifetime of Solomon, at the time of the dedication of Solomon's Temple.

After the temple was dedicated, God appeared to Solomon and gave him this warning:

> But if you turn aside from following Me, you or your children, and do not keep My commandments and My statutes which I have set before you, but go and serve other gods and worship them, *then I will cut off Israel from the land which I have given them; and the house which I have consecrated for My name I will cast out of My sight*; and Israel will become a proverb and a byword among all peoples. *And this house will become a heap of ruins*; everyone passing by it will be astonished, and will hiss; and they will say, *"Why has the Lord done thus to this land and to this house?" Then they will say, "Because they forsook the Lord their God who brought their fathers out of the land of Egypt, and laid hold on other gods, and worshiped them and served them; therefore the Lord has brought all this evil upon them."* (First Kings 9:6–9)

From the time of the building of Solomon's Temple until that same temple was destroyed as a divine judgment was nearly four hundred years.

Four hundred years saw a lot of innocent blood spilt.

When Jonah announced the destruction of Ninevah, they repented, and God forgave them. However, one hundred years later, Nahum prophesied the total destruction of Ninevah, and no reprieve was given.

If nations are spared, perhaps it will be because God found "ten good men." He offered to spare Sodom and Gomorrah if He found but ten good men, which He did not (see Genesis 18 and 19). As God said in Jeremiah 18, the severity and longevity of the judgments will depend in part on a nation's citizens and leaders.

Will Western democracies be like King Zedekiah—the last King of Judah—who rejected God's offer of mercy and refused to heed the Lord's warnings? Right up until the end—even after God had threatened the destruction of Jerusalem and the temple—God offered to spare the city from destruction if King Zedekiah would but surrender to the armies of Babylon.

> King Zedeki'ah sent for Jeremiah the prophet and received him at the third entrance of the temple of the LORD. The king said to Jeremiah, "I will ask you a question; hide nothing from me." Jeremiah said to Zedeki'ah, "If I tell you, will you not be sure to put me to death? And if I give you counsel, you will not listen to me." Then King Zedeki'ah swore secretly to Jeremiah, "As the LORD lives, who made our souls, I will not put you to death or deliver you into the hand of these men who seek your life."
>
> Then Jeremiah said to Zedeki'ah, *"Thus says the LORD, the God of hosts, the God of Israel, If you will surrender to the princes of the king of Babylon, then your life shall be spared, and this city shall not be burned with fire, and you and your house shall live. But if you do not surrender to the princes of the king of Babylon, then this city shall be given into the hand of the Chalde'ans, and they shall burn it with fire, and you shall not escape from their hand."* King Zedeki'ah said to Jeremiah, "I am afraid of the Jews who have deserted to the Chalde'ans, lest I be handed over to them and they abuse me." Jeremiah said, "You shall not be given to them. Obey now the

voice of the LORD in what I say to you, and it shall be well with you, and your life shall be spared. But if you refuse to surrender, this is the vision which the LORD has shown to me: Behold, all the women left in the house of the king of Judah were being led out to the princes of the king of Babylon and were saying,

"'Your trusted friends have deceived you
and prevailed against you;
now that your feet are sunk in the mire,
they turn away from you.'

"All your wives and your sons shall be led out to the Chalde'ans, and *you yourself shall not escape from their hand, but shall be seized by the king of Babylon; and this city shall be burned with fire.*" (Jeremiah 38:14–23)

If King Zedekiah had but repented, Jerusalem would have been spared. At some point, a remnant of righteous reformers may emerge that bring forth the fruits of repentance of ending child killing and restoring the covenant of marriage. Perhaps those happy, brave few will give God reason to show mercy in the midst of judgment. Perhaps in the midst of His wrath, God will remember mercy.

If certain nations of the West are not spared, history will certainly record it was because they, like Zedekiah, hardened their hearts and refused the offer of mercy from the hand of God.

When will those judgments fall? Perhaps in a decade; perhaps in one hundred years; perhaps on the "installment plan" over multiple years.

The point is this: sometimes divine judgment is slow in coming, but be assured—there will be a reckoning from the hand of God for the crimes and sins committed against Him.

Even now, North America and Europe are experiencing the "first fruits" of divine judgment. You can see it all around you.

Of this one can be sure: God hears the cry of blood. God hears the cry of sins that reach to heaven, like those of Sodom and Gomorrah and the Western democracies.

God is not mocked. What a nation sows, it will reap.

ABOUT RANDALL TERRY

Randall A. Terry is an internationally known activist, author, and artist.

He was the founder and leader of Operation Rescue, the largest peaceful civil-disobedience movement in United States history. His leadership led to over 70,000 arrests during Operation Rescue demonstrations in the United States, as Christians of all denominations took to the streets to defend the lives of unborn children. He has personally been arrested forty-nine times for peaceful protest and has spent over a year in different jails and prisons around the country.

As an artist, Mr. Terry has written and produced five original music albums, seven documentaries, and two feature-length live-action films.

As an author, he has written seven best-selling books, with nearly 400,000 copies in print.

Mr. Terry has been featured in the *Rolling Stone*, the *New York Times*, the *Washington Post*, the *Washington Times*, the *Los Angeles Times*, *Time Magazine*, *Newsweek*, *U.S. News & World Report*, *People Magazine*, *Roll Call*, *der Spiegel*, *Christianity Today*, and most major newspapers in the United States.

He has been a guest on: *Oprah, 60 Minutes, Meet the Press, Nightline, Hannity, Larry King Live, Good Morning America, 20/20, 48 Hours,* TBN, *Scarborough Country, Crossfire, Sonya Live, Donahue, Sally Jessy Raphael,* BBC, Italian television, Niko Television, Telemundo, *ABC World News Tonight, CBS News, NBC News,* and more. He has appeared on major TV broadcasts on six continents.

Mr. Terry has a B.A. from the State University of New York in Communications and a master's degree in Diplomacy with a concentration in International Terrorism from Norwich University. He is also a graduate of Elim Bible Institute, where he majored in the Bible.

Originally from Rochester, New York, Mr. Terry is the father of seven children and currently resides in Tennessee with his wife and four teenage sons.

Howl ye; for the day of the LORD is at hand; it shall come as a destruction from the Almighty. Therefore shall all hands be faint, and every man's heart shall melt: and they shall be afraid: pangs and sorrows shall take hold of them; they shall be in pain as a woman that travaileth....

Behold, the day of the LORD cometh.... And He shall destroy the sinners thereof out of it [the land].... And I will punish the world for their evil, and the wicked for their iniquity; and I will cause the arrogancy of the proud to cease....

And Babylon, the glory of kingdoms, the beauty of the Chaldees' excellency, shall be as when God overthrew Sodom and Gomorrah.

Isaiah 13:6–19 KJV

PUBLISHER'S WORD

The warning of God's judgement upon Babylon is both physical/geopolitical and spiritual. It is both site oriented and spirit oriented. The Apocalypse (book of Revelation) speaks poignantly of God's purposes and Babylon's defilement of those purposes, as an angel cries out:

> Babylon the great is fallen.... For all nations have drunk of the wine...of her fornication.... Come out of her, My people.... For her sins have reached unto heaven, and God hath remembered her iniquities. (Revelation 18:2–5)

The picture is both powerful and prophetic. There will be no exit from the calamitous judgment soon to fall, with the sole exception of those who, in humble repentance, repudiate the iniquitous spirit of Babylon and turn, in faith, to embrace JESUS CHRIST, YESHUA the MESSIAH, in joyful obedience to HIS will—and HIS alone. Judgment will be swift and complete, "for in one hour is Thy judgment come" (Revelation 18:10).[1]

---

1. Chuck Crismier, *King of the Mountain: The Eternal, Epic, End-Time Battle* (City: Elijah Books, 2013), 308–9.

All of the above is from Charles Crismier's book *King of the Mountain*. Charles has given me permission to use his words to introduce this worthy book by my dear friend, Randall Terry. They are suitable for this book because they speak succinctly to the problem of God's judgment, which Terry grapples with here in depth and with a wealth of Biblical support for his assertions. Nations today have reason to be concerned about the wrath of God.

I am very pleased with the work of this book from Randall Terry, whom I have known for well over a quarter of a century. Randy and I have met in person only once, since he was asked by yours truly to be the guest speaker at one of my twenty-five prayer breakfasts. Randy was the first person to fly out after Gail and I moved from the San Fernando Valley. I asked Randall to be the first speaker at our new location due to his precious love of family. He was the founder of Operation Rescue, the organization dedicated to saving babies from murder, dating to way back before many others in America were concerned with saving the lives of babies in the womb. Over the years since then, I have respected Randall for his courage and wonderful heart for the unborn babies, put into practice long before others stepped up to the plate.

Some in America say they love the USA, but they're not willing to take the brunt of cultural resistance on issues such as the murder of babies in the womb. But we must act, wise as serpents and gentle as doves, to insure that all the citizens of our beloved nation, including those in the womb, enjoy the liberties promised by our founders.

Let us take hope in our Declaration of Independence, the only government document in world history that is a creedal statement of Bible-based ideals:

> We hold these truths to be self-evident, that all men are created equal, that they are endowed by their Creator with certain unalienable Rights, that among these are Life, Liberty

and the pursuit of Happiness.... Appealing to the Supreme Judge of the world for the rectitude of our intentions,... with a firm reliance on the protection of divine Providence, we mutually pledge to each other our Lives, our Fortunes and our sacred Honor.

I honor Randall Terry, our beloved, courageous friend for decades. I do not know of anybody that has more drive, courage, and chutzpah than Mr. Terry. His book is so very important in this particular time in the USA and beyond. I hope Americans and others in the world will always have a heart to save babies in the womb.

A Psalm of David. Fret not thyself because of the wicked men, neither be envious for the evil doers.
For they shall soon be cut down like grass, and shall wither as the green herb.
Trust thou in the LORD and do good: dwell in the land, and thou shalt be fed assuredly:
And delight thyself in the LORD, and He shall give thee thine heart's desire.
Commit thy way unto the LORD, and trust in Him, and He shall bring it to pass.
And He shall bring forth thy righteousness as the light, and thy judgment as the noon day.
Wait patiently upon the LORD and hope in Him: fret not thyself for him which prospereth in his way, nor for the man that bringeth his enterprises to pass.
Cease from anger, and leave off wrath: fret not thyself also to do evil.
For evil doers shall be cut off, and they that wait upon the LORD, they shall inherit the land.
Therefore yet a little while and the wicked shall not appear, and thou shalt look after his place, and he shall not be found.
But meek men shall possess the earth, and shall have

their delight in the multitude of peace.

The wicked practiceth against the just, and gnasheth his teeth against him.

But the Lord shall laugh him to scorn: for He seeth that his day is coming.

The wicked have drawn their sword and have bent their bow, to cast down the poor and needy, and to slay such as be of upright conversation.

But their sword shall enter into their own heart, and their bows shall be broken.

A small thing unto the just man is better than great riches to the wicked and mighty.

For the arms of the wicked shall be broken: but the LORD upholdeth the just men.

The LORD knoweth the days of upright men, and their inheritance shall be perpetual.

They shall not be confounded in the perilous time, and in the days of famine they shall have enough.

But the wicked shall perish, and the enemies of the LORD shall be consumed as the fat of lambs: even with the smoke shall they consume away.

The wicked borroweth and payeth not again. but the righteous is merciful and giveth.

For such as be blessed of God shall inherit the land, and they that be cursed of Him, shall be cut off.

The paths of man are directed by the LORD: for He loveth his way.

Though he fall, he shall not be cast off, for the LORD putteth under his hand.

I have been young, and am old: yet I saw never the righteous forsaken, nor his seed begging bread.

But he is ever merciful and lendeth, and his seed enjoyeth the blessing.

Flee from evil and do good, and dwell forever.

For the LORD loveth judgment, and forsaketh not His

Saints: they shall be preserved forevermore: but the seed of the wicked shall be cut off.

The righteous men shall inherit the land, and dwell therein forever.

The mouth of the righteous will speak of wisdom, and his tongue will talk of judgment.

For the Law of his God is in his heart, and his steps shall not slide.

The wicked watcheth the righteous, and seeketh to slay him.

But the LORD will not leave him in his hand, nor condemn him, when he is judged.

Wait thou on the LORD, and keep His way, and He shall exalt thee, that thou shalt inherit the land: when the wicked men shall perish, thou shalt see.

I have seen the wicked strong, and spreading himself like a green bay tree.

Yet he passed away, and lo, he was gone, and I sought him, but he could not be found.

Mark the upright man, and behold the just: for the end of that man is peace.

But the transgressors shall be destroyed together, and the end of the wicked shall be cut off.

But the salvation of the righteous men shall be of the LORD: He shall be their strength in the time of trouble.

For the LORD shall help them, and deliver them: He shall deliver them from the wicked, and shall save them, because they trust in Him. (Psalm 37 Geneva Bible)

JERRY NORDSKOG, Publisher
New Year's Day, January 1, 2023

About Nordskog Publishing...

Publishing meaty, tasty, and easily digestible Biblical treasures on Christian theology, American and Church history, and Christ-honoring true stories of men and women of great faith.

NORDSKOG PUBLISHING'S PRIMARY MISSION is to enhance the spiritual growth of Christ's redeemed people through understanding of His Laws, and all Truth, as found in His Holy Scriptures. We seek to illustrate His power in all believers through application of the Bible to every subject and every aspect of life and living.

Nordskog entered Christian book publishing in 2006, specializing in Biblically grounded, *"Meaty, Tasty, and Easily Digestible Biblical Treasures."* Nordskog Publishing has published over fifty titles, exploring various genres. Thus far, we have published children's, devotional, inspirational novels, personal growth, Christian history, and unique, applied-Biblical-faith categories—including several translations into Mandarin, Portuguese, Spanish, and Indonesian. Most titles have eBook versions available. The company continues to search for the best in inspiring, stimulating, Christian-growth-inducing themes.

Sign up for our E-Newsletter, *The Bell Ringer*, for timely articles, recent releases, discounts. NordskogPublishing.com/newsletter/

staff@NordskogPublishing.com • 805-642-2070

More from Nordskog Publishing…

Rebuilding Civilization on the Bible:
Proclaiming the Truth on 24
Controversial Issues

BY JAY GRIMSTEAD &
EUGENE CALVIN CLINGMAN
COALITION ON REVIVAL

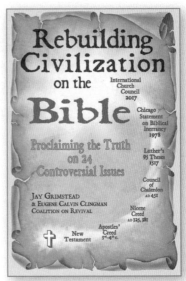

Anything that waters down, neglects, or rejects God's Word as the sole source of ultimate truth, goodness, and life undermines the faith of Jesus Christ in the world. Ready to fill any spiritual vacuum, the forces of godlessness will create a world of horror like those of the ancient pagan cultures. If successful, such could undo centuries of Christian progress toward true civility, liberty, and prosperity.

Using historic tools, with the contribution of dozens of Christian leaders, Dr. Jay Grimstead answers 24 controversial doctrinal questions, defending the historic Biblical faith with Scripture.

Nordskog Publishing urges every Christian to join this effort to defend the inerrancy and authority of the Bible and to restore it to its proper place as the sole rule of faith over all of life.

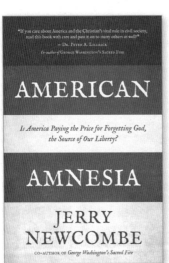

American Amnesia: Is America Paying
the Price for Forgetting God, the Source of
Our Liberty?

BY DR. JERRY NEWCOMBE

Dr. Newcombe continues to press the cause of Christ through his powerful commentary on current affairs from a Biblical worldview. He wields the mighty weapons of God's grace, love, and wisdom in this compilation of his essays.

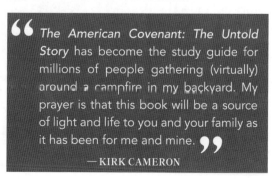

More from Nordskog Publishing...

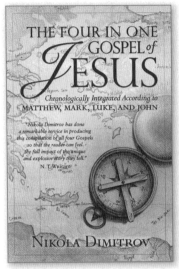

The Four in One Gospel of Jesus:
Chronologically Integrated According to
Matthew, Mark, Luke, and John

COMPILED BY NIKOLA DIMITROV, DMIN

Have you ever wondered about the order of events in the life of Jesus Christ on the earth? *The Four in One Gospel of Jesus* is your book. This bold, decade-long effort places all the events recorded in the four New Testament Gospels into a single chronological narrative according to the best historic scholarship.

Written in the exact words of the venerable King James, varying only to remove archaic spellings, Nordskog Publishing presents a thoroughly readable and accessible harmony perfect for seekers and accomplished scholars alike.

Land That I Love:
Restoring Our Christian Heritage

BY BOBBIE AMES

With the gracious forthrightness of a true Southern lady, Bobbie Ames confronts us with our current societal dilemma, traces its development, reminds us of our compelling history at God's Hand, and leads us toward the solution to the recovery of America's great heritage. This overview of four hundred years of American spiritual struggle and victory should grace every home and educational institution, to read and re-read for decades to come.